The Royal Horse of Europe

The Royal Horse
of Europe

THE STORY OF THE ANDALUSIAN
AND LUSITANO

Foreword by
Fernando d'Andrade

Sylvia Loch

J. A. Allen
London

For Allegra

First published in Great Britain by
J. A. Allen & Co Ltd
1 Lower Grosvenor Place
Buckingham Palace Road
London SW1W 0EL
1986

British Library Cataloguing in Publication Data

Loch, Sylvia
    The royal horse of Europe.
    1. Horse breeds—Spain
    I. Title
    636.1'00946   SF290.S7
    ISBN 0-85131-422-8

Typeset and printed by
BAS Printers Limited, Over Wallop, Hampshire
Bound by Hunter and Foulis, Edinburgh

Contents

FOREWORD by Fernando d'Andrade   9

ACKNOWLEDGEMENTS   9

SPECIAL ACKNOWLEDGEMENTS   11

INTRODUCTION   12

CHAPTER I   **THE HORSES OF SPAIN AND PORTUGAL**   17

All the Horses of the Peninsula   17

The Garrano Pony   18

The Asturian   20

The Sorraia — Early Ancestor to the Iberian Saddle Horse   21

The Iberian Saddle Horse   22

A Plethora of Names for the Same Horse   24

Andalusian   25

Spanish   27

Carthusian   28

Lusitano   30

Portuguese   31

Alter Real   31

Jennet or Ginete   32

Peninsular   33

Castilian   33

Extremeño   33

Zapatero   34

Iberian   34

Dismissing the Villano   34

CHAPTER II   **THE ORIGINS OF THE IBERIAN HORSE**   35

The Very Earliest European Saddle Horse   36

Invaders and Traders   39

The Greeks   41

The Celtiberians   41

Iberia Under the Romans   43

CHAPTER III   **THE DEVELOPMENT OF THE BARB OR BERBER**   49

The Arab Horse and His Influence on the Barb   54

The Moorish Invasion of the Iberian Peninsula   57

Moorish Civilisation and Culture   60

CHAPTER IV   **THE GREAT HORSE AND THE AGE OF CHIVALRY**   62

Horses in Ancient Britain   62

The Emergence of the Destrier or Great Horse of War   64

The Norman Invasion of 1066   66

The Crusaders   67

Pilgrimages   69

The Great Tournaments   70

	The Heavy Horse	72
	The Demise of the Weight-carrying Cavalry Horse	75
CHAPTER V	THE AGE OF REVIVAL AND THE BAROQUE HORSE	77
	A Change in the Role of Cavalry	77
	The Development of Riding Academies	79
	Naples and the Neapolitan Horse	79
	The Age of Splendour in France	83
	The Classical School in Germany	85
	The Foundation of the Spanish Riding School of Vienna	85
	Other Famous Breeds within Europe	88
	The Royal Horse of England	90
	The Duke of Newcastle	90
	Renaissance and Post-Renaissance Horsemanship in Spain and Portugal	93
	A Horse Fit for a King	94
CHAPTER VI	THE CAVALRY HORSE AND THE SPORTING HORSE	97
	A Forward-going Horse for the Professional Soldier	98
	The Demise of the Iberian Horse	99
	Equestrian Sport in the Field	99
	The Growth of Hunting Amongst the Middle Classes	100
	A New Style of Riding	100
	The Rejection of High School	101
	The Survival Against All Odds of the Iberian Horse	102
	Iberian Equestrian Sport	103
	The Development of Bullfighting	105
CHAPTER VII	SPAIN — AN INSIGHT INTO HER HISTORY AND CULTURE	108
	The Essential Differences within Iberia	108
	The Spaniard and His Horse	108
	Spanish History Creating a Special Dependence upon the Horse	110
	The Inquisition, Bloodshed and American Gold	111
	Spanish Wars in Europe and the Steady Drain on Spanish Horses	112
	The Dispersal of Breeding Stock during the Peninsular Wars	113
	Revolution!	114
	The Modern Church and the Role Played by the Horse	114
	The Great Horse Fairs of Spain	117
	The Gypsies, the Music and the Dancing	120
CHAPTER VIII	PORTUGAL — AN INSIGHT INTO HER HISTORY AND CULTURE	121
	The Atmosphere of Portugal	121
	The Portuguese Temperament	122
	Portuguese Cavalry	122
	Friendship with England	123

The Period of Discoveries   124

The Portuguese Empire, 1499–1580   125

Troubles with Spain   126

Political Unrest and Revolution   128

Democracy Restored   129

The Horse Fairs of Portugal   130

CHAPTER IX   **THE CORRIDA**   132

The Ancient Art   133

The Sequence of the Fight   134

Tackling the Bull by Hand   137

Unforgettable Moments   138

CHAPTER X   **PRESENT-DAY HORSE BREEDING IN THE PENINSULA**   141

The Great Families   141

The Hidden Life of the Interior   142

Husbandry and Care   142

The Iberian Foot   143

A Surprise Display   144

Where the Herd Roams   145

Care of the Herd   146

Selection of the Colts   148

Brave Bulls   149

The Life of the Stockman   149

The Rationale of Traditional Breeding   151

CHAPTER XI   **BREEDING FOR A PURPOSE**   152

The Old Iberian Factor   152

The Theory of Use Determining Physical Appearance   153

The Emergence of Two Types within One Breed   154

The Influence of Arab Blood in Spain   154

Military Control of State Breeding   155

The Warning of Dr d'Andrade   157

Conflicting Arguments   158

A Change of Course   159

The Selection Process in Portugal   160

The Veiga Horse   162

Breeding for the Future   163

CHAPTER XII   **CLASSICAL HORSEMANSHIP AND THE GREAT IBERIAN SCHOOLS**   165

Iberian Horsemen   165

The Doma Vaquera   168

The High School of the Picadeiro   169

The Young Lusitano   170

Training for the Bullring   172

The Classical Schools of the Peninsula   175

    Nuno Oliveira's School   175

    The Portuguese School of Equestrian Art   176

    The Andalusian School of Equestrian Art   178

CHAPTER XIII	THE ROYAL MARES OF ENGLAND	180
	The Development of the Racing Horse from Early Times	181
	Henry VIII and His Love of Fine Horseflesh	182
	Elizabeth I and Her Master of the Horse	184
	The Royal Mares	184
	The Establishment of Newmarket	186
	The Great Duke of Buckingham	186
	The Abolition of Race Meetings and the Dispersal of the Royal Studs	188
	Resolving a Myth	191
	Enter the Orientals	193
	The Male Foundation Line of the Thoroughbred	193
	'They are Bred out of All the Horses of All Nations'	194
CHAPTER XIV	BRITISH BREEDS WITH IBERIAN INFLUENCE	196
	Britain's Rich Heritage	196
	The Cleveland Bay	197
	The Welsh Cob	199
	The Irish Draught and the Connemara Pony	200
	The British Appaloosa	204
CHAPTER XV	THE CONQUISTADORES AND THE HORSES OF THE AMERICAS	205
	Against All Odds	206
	The Very First Horses	208
	The First Colonial Stud Farms	209
	Cortés and His Horses	210
	The Horse's Role in the Conquest of Mexico	211
	Brazil	213
	Peru	214
	Argentina	218
	The United States	219
	The Quarter Horse	223
CHAPTER XVI	A LOOK INTO THE FUTURE	225
	Special Contributions	225
	Our Research to Date	226
	A Logical Contribution to Breeding	227
	Nature's Authentic Schoolmaster	231
	The Ennoblement of the Art of Dressage in Competition	236
	Versatility in All Spheres	239
APPENDIX	THE ROYAL STUDS OF ENGLAND, 1576–1624	242
REFERENCES		248
INDEX		255

Foreword

by Fernando d'Andrade

The Royal Horse of Europe is a very special book written by a knowledgeable horse-woman who lived in Portugal for many years. She was able not only to admire but also to understand the Iberian horses, breeders and riders.

My father, Ruy d'Andrade, was acknowledged to be the most important researcher of the Iberian horse, and as a writer myself, a breeder of Lusitano horses and President of the Stud Book, I am grateful to the author for this beautifully presented book. She has not only explored and developed the fundamental truths but has also so clearly explained my father's thesis about the origins of the Hispanic Jennet. This book will fill a great gap in the equestrian literature of the world, especially for the English-speaking nations where inconsistencies in existing reports have led to erroneous concepts about the true origins of the Hispanic Jennet and the Barb horse.

I am convinced that *The Royal Horse of Europe* will make an impact on all cultivated people and that the author's original research into our horse's influence in England and all over the world, will restore the noble Hispanic Jennet to his place as one of the most important hot-blooded horses of all time.

July, 1986
Monte Estoril, Portugal

Acknowledgements

The writings of the late Ruy d'Andrade were the strongest influence on this book's conception; the letters and patient assistance of his son Fernando have indebted me to this great horse-breeding family, and I am deeply grateful for permission to reproduce certain photographs and quotations from the d'Andrade library. This *oeuvre* can only be a part payment of my appreciation. My late husband, Henry Loch, had already recognised the need for an English narrative with particular emphasis on the early Iberian influence in Great Britain.

The enthusiastic support received from all over Portugal and Spain has been inspirational. From Lisbon, I would especially like to thank Alfredo Coelho, breeder and equine historian, who uncomplainingly satisfied again and again my quest for the historical truth with original information from his own forthcoming book (see page 254); also, Arsenio Raposo Cordeiro, Director of the Lusitano

Breeders' Association. In Spain, I am indebted to Mr and Mrs Klaas Mesdag, and to Johanna Beattie Baptista for her unstinting research and translations; likewise to Carmen Lopez de Tejada at the Ministry of Tourism in Madrid for permission to reproduce some invaluable photographs. My thanks also to the Domecq and Gonzalez families in Andalusia, and to Nicholas Luard.

Daphne Machin Goodall, author of so many definitive equestrian books on the breeds of the world, was painstakingly enthusiastic as she checked and rechecked my manuscript for historical accuracy, as was Tim Young, history master at Eton College. Anthony Dent gave me valuable historical perspective. In London, the Embassies of Portugal and Spain and their respective Tourist Offices afforded me assistance and encouragement beyond my wildest hopes. Their Excellencies João Hall Themido and D. José J. Puig de la Bellacasa have treated me with great consideration. TAP Air Portugal generously helped me on my last photographic tour; the Austrian, Italian and Moroccan Tourist Boards invaluably assisted throughout my research.

In other countries, it is impossible to thank everybody individually by name, but I would particularly like to mention Pat Boyle in New South Wales, Gilbert H. Jones in Oklahoma, Juan Antonio Azula de la Guerra in Lima, Eileen Craig in Texas, Pamela Reeve Kelly and Barbara Currie in California, and Bent Branderup in Denmark.

At home, the British Museum, the National Army Museum and the British Library, the Newmarket and Sudbury Librarians, Sir John Miller, Dr John Hemming, Charles Harris, Elizabeth and Madeleine McCurley, Neill Dougall, Anthony F. J. Fox, Tom Thompson-Jones, Irene Benjamin, Zoe Lindop, Lewis Champion, Pat Dyke, David Fuller at Ackermann's, Major John Watson at *Country Life*, Colonel Anthony Crossley and Lucinda Green with *Riding Magazine*, have not only given me the assistance I needed but at every turn enthusiasm abounded which was greatly sustaining. I must make special mention of the high quality work of Charles and Jane Hodge at their Lowestoft Photographic Studios, of Bob Rowland for his cartography and line drawings; and gratitude to Sue Angel for her secretarial help.

Mere thanks to Caroline Burt of J. A. Allen's for her belief from the very beginning in this book would be quite inadequate; something more profound is owed to her and to Lesley Gowers my editor who put heart and soul and then *more* into completing *The Royal Horse of Europe* within the tightest of schedules.

Finally, I must thank my husband Richard from the bottom of my heart. After only a year of marriage, he found the equestrian pulse of the Iberian Peninsula beating through all the rooms of our house and yet uncomplainingly he provided me with the discipline and support from his own successful writing experience to sustain me through those recurring crises so well known to every author. Throughout this time, my mother has brought calm consistency to our family life which can never be requited. To my late father whose love of beauty, historical perspective and creative energy inspired me on my journeys through Spain and Portugal, may he please receive the true thanks of a loving daughter.

Sylvia Loch
July, 1986

Special Acknowledgements

The author and publishers are indebted to a small number of distinguished international sponsors who have most generously funded part of the production costs for the artwork of *The Royal Horse of Europe*.

Our immense appreciation and gratitude is owed to:

Mrs Frances Beveridge of Portugal who contributed towards the production of the British sporting plates and the English equestrian portraits and pictures.

Mr and Mrs Richard P. Mellon of the United States of America, who have contributed towards the American pictures, the Spanish photographic plates and the superb equestrian portraits from the Prado.

The Calouste Gulbenkian Foundation of Lisbon who have kindly contributed towards the Portuguese art and photographic work.

Sr Alberto Salema Reis of Lisbon whose present to the author of an original copy of *Luz da Liberal e Nobre Arte da Cavallaria* not only provided some beautiful engravings for reproduction but also enabled the completion of the sponsorship funds required for this book.

Without such magnanimous support *The Royal Horse of Europe* would not have been so completely illustrated. Our renewed thanks to all four sponsors.

Introduction

Noble king! Noble horse! Horses and kings! Royal horses!... However hard I try to picture another king, another horse, another royal equestrian portrait, it is always Van Dyck's image of Charles I on his charger that leaps across the mind's eye when my thoughts turn to art and horses.

For years I studied the history of art, wandering through the great galleries of London, Edinburgh and Glasgow with my father who was a portrait painter in the classical manner. Together, we would explore the portraits of the pre-Renaissance, through the rich delights of the Florentine, Venetian and Flemish schools to the English school of Gainsborough and Reynolds, the French Impressionists, and the modern day. Whilst I grew to love and admire many portraits from many periods, it was always the same Van Dyck portrait, with its curious haunting quality, which imprinted itself upon my brain with such clarity and forcefulness.

It was not, however, until I went to live in Portugal that a strange feeling of déjà vu began to engulf me. The horse of Van Dyck's time did not merely belong to art galleries and history books, it was there before me, in the flesh and very much alive. As I explored the Portuguese interior, especially those remote *quintas* (country houses) built by aristocratic *fidalgos* (noblemen) whose allegiance to the crown had earned them vast estates of cork forest and endless plains where horses and bulls had been bred for centuries, I became more and more excited by this discovery of a horse which most people at home believed had ceased to exist at least two hundred years ago.

From Portugal I went to Spain, and the story was the same. Away from the coast, and far removed from the bullfights so vividly described by Ernest Hemingway, there existed another way of life which centred round a form of horsemanship dating back to pre-Roman times.

I have lived with horses all my life. From early childhood on a lowland Scottish farm where two Clydesdales and a tractor were responsible for tilling the rich arable acres of Midlothian, through a background of hunting and pony-clubbing filling every moment of school holidays, to running a small riding school prior to disappearing to a demanding administrative job in the City of London, horses have been a way of life. For a time I rode out in charge of rides at Hyde Park's Rotten Row in London and there were always polo ponies at nearby Richmond, and a flatmate's brother in the Household Cavalry who would arrange an early dawn exercise before London had sprung to life.

It was not, however, until I came to understand the horses and horsemen of the Iberian Peninsula that my imagination was truly gripped and I realised that those Portuguese *cavaleiros*, bullfighters on horseback who combat the bull according to fixed rules and do not kill him, may be described as the last survivors of mediaeval chivalry in the literal sense of the word, and the last exponents of equestrian art with a practical purpose. This was in striking contrast to the dressage we see on the showgrounds of Goodwood, Fontainebleau and Aachen, and even in the noble hall of the Spanish Riding School where dressage is performed for its own sake – the exercises developing into an art in themselves, culminating in a beautiful spectacle. In the Iberian Peninsula these graceful movements and airs above the ground have retained their original meaning and use – that is, as a combat technique. Martial arts of fighting a mounted enemy have, over the centuries, been replaced by fighting a bull, and to prepare for this deathless combat in the Portuguese bullring, years of painstaking schooling of the horse in High School dressage must be undertaken.

The revelation of finding that the horse of the Van Dyck portrait was none other than the great Iberian war-horse was so exciting and so extraordinarily significant, that I knew a book had to be written to fill the great vacuum of knowledge that exists about this type of horse.

Van Dyck Revisited

I now invite the reader to come with me on an imaginary trip to London's Trafalgar Square to share in this equestrian quest of discovery. As we mount the great marble steps of the National Gallery, we shall find a turning half-way up the second flight of stairs which will lead us eventually to Room 21. There, hanging in splendour, taking up a whole wall of its own, is the inspiration for this book. Over eight-foot square and vibrant with colour and verve, the portrait captures a golden moment in the age of chivalry and the history of the horse. The dun-coloured charger is more than just an impressive steed, fit to bear a Stuart king for the execution of his portrait. It is a special type, a breed, which was loved and revered by every court of Europe. Throughout this book we shall discover how such a horse came to be at the court of St James and what role he played in moulding the shape of modern breeding and equestrian sport. But before we trace him to the country of his origin, let us gaze once more on the immortal brushwork of Van Dyck, the Flemish court painter appointed by Charles I in 1632, whose prolific works of the King and his courtiers were to form an elegant and exquisite record of that doomed court and provide an inspiration for British portrait painters of later generations.

Somehow, the gathering clouds blend too easily against the background of turning leaves on the ochre-coloured tree where a tablet, 'Carulvs Rex Magnae Britainiae', proclaims the identity of the white-faced king. As we stand and gaze we cannot help wondering if Van Dyck, in some unsuspected moment of vision, felt the chill wind of change as he worked his brush over the storm-threatened sky. There is a look of apprehension in the eyes of the king, whilst the troubled eye of the great stallion mirrors his master's unrest. The days of the Stuarts were already numbered; so too were the days of the great chargers, the Spanish and Portuguese horses brought in from the Iberian Peninsula as the fitting mounts for monarchs and noblemen.

Everyone knows that this horse has long disappeared from our island shores. What many of us do not know is that 350 years on, in the land from whence he came, this horse still exists, pure and unchanged.

Threatened by harsh economic times, wars, revolutions, assassinations and the collapse of an empire, miraculously he has survived. You may find him still in the warm southerly plains of the Iberian Peninsula. He is the Iberian horse.

The Iberian Horse Throughout History

History has changed the role of horses throughout the ages, but never so dramatically as in the past four hundred years. The advent of the Thoroughbred has overshadowed the memory of the great breeds of the past, but we should remind ourselves that the Thoroughbred would not exist in its present splendid form had it not been for those noble ancestors with their hot-blooded ancient line. The majority of Europe's modern breeds can be traced back to an Iberian ancestor, and whilst the Arab, Barb, and Turkish horses of the orient cannot be underestimated in their influence, pure-bred Spanish and Portuguese horses were being prolifically used in England to inject new blood into the heavier breeds long before the famous Byerley Turk or the Godolphin Barb ever set foot on English soil.

There is much evidence that as early as the holy Crusades, the armoured knights had begun to bring back a lighter, more athletic horse, and the huge, ponderous carthorse type so often depicted in twentieth-century films and artists' impressions of these religious wars are erroneous.

By the end of the Crusades an altogether more compact horse was proving himself in battle, and as Europe turned in on itself and the cause of the holy campaigns ebbed away towards the end of the thirteenth century, so the Iberian horse became more and more the mount of military leaders as the perimeters of battle moved further from the Holy Land and closer to home.

There was much movement of horses by land and by sea. As early as 1147, England and Portugal had begun their oldest alliance. This was reconfirmed in the historic Treaty of Windsor in 1386 which is being celebrated at a sixth centenary ceremony at Windsor Castle by the heads of state of the two countries, even as this book goes to press.

With the expansion of the great Spanish–Hapsburg empire throughout the Continent, the irruption of the Thirty Years' War and the employment of small firearms necessitating new cavalry tactics, Iberian horses were in demand by every European military leader. They were also arriving by the shipload in the New World, spreading into the interiors of the newly claimed territories and laying down the foundations for all native American breeds.

As their qualities in battle came to be recognised as unsurpassable, so they rose in status, and where once only kings and emperors had ridden them into battle, it was now the turn of all the nobility and officers of rank. But primarily, they were the darling of the courts. The 1st Duke of Newcastle, England's leading exponent of classical horsemanship, wrote in 1658: 'I have seen Spanish horses and had them in my own possession which were proper to be painted after, or fit for a king to mount on a publick occasion.'

The disbeliever might claim that vanity and narcissism were responsible for the popularity of the Iberian horse. One could argue that those physical aspects so revered in the horse of this time were equally desirable in a perfect specimen of manhood. Study again the Van Dyck and the implications are understandable.

There is no doubt at all that this horse is an aristocrat: the long, chiselled, noble head with aquiline and slightly hawked nose, the blazing nostrils and generous eye; the powerful shoulder and proud, arched neck; the finely shaped but sinuous legs, clearly not built for burden but for speed and agility. This horse is a spectacular example of athleticism as well as nobility. But is not this merely a reflection of the laws of Nature? Good breeding goes hand in hand with leadership and performance? As it is with man, so it is with horses.

About the time that the Iberian horse had reached his zenith in the courts of Europe, having proven himself on the battlefield, so the Renaissance had burst upon the cultural scene, awakening in men a love of classical beauty in art, sculpture and poetry and music. We are fortunate indeed that great painters of the calibre of Leonardo and Michelangelo, and soon afterwards Velasquez and Van Dyck, should be so prolific and so accurate in their portrayal of *equus* at that time. Thus we may never be allowed to forget the type of horse which so thrilled our forefathers.

Neither should we forget how our very freedom and development as a nation depended on the courage of our horses. Empires were built from on horseback; battles throughout the ages were won or lost because of the strength or lack of good cavalry. The effulgent Newcastle spoke sobering words when he described the Iberian horse's great courage on the battlefront: 'Fame still adds something surprising, relating to the courage of these horses, which is, that they have carried an officer safe from the field of battle, after their guts have been hanging on the ground and with the same courage and vigour as when he first mounted him.'

In those far-off unmechanised days, suffering by horses in the pursuit of men's bitter quarrels was taken for granted. Horses have died in their unrecorded millions in the service of their country from the first cavalry horses of the Celtiberians, scaling the rocks of Spain and Portugal in support of Hannibal, to the selfless sacrifice of the British horses which galloped undemurring into the Russian guns at Balaclava.

So many horses of diverse breed have played an equally important role in the guardianship of our land, it would be wrong to say one breed was nobler or more courageous than another. Horse lovers all over the world believe their very own particular horse to be the bravest and best, and that is how it should be.

In this book I have tried first and foremost to fill a gap in the bookshelves of the equestrian library of the English-speaking nations, and to clarify and put right a number of popular misconceptions about the horse in history for it is rare that the equestrian public realises just how important a part the Iberian horse has played outside his own special corner of Europe. I have also endeavoured to illustrate how this horse is bred today in the land of his origin, how his perfect manners make him the ideal stock horse on the great *haciendas*, and how in the bullring and the indoor school he transforms into a mythical beast with all the natural choreography and art of a ballet dancer.

In my enthusiasm for this beautiful breed of horse with which I have enjoyed almost two decades of extremely close association, I hope the reader will forgive me if I sometimes eulogise. My defence is that every person I have come across who has spent some time with these horses, particularly on their backs, has felt the same awe and longing to learn more. The Iberian horse has many *aficionados* the world over, particularly in France, Australia and America.

The time has come I feel to introduce this horse to those who do not yet know him. To capture the mood of this book, I have chosen an extract from the moving tribute Ronald Duncan wrote in 1954 for London's Horse of the Year Show. This poem was written for the horse in general; it can with truth and accuracy be applied as an acclaim also to the Spanish and Portuguese horse.

> He serves without servility; he has fought without enmity.
> There is nothing so powerful, nothing less violent,
> There is nothing so quick, nothing more patient.
> England's past has been borne on his back.
> All our history is his industry;
> We are his heirs,
> He is our inheritance.

Left: *Andalusian stallion – Nevado III, from the distinguished Terry stud. (Photo by Arnaiz)*

Below: *Lusitano stallion – Xavante, from the Cordeiro stud, winner of the supreme championship at Lisbon as a three-year-old in 1983. (Photo by Jane Hodge)*

An Alter Real stallion being driven in long reins during a visit to England by the Portuguese School of Equestrian Art. (Photo by Peter Hogan)

Asturians. The green mountain valleys to the north of the Iberian Peninsula have always produced a different type of horse. The Asturians or Galicians shown here were popular long ago with the Romans. (Photo by Ontañón)

CHAPTER I

The Horses of Spain and Portugal

Mas vale caballo que caudal . . . a horse is worth
more than riches.

OLD SPANISH PROVERB

Spanish? Andalusian? Arab? Lipizzaner? Barb? Lusitano? Are these all the same
horse or six separate breeds? If they are separate then why do many of us generally
think of them as one? We are certainly not helped by the conflicting opinions of
reference books and sometimes the statements of our contemporaries abroad.

The old books talk of the Spanish Jennet, and the new of the Iberian horse.
What really is the Iberian horse? Is it a relation of those palfreys, pacers, parade
horses or even ponies we read about in history and which we are encouraged to
think came out of the Iberian Peninsula – i.e. Spain and Portugal? Again, are they
all descendants of the Arab?

It certainly is confusing until the skeins are unravelled, and that is the purpose
of this book. In the first two chapters, we shall define the indigenous horses of
the Peninsula and trace their development from prehistory itself. In Chapter III
we shall investigate the origins of the Barb or Berber horse and explain the relationship of the Arab horse to our story – a much misunderstood subject. In Chapter
IV the significance of breeding for cavalry will be explained. The famous
Lipizzaner, together with other, less celebrated descendants of the Iberian horse,
is discussed in Chapter V, and from the subsequent chapters which delve into
the countryside and traditions of Spain and Portugal, we are led to the modern
Thoroughbred, the horses of America and all the British breeds which owe much
of their quality to the genetic influence of the blood horse of the Peninsula.

All the Horses of the Peninsula

Excluding imported stock and the development of the Arab horse, there have
always existed in the Iberian Peninsula two, if not three, distinct equine types
which date back to Palaeolithic times. These are:

> the Iberian Saddle Horse from the southern half of the Peninsula;
> the Garrano pony from North Portugal; and
> the Galician or Asturian pony/cob from north-west Spain which is
> thought to be a mixture of the first two types.

The Iberian Saddle Horse is the principal subject of this book. As we shall discover
further on in this chapter, he is known by many names, each of which will be

discussed in detail so that, from now on, there will be no confusion. This horse, with his distinctive sub-convex profile, high wither and short-coupled, powerful conformation, was developed first and foremost by ancient man as a war-horse. He originated in the river basins of the hot mountainous regions of Andalusia and the Ribatejo and Alentejo, and gradually spread northwards and eastwards until he became famous throughout the whole Peninsula. So often confused with his probable descendant, the Barb of North Africa, he came to be coveted by all the invading peoples who came to Spain and Portugal along the Mediterranean sea routes, who when they left, carried him away for use in their own cavalries. Thus, throughout history, he was distributed far and wide, reaching, we believe, as far east as Syria long before the birth of Christ.

The Iberian horse with his extraordinarily dominant genes, has survived all manner of change and adversity and still today has a place in breeding for the future. Not only does he excel as a fighting horse, a High School horse, or a horse to work the cattle of Australia, Argentina or the Peninsula, but he is also first and foremost a mount of pure pleasure, a superb riding horse. Europe's oldest and purest saddle breed, he is truly a Great Horse.

Although we shall not dwell for long on the horses of the north, it would be misleading to omit this distinctively different indigenous type altogether, but it should be understood that this second type bears little or no relation to our story of the royal horse of Europe.

The Garrano Pony

In the northern hilly regions of Portugal and in the extreme north-west of Spain, where the wet green mountain valleys are rich in grass, there exists in direct contrast to the Iberian Saddle Horse, a pony type of concave profile. From early cave paintings which have been radiocarbon-dated to Palaeolithic times, we know that this pony breed has occupied the Iberian Peninsula for roughly the same length of time as the Iberian Saddle Horse. Despite inevitable cross-breeding, this breed has remained remarkably unchanged from those early days and is probably put to the same purpose today as he was then. Largely used as a beast of burden, for turning the water wheel on remote homesteads, for moving timber and cork deep within the forests, he is also occasionally used as a mount for the country people. This 'little horse', as I prefer to call him, for he does not have the kind, sweet temperament to which we in Britain have become accustomed in our mountain and moorland breeds, is not ridden for pleasure or sport, but used rather as a donkey or mule. He is to be seen winding up and down the steep narrow paths of the thickly wooded countryside of the colder, wet climate of the north, often pulling a small cart.

He ranges in size from 11 to 13 h.h. and is often bay or brown in colour. Chestnuts are normally cross-bred and are not the indigenous pure type. His conformation is pleasing although a little light, but he has proved himself to be surprisingly hardy. The Portuguese Army, for example, uses a number of these little horses as pack ponies for machine guns on military exercises.

Over the last century the breed has undergone certain changes due to a steady infusion of Arab blood organised by the Portuguese Ministry of Agriculture. However, there still remain a large number of the original, pure type.

Known as the Garrano after the Garrano do Minho and Trás-os-Montes province where he is principally bred, it has been suggested by several equestrian researchers that the word 'garron' used in Scotland for Highland ponies came from the same Celtic background. Dr Ruy d'Andrade, the great Portuguese hippologist, was convinced after a lifetime of study and research particularly on teeth and the facial structure[1] of the horses of the Peninsula, that all the ponies of Europe came from one common ancestor, and it would appear that these migrated down into France and Spain from northern Europe after the Ice Age. Why this breed should become concentrated in the north-west of the Peninsula can be explained by the fact that the early Celtic traders of ancient Britain and Ireland, Belgium, France, Portugal and Spain may have encouraged the breeding of these horses in the areas closest to their ancient sea routes, as horses were exchanged for meat, hide, fat and wool. (See Chapter IV.)

CONVEX AND CONCAVE PROFILES

A typical Iberian head showing a slight convexity of forehead and of profile. Note the long tapering nose (sometimes this is referred to as Roman-nosed). The eye is almond-shaped. The whole appearance is fine and noble.

A typical concave profile as found in the pony breeds of the north of the Peninsula. Note the angle of mouth and cheek compared to those of the Iberian. The eye is rounded.

The true Roman nose of the cold-blood draught horse. In contrast to the Iberian head, the forehead is flat and convexity sudden and pronounced. The nose is coarse and fleshy at the base. The eye is somewhat angular. Overall appearance is heavy.

In her book, *A History of Horse Breeding*, Daphne Machin Goodall suggests that in some Garranos 'it is not difficult to envisage the future Andalusian or Lusitano'. I am unable to agree with the principle behind this, for the pure-bred Garrano is of concave profile, whilst the pure-bred Lusitano or Andalusian has always been of sub-convex or straight profile, but it is a confusing issue as the two types have been sucessfully crossed from time to time. There is the possibility that some of the wild horses of South and North America stem from just such a horse, although in the majority of opinions these are more likely to have descended from the Sorraia, the primitive forebear of the Iberian Saddle Horse.

The Garrano is often to be found trotting behind gypsy caravans and wagons, taking the itinerant people of the Peninsula from fair to fair, where there is always

1. The subject of facial structure is researched in all Dr d'Andrade's books. Similar remains of Celtic ponies to those found in the Iberian Peninsula (Garranos) have been found in England and dated at approximately 10 AD. The main features being a narrow, slightly dished profile.

a great demand for these little horses. At one time they were extremely popular for trotting races, but interestingly enough have never been prized as children's ponies despite their handy size.

Ponies in Spain are sometimes referred to as *jacas*. This is misleading, for the word *jaca* is more often used to indicate a cross-bred working horse (see Chapter X) and from *jaca* comes the word *hacané* in French, and hackney in English.

Before we leave the Garrano, it is important for those readers interested in breeding to remember the significance of the convex-shaped head. In the rare instance of a supposedly pure-bred Iberian horse appearing with a dished face, Arab blood is normally blamed but research has shown that this is often caused by a throw-back to some early crossing with one of these little horses from the north of the Peninsula.

The Asturian

Time and again, we read in history of a breed of horse originating in the north-west tip of Spain, particularly concentrated in the Asturias, which is neither war-horse nor pony. These horses were well-known to the Romans, who called them Asturcones, and Pliny (23–79 AD), the Roman naturalist, describes them thus: 'the Galician and Asturian tribes of the north breed a kind of horse which they call *thieldones* or *celdones* in their language. This smaller strain [one imagines he is comparing them to the Iberian Saddle Horse] do not trot but have a special easy pace produced by alternately moving both legs on the one side.'

Not only were these horses popular with the Romans, who did not use stirrups, but they also became extremely popular in France during the Middle Ages. Easily trained, or naturally inclined to other gaits, they were comfortable to sit to and became ideal presents for knights to give their ladies at court. Known as palfreys in England, the French word for these lightweight hacks was *haubini*. For centuries, the Irish had been importing these horses across the Bay of Biscay, and *haubini* gave rise to the anglicised version of hobbye, later hobby-horse, which generally depicted a comfortable pacing nag.

It is almost certain that the Asturian developed as a result of crossing between the pony type of the north, and the Iberian Saddle Horse, from which would be derived the kind temperament and feeling of comfort in the saddle. The larger palfrey (he was unlikely to have been more than 14 h.h. in the Middle Ages) would have had more Iberian blood, and the smaller one, more Celtic blood.

Today the Asturian appears to have degenerated, and in those remaining wild herds centred round Mount Sueve, the purest animals are no more than 12 to 13 h.h. and are almost all black. Sadly, many are slaughtered for meat, despite the concern that has been shown by horse lovers.

Their first cousin, the Galician pony, which is roughly the same height, is normally brown, chestnut or bay. These animals also run in semi-feral herds and the people of Spain's Pontevedra district make a festive occasion of rounding them up at certain times of year where much ceremony accompanies the branding and culling of this little-understood race of horse.

It is a pity that history does not record more about the Asturian, for Spanish palfreys or amblers were highly prized before the Iberian war-horse became so famed, and no doubt these little horses have a story all of their own to tell.

Having left the other indigenous breeds of Portugal and Spain behind us, we may now concentrate on the Iberian Saddle Horse, but before we discuss today's Andalusian and Lusitano, let us first look at his early ancestor.

The Sorraia – Early Ancestor to the Iberian Saddle Horse

It is now recognised without doubt by hippologists and natural historians specialising in *equus*, that the Sorraia is the primitive ancestor of the Iberian Saddle Horse. Still to be found in Portugal today, having been carefully preserved and cultivated from a last-remaining herd by Dr d'Andrade, the Sorraia bears the strong dominant genes of the sub-convex profile, the high trotting action, and the close-coupled compact body of his modern descendants. Except in profile, he closely resembles that other primitive horse the Tarpan, which is the prehistoric ancestor of the Indo-European domesticated horse. The Sorraia represents *equus stenonius*, one of the six types of original wild horse known to man.

This horse takes his name from the Rivers Sor and Raia, small tributaries of the Sorraia (see map) which waters the plains where these horses are bred. The breed is extremely hardy and noted for its ability to survive on very little food of the poorest quality. Rarely exceeding 13.2 h.h. but being tough and wiry, the Sorraia was popular with local stockmen and for centuries was the mount of cow-

Sorraia stallion – the Sorraia is the ancient ancestor to the Iberian Saddle Horse. After thousands of years this primitive type still retains all the characteristics that we find in cave paintings in the south of the Peninsula. (Photo by Sally Anne Thompson)

The Tarpan. This primitive horse, similar to the Sorraia, is bred in Poland in semi-domestication for zoological research. (Photo by Daphne Machin-Goodall)

boys who slept rough with their herds or horses and bulls, moving them round the Ribatejo and Alentejo estates. Nowadays greatly reduced in numbers, it is still maintained as a pure herd by the d'Andrade family not only for national interest but also for purposes of research by zoologists and geneticists from all over the world. Moreover, a number of historians are convinced that the Sorraia horse, prolific also in Spain at that time, played a greater part in the ancestry of the mustangs of South America than the more refined Andalusian.

The colouring of the Sorraia is of special interest, being a distinctive yellow or mustard dun, or mouse grey with a black dorsal stripe, black-tipped ears and a heavy, luxuriant black mane and tail, often streaked with the blonde or mouse colour of the main body. The legs are invariably striped horizontally (*zebrado*) and in the summer when the coat lightens, pale spots are often apparent on the belly. It is evident that in the Sorraia there has been no introduction at any time of oriental or north European blood. This helps to show the influence of other genes which over the millennia were to refine the Iberian Saddle Horse as he crossed and re-crossed into North Africa during his early evolution.

The Iberian Saddle Horse

From the primitive forebear of the Sorraia, we have now arrived at the point in our text where we may pursue the subject of our story, the great Iberian war-horse or saddle horse. Before we go on to discuss the legion of names by which he is known, and the changes in his evolution which brought about the metamorphosis from the humble Sorraia to the full-blooded charger, let us first examine his appearance so that a firm picture of today's modern Iberian horse may be established in the mind's eye:

> The Iberian horse should be of noble proportions constituting a spectacle of beauty combined with efficacy of performance as a suitable mount for work with bulls and cattle, manège work and as a versatile, comfortable riding horse.
>
> His height should be between 15 and 16.2 h.h.
>
> His colour[2] may be any true colour, including dun and chestnut, and there is a traditional preponderance for darkly dappled grey.
>
> His head should be of noble aspect, with a slightly rounded forehead; alert, vivid eyes inclined to be almond-shaped; generous well-shaped ears; a straight or sub-convex profile lengthening into a finely tapering muzzle. The cheek is normally deep and well rounded.
>
> The mane and forelock is heavy and luxurious.
>
> The neck is well proportioned, deep and muscular with a pronounced arch on the upper line, set into a powerful, sloping shoulder. The wither is long and high allowing excellent forward and upward movement from the forelimbs.
>
> The back is short, with strong, broad loins; the rib cage is deep and inclined to be flat at the sides thus enabling good elevated movements.
>
> The hindquarters are rounded on top with a sloping croup and low-set tail which is heavy and held tightly when in movement.
>
> The extremities are slender but muscular with excellent dense bone. The cannon bones and hocks are somewhat longer in relation to the forearm than is normal in other breeds, and the stifles have a slightly elbowed appearance. The pasterns are sloping and elastic giving spring to the gaits especially over hard ground. The second thigh is often well developed. The hooves are neat, round and high.
>
> The gaits are powerful, rounded and lively and the horse is noted particularly for his excellent trotting ability which stems from his energetic forward-going hock action. The horse is famed for his acceleration over a given distance and his ability to collect and gather himself into a position of supreme balance. It is this athletic control of his compact frame which has led to his success as a fighting horse and enables him to enjoy the demands of school work.
>
> Strong and hardy of constitution he survives well on relatively modest feeding, and the adult horse should give an overall impression of roundness, particularly in the back and quarters when ridden.
>
> His outstandingly fine temperament makes him easy to school and train; he is sweet and gentle in the stable, and combines gaiety with courage and obedience in all his work.

---

2. Since the introduction of the Spanish Stud Book in 1912 many of the traditional old colours of the Iberian horse became unacceptable. Today in Spain it is not possible to register chestnuts, palominos, pieds or skewbalds. By contrast, in the Portuguese Stud Book for the Lusitano or Lusitano-Andalusian horse, no colour is ineligible. At present a number of chestnut horses are registered, but so far there have been no registrations of pieds or skewbalds although technically they are not disallowed.

Stallions and mares tend to build up a very strong relationship of trust and fidelity with their owners.

All these characteristics form the basic genetic inheritance of the Iberian Saddle Horse. As with all breeds, however, different studs have over the centuries selectively bred for different purposes. Thus in some Iberian horses we find a heavier or a lighter strain, depending on the purpose for which they have been bred, e.g. war, bullfighting, parade, carriage driving, work with cattle, showing in hand and so on. There is no doubt that some of the horses in the extreme south of Andalusia have a greater preponderance of oriental blood than horses further north in Castile and to the west in Portugal. Basically, however, the overall look of uniformity is firmly fixed except where outcrossing has occurred in recent times and brought in other characteristics.

Iberian mares are smaller and lighter in build than stallions, but those few that are used for riding will often make up physically until they have all the appearance of the Iberian stallion, even to the extent of developing a highly crested neck which is normally only associated with the male of the species.

A Plethora of Names for the Same Horse

Iberian Saddle Horses are bred in four different regions of the Iberian Peninsula. Historically and genetically, they are all the same horse.

Andalusian, Spanish, Carthusian, Lusitano, Portuguese, Alter Real, Ginete or Jennet, Peninsular, Castilian, Extremeño, Zapatero, Iberian . . .

It is ironic that a horse, which until recent times was in danger of becoming a rare breed in its original form, and which has receded from the mainland mass of Europe where it was once so esteemed into that isolated south-westerly corner from whence it first emerged, should possess such a legion of names. Confusion abounds amongst the most distinguished of equestrian scholars; even in the two countries concerned, Spain and Portugal, there are some who are unwilling to face the unquestionable historical facts: that all these horses are basically the same breed.

Why, then, has he acquired so many names? There are many reasons.

The name of this horse depends mostly on the geographical name of the breeding area and little more. Due to historical events, however, these names have changed from time to time. Sometimes, as will be seen, the name has remained the same, but the geographical area to which it originally referred, changed both in size and ownership. No wonder this has baffled the experts. There has arisen an artificial differential within a breed which was never genetically divided. The importance of the breed in the eyes of the world has been reduced, and its impact today in terms of status and popularity has diminished as a direct result. Let us untangle the threads of the mystery and we shall see that the situation is perfectly straightforward. All these horses are quite clearly one and the same noble breed.

Andalusian

In this name lies the greatest complexity of all. We know from the map below where Andalusia is today. What very few scholars realise is that at the time of the Moorish invasion in 711 AD the Arabs termed the whole of the Iberian Peninsula – with the exception of the Asturias – Andalus (see map on page 40). This name is thought to have originally been Vandalus, i.e. Land of the Vandals. Andalusia is most likely therefore to be a derivative of the Moorish name which in the eighth century was used by the Moors to indicate the entire Peninsula.

Gradually, however, Andalus came to refer to the southern provinces. As the Moors were forced back by the Christian knights, first out of Lusitania or Portugal, and then gradually from Castile, their whole empire of Andalus retracted its

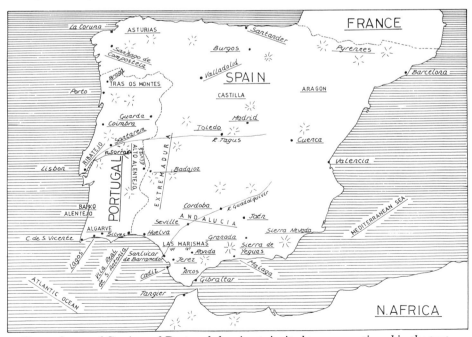

General map of Spain and Portugal showing principal towns mentioned in the text.

borders. Eventually, only that area around Seville, Cordoba and Granada, with the pleasant lands to the south, were included. This today constitutes Andalusia.

Thus while the term Andalusian horse generally indicates a horse whose fore-bears were bred in Andalusia as we know it, it would be technically correct to term the following horses as Andalusian:

an Iberian Saddle Horse bred in Lisbon;
an Iberian Saddle Horse bred in the Basque country;
an Iberian Saddle Horse bred in Valença;
an Iberian Saddle Horse bred in Malaga.

Breeders of the old school recognise the all-embracing nature of the name, and perhaps it should not have been dropped from the official Stud Book within Spain. Others argue, however, that the term Spanish was always recognised worldwide whilst the term Andalusian was peculiar to the Peninsula.

Foreign admirers of the Iberian horse generally consider that the name Andalusian indicates only the horses specifically bred in the rural area of the plains round the River Guadalquivir. Certainly it is accepted that the early Iberian horse in Spain developed principally in this area, before migrating in all directions. Even today, there is a greater concentration of animals in this region (as there is round the River Tagus in Portugal) than in any other province of Spain. But the name Andalusian is more far-reaching than most people imagine.

Pure-bred Andalusian stallion – an overall picture of symmetry. Note the powerful neck, chest and shoulder, and the fine limbs typical of the blood horse. As with many examples of the modern Andalusian, the quarters are slightly more horizontal and the tail is set higher than in the Lusitano.
(Photo by Sally Anne Thompson)

Al-Andalus. The name has a moonlight, magical quality about it. This last outpost of the Moors so transformed the culture of that fertile land that it is still the undisputed centre of horse breeding. While the rest of Spain has become industrialised to the north and east, Andalusia has benefited from the superb system of irrigation organised by the Moorish invaders and it is here that sherry, the fortified wine which takes it name from Jerez de la Frontera, is made, preserving the rurality of the province and its independence from so many of the demands of the twentieth century.

Andalusia has always attracted foreigners. At the heart of the sherry industry are many Anglo-Spanish families, and names such as Croft, Sandeman, Williams and Humbert, Terry and Osborne abound, reminding us of the English families who first came over to this part of Spain in the eighteenth century to organise the production of the special white grape for the then highly lucrative export of sherry.

It was, however, the ancient monasteries of Andalusia which first became the organised centre of horse breeding in the province. Alongside their carefully tended vineyards, the Catholic monks were responsible for the establishment of a planned breeding programme for the Iberian Saddle Horse, and from the fifteenth century onwards, the monasteries developed horses of pure blood as a work of dedication to the Church and the Crown. Spain's might as a great Catholic power had always been recognised as being attributable to her horses and cavalry, and the monks of Andalusia preserved the excellence of these horses as an act of devotion. This was further encouraged by the Inquisition.

In recapitulation, therefore, the term Andalusian – even in 1986 – may refer to an Iberian Saddle Horse bred by one of the Andalusian families with bloodlines dating back to the records of ancient monasteries built in the reign of Ferdinand and Isabella (1479–1516). It may also refer to a Portuguese-bred Iberian horse, or an Iberian horse bred as far north as Santander.

Spanish

Because of the misinterpretation of the term Andalusian, it was decided by the Spanish Breeders' Association in 1912 that with the introduction of a national Stud Book, from this date onwards all pure-bred Iberian horses, which previously had been called Andalusian should be known as Spanish. This was largely augmented to appease breeders from areas outside Andalusia who felt that the stud farms within the Andalusian belt enjoyed an unfair advantage, particularly as regards foreign trade.

Many breeders were against the adoption of the term Spanish, for within the country the name Andalusian was traditional and its historical significance dated back over a thousand years. It was also felt that the term Spanish could imply any type of horse bred in Spain, including the Galician or the heavy Breton horses popular in the north. Despite much controversy, the Spanish advocates won the day, and today the official term in the Stud Book is *Pura raza espanola* – Spanish pure breed.

Outside the Peninsula, however, the term Spanish has always been popular. Extraordinarily enough, it was also used much earlier, well into the seventeenth century, to encompass Portuguese horses as well. This is easily explained by the fact that from Roman times – approximately one thousand years before the Moorish invasion – Hispania (from whence came our modern term Spain) was one dominion. This included the whole bloc of modern Spain and Portugal with the Peninsula being divided into three provinces.

Anything that came out of any one of these provinces was termed Hispanian, or more latterly Spanish; even if it came from Lusitania (which corresponded to modern Portugal).

Although Portugal became a separate kingdom in the early twelfth century, she was to join herself to Spain under the crown of Castile in 1581, and therefore, in the eyes of the rest of the world, for the greater part of the sixteenth and seventeenth centuries, the two countries were as one. Such was the dominance of the larger country that the word Spanish became all-encompassing, regardless of whether it referred to Portugal or to Spain. This included references to horses, one of the most prized acquisitions collected from the Peninsula during legitimised plundering raids of war and conflict. Whilst Spanish horses could be easily moved by land to France and the Hapsburg countries, and via the Mediterranean to Italy and further east, Portuguese horses and Spanish horses from the north west of Spain had to travel by sea to England and Ireland, and on many occasions contributed to the dowries of Spanish and Portuguese princesses en route to wed English princes or kings.

Thus, for example, the Spanish coursers (see Chapter V) imported by Elizabeth I could have been Spanish or Portuguese, as could have been the Spanish Jennets ridden by the Duke of Newcastle after his patron, Charles II, married the Portuguese princess Catherine of Braganza. It is known from research, however, that the majority of horses came from Cordoba in Spain, as it was here that the court was established, but excellent horses of the same type were always bred in both countries. Since Spain officially recognised Portugal's independence in 1668, the problem of nomenclature begins to resolve itself in this area, and certainly today, the term Spanish only refers to Iberian Saddle Horses bred in the country of Spain itself.

Carthusian

The Carthusian is not a separate breed but is clearly recognised as an important offshoot of the Iberian Saddle Horse or Andalusian. Referred to by the Spanish as *Cartujano*, the main difference between this type and the other Andalusians is that successive breeders have selectively bred for an oriental look in an attempt to recapture the appearance of the early Berber horses which came to the Peninsula long before the birth of Christ. The *Cartujano* is one of Spain's most prestigious lines of saddle horse coming as it does from one of the oldest recorded stud books in the world.

In 1476 Don Alvaro Obertus de Valeto left ten thousand acres of land to the fathers of La Cartuja, the Carthusian monastery lying by the Guadalete River, just to the south of Jerez de la Frontera. This led to the establishment of a particularly fine herd of Spanish mares said to be comprised of the purest descendants of the early Andalusian. A translation from *El Caballo en Espana*, a magnificent book compiled by the Spanish government in 1976, describes the *Cartujano* in the following glowing terms:

> 'The monks of the Cartuja in Jerez, with deep vision and an understanding of the importance of the Spanish horse in their region, taking advantage of the magnificent quality of the earth, with their pastures and facilities, devoted themselves completely to the production of the Spanish horse, eliminating as far as possible the crosses with other breeds, going back to its origin in the African-Berber which lacked the height of the other Africans and the Andalusian Spaniard, but due to its great quality the size was compensated for by its lightness, temper and rapidity.'

All through the centuries that followed, the Carthusian monks jealously guarded these horses and even defied a royal edict which the studs at Seville and Cordoba had been forced to obey to introduce Neapolitan and central European blood at one period just after the Reconquest, when attempts were made to heighten the Andalusian.

A certain amount of mystique built up around the closely guarded secret of selective breeding which only the monks understood. Not only were the Carthusian fathers guardians of the purity of line, they were also strong supporters of the Spanish system of equitation. For when – as we shall read in Chapter V – the French riding style *École à la bride* became fashionable, the Spanish monks energetically opposed it, even threatening to excommunicate those who rode in the 'style of the bastard school, forgetting that of *gineta* [the traditional Spanish horse] which has given so many days of glory to Spain and to Religion.'

The buildings of the ancient stud farm still exist in Jerez in front of the old monastery, which is closed to the public but still operates quietly behind its huge heavily ornate locked gates. There are no horses left today, for all the *Cartujanos* were removed from La Cartuja in 1835, but over the gate the name *Salto el Cielo* (Leap into Heaven) remains.

Andalusian-Carthusians are still bred in Spain although the original stock was greatly depleted. Some horses managed to escape the raids of Napoleon's rapacious armies during the Peninsular Wars, and had it not been for the Zapata family who intervened and continued to breed on the guidelines laid down by the Carthusian monks, the line would have been lost. Church properties were dissolved throughout Spain in 1835 (see Chapter VII) and all the horses went into private hands. In recent times the Carthusian branch of the Spanish horse has been continued by the Terry family, Don Vincente Romero and more latterly by Don Francisco Chica Navarro.

Typical of this celebrated horse is a wide front and a smaller lighter body than the average Andalusian. It is the face which is particularly distinctive: broad of brow and straight of profile in the upper part, the head is somewhat smaller than usual, but the nose is long and finely tapering with a slight depression at the base of the nostrils which makes a small 's' along the lower profile. Spaniards are also proud to point out two tiny horns which exist in some *Cartujano* horses between the ears; this is always the subject of much interest and speculation about the breed's ancient past. Despite their lack of height, Carthusian horses are always greatly in demand and fetch extremely high prices in Spain to this day.

Lusitano

From the old Latin came the names *Lusitania* for Portugal and *Hispania* for Spain. Curiously, while the term Hispanico[3] is rarely used by itself in Spain, Lusitano has become the everyday adjective and proper noun to describe Portugal's Iberian Saddle Horse.

Only in recent years has the term Lusitano become so popular. Previously – as we have seen – Andalusian was used throughout the Peninsula to denote the breeds of Spain and Portugal. When the Spanish Stud Book dropped the name Andalusian as an official title, Portugal in turn took up a more nationalistic name for her horse, although this was not used officially until 1966. The name Lusitano means nothing more nor less than Portuguese, and a male horse is described as a Lusitano; a mare, a Lusitana. As the word for breed in Portuguese is a feminine noun, i.e. *raça*, the adjective in this case is Lusitana. Therefore *pura raça lusitana* means pure-bred Lusitanian.

The Lusitano horse, or, as it was often called in the past, the Portuguese-Andalusian, is identical to the Spanish-Andalusian in appearance. They are both pure-bred Iberian Saddle Horses sharing the same heritage and evolution. Any differences which occur between the two breeds today are the result of selective

Pure-bred Lusitano stallion. The short-coupled body conformation with deep shoulder, powerful chest, high wither and sloping croup are typical of the Iberian Saddle Horse. The limbs are long and slender, and the head distinctive in its convexity. (Photo by Sally Anne Thompson)

3. *Hispanico* is more usually used as a term for horses in conjunction with other names, e.g. cross-breds are referred to as Hispano-Arabs, Hispano-Anglo-Arabs, etc.

breeding in modern times, with horses nowadays being bred for new purposes. The most noticeable difference today is that the Lusitano has retained a more convex profile in the head, whereas recent selection in Spain has favoured the oriental look, and in many lines this old characteristic of convexity has been bred out. Like the Andalusian, the Lusitano is one of the world's most ancient breeds and is bred principally in the undulating Ribatejo and Alentejo districts which are well watered by the River Tagus to the east of Lisbon and spread deep into Portugal's agricultural heartland.

The breeding of the Lusitano is inextricably tied up with the breeding of bulls, and large sales and horse fairs are held annually at the old fortified market town of Santarem, and at Golegã, which lies in the centre of the horse-breeding district. Many Spaniards come to Portugal to buy Lusitanos, which are bred all the way through this fertile strip to the Spanish border at Badajoz. As in Spain, horses have been bred in Portugal in the same areas since prehistory, but being a poorer country Portugal has never produced as many horses as her more powerful neighbour and at one time (see Chapter VIII) had to import from Spain to improve her bloodlines. Since that period, in the early seventeenth century, Portugal has concentrated on preserving the purity of her horses and many claim that the Lusitano today is probably the closest descendant of the famous horses which spread throughout Europe in the Renaissance from the Spanish empire.

Portuguese

This term is rarely used on its own but invariably it implies horses of the Iberian saddle type and not of the other breeds which exist in the north.

Alter Real

Alter do Chão, a small town which gives its name to the Alter breed of horse, lies in a corner of the Portuguese Alentejo province and boasts a national stud where this Portuguese offshoot of the Andalusian horse is found. *Real* is Portuguese for royal, and indeed this stud was founded by the Braganza royal family for the purpose of supplying the royal manège in Lisbon with suitable High School and carriage horses. In 1748 a herd of approximately fifty of the best Andalusian mares was imported from Spain, and land was made over from one of King Dom João V's royal estates for the purpose of serious breeding. After the accession of his son, Dom José I, the royal stud at Alter benefited greatly from this king's ardent enthusiasm for classical equitation, and in order to expand the stud, various neighbouring properties were rented to accommodate the increasing stock. The best Iberian horses had always been bred in the last frontiers between Portugal and Spain where war had continued intermittently for centuries, and the grazing at Alter promoted a very fine line of horse which became respected all over the Peninsula. It was here that Portugal's most famous Master of the Horse, the Marquis of Marialva (see Chapter V) presided, administering selective breeding and laying down the principles of the High School work.

During the Peninsular Wars, the Portuguese studs suffered in the same way as the Spanish. Many of Alter's best horses were swept away between 1807 and

1811 by Napoleon's pillaging army as they desecrated the Portuguese countryside, and breeding went into a decline. In the following years, various attempts were made to re-establish the stud to its former state of glory, and English, Norman and German blood was introduced with poor results. There was a later attempt to 'Arabise' the Alter, but it was not until new Andalusian blood was reintroduced near the end of the nineteenth century that the breed really began to improve.

Matters looked grave again for the Alter Real horses at the beginning of the twentieth century, when Portugal renounced her monarchy. The archives at Alter were almost completely destroyed and with a government decision to discontinue the stud, stallions were taken away for gelding. Had it not been for the last-minute intervention of one man, the Alter Real line would have been lost to posterity. Dr Ruy d'Andrade arrived at Alter just in time to save two stallions and a handful of mares. By 1942 he was able to hand over to the Ministry of Agriculture a small but thriving stud of this original line.

Today, although small compared to its former position of prestige, the stud is state owned and is well maintained and respected throughout the Peninsula. As we shall read in Chapter XI, the Portuguese select their best stud stallions from working stock and therefore Alter Real horses are trained for High School.

Typical of the Iberian Saddle Horse described on page 23, this offshoot of the breed is always bay in colour, and due to in-breeding was at one time smaller than the average Lusitano, but now stands around 15–16 h.h. They are immensely strong and powerful however, with a high breast and a broad, muscular back which appears slightly swayed. Their long pasterns and strong hocks give them a spectacular, high-stepping action and under saddle they look very much bigger than they actually are. The stud is one of Portugal's few cultural extravaganzas and represents a living monument to this small country's equestrian heritage.

Jennet or Ginete

The Iberian Saddle Horse of either Spain or Portugal is often referred to in historical terms as a Jennet[4] (anglicised version) or *Ginete* (Spanish version). The name is a colloquial word derived from the adjective *gineta* which describes the type of horsemanship employed in the execution of the various equestrian exercises which has made this horse so famous over the centuries. Riding *à la gineta* therefore implied the Iberian style of horsemanship adopted in the battlefield or in the Spanish or Portuguese countryside for work with bulls and cattle. In England, France, Germany and Portugal, the term came to imply the Iberian horse itself, but in Spain a *ginete* indicated the rider. Many historians take the view that the *ginete* style of riding was brought to the Iberian Peninsula by the Moors in the early eighth century. This we know to be incorrect by examining early engravings of mounted Iberian horsemen dating back to the fourth century which show a bent leg in the saddle, indicating that stirrups were already being used during that early period.

The term *ginete*, implying a horseman, dates back to an ancient Greek word

---

4. The last reference for Jennet in everyday parlance in England comes in Disraeli's novel *Lothair*, published in 1870: 'The dames and damsels vaulted on their barbs and genets.'

Top: *Cerbero, a renowned Spanish 'springer', painted by J. G. von Hamilton. 'Springer' in those days did not indicate a jumping horse in our sense of the word but rather a horse which performed good leaps and airs above the ground. (See Chapter V.)*
Above: *One of the fifty-five equestrian portraits in the Wilton House Riding School collection by Baron Reis d'Eisenberg. As with many of the horses featured in the collection he was probably of pure Spanish blood. (See Chapter V.) (Courtesy the Earl of Pembroke)*

Emperor Charles V (King Charles I of Spain) at the Battle of Muhlberg, 1547, by Titian, Prado Museum, Madrid.

meaning light-armed soldier and through Byzantine influence çame to be used in the Berber vocabulary as *zenete* meaning cavalryman. The root of this word, however, goes back further. From approximately 4000 BC, all Portugal and northern Spain was known as the land of the *Cynetes* – long before the Roman name Lusitania was adopted. There also existed an ancient tribe far to the east of Spain, near Valencia, which were named the *Gymnetes*. As both these peoples were skilled in mounted combat on their nimble Iberian horses, it seems clear how the word came into the language. The Greeks, during their occupation of the Peninsula in or around 2000 BC, would have incorporated the term into their own language, and by the time it was used by the Moors of the eighth century, it had already been in existence for several thousand years.

The word Jennet in English was first used in the sixteenth century. In a report on the Royal Studs of England by Prospero d'Osma (see Chapter XIII) in 1576, we read of Jennet mares from Spain; the name occurs again and again in the Duke of Newcastle's book on classical equitation, *A General System of Horsemanship* (first published in 1658); and Thomas Blundeville, a prolific writer on equestrian affairs from Norfolk, in *The Fower Cheifest Offyces of Horsemanshippe*, published just under one hundred years earlier, describes the Jennet thus:

> 'I have heard some of the Spaniards to set such praise on their jennet's courage, as they have not letted to report, that they have carried their riders out of the field, I cannot tell how manie miles, after the jennets themselves have been shot cleane through the bodies with harquebushes.'

This praise of the Jennet in war is in much the same vein as Newcastle's descriptions, and until the end of the eighteenth century the word was used fairly prolifically in the English language. It is a useful term for, similar to the word 'hunter', it is more than just a name but indicates the purpose for which the horse concerned is bred. It sums up the Iberian Saddle Horse extremely expressively.

Peninsular

This is a very loose term, popular in the early twentieth century in both Spain and Portugal, again signifying the Iberian Saddle Horse.

Castilian

This term, not often used today, denotes a typical Iberian Saddle Horse bred in the province of Castile. Castilian war-horses were renowned for their courage and during the reign of King Ferdinand and Queen Isabella of Castile (1474–1516) were prominent during the wars of the Reconquest. Breeders of the Castilian encouraged weight-carrying ability as well as agility, and today the Castilian or *Castellano* is heavier than the Andalusian from the south of the Peninsula.

Extremeño

The Extremeño horse from Extremadura is again an Iberian horse from the province of the same name, and like the Castilian is a heavier horse than, for example, the Carthusian.

Zapatero

Some English and American horse encyclopaedias refer to the Zapatero or Zapata as a separate breed in Spain. This is incorrect. The Zapata family, as we have read, did much to assist in the continuity of the Carthusian horse, and a Zapatero horse would merely indicate that it had come from the Zapata stud. In 1858 the stud of the Zapata brothers was bought by Vicente Romero Garcia, a Jerez land-owner, and some horses from the Zapata strain later passed into the hands of Fernando Terry just after the Spanish Civil War. One of the best known Zapata horses from Spain, Honroso IV, was sent to the Spanish Riding School of Vienna to infuse new blood into the Lipizzaner stud at Piber.

Iberian

This is the anglicised version of the term *ibérico* in Spanish and Portuguese. Although not extensively used in the Iberian Peninsula itself, it is a very useful term for collectively indicating the indigenous saddle horse of the two countries, be he Andalusian, Carthusian, Alter Real, Lusitano or old-fashioned Jennet.

From now on in this book, for the purposes of clarification, the term Iberian will be used when talking of these horses in a general sense. When, however, it is possible to specify the horse concerned and from whence he comes, this will be accomplished. It is hoped, however, that it will be less confusing for the reader if this general rule is applied within these pages, and the words saddle horse will be dropped, so that Iberian stands clearly on its own with all its incorporated meaning.

Dismissing the Villano

One other name which appears in an ancient Italian book about the horses of the Peninsula and has consequently been taken up by modern researchers, is the Villano horse or *Villani di Spagna*. The translation of a similar word in Portuguese (*vilão*) and Spanish (*villano*) means rustic, and it would appear that the original Italian writer who used this word found certain heavier horses of part-Spanish blood in the mountainous areas to the north of Jaen which were used on the land. As this term is not used in either Spain or Portugal today and concerns a cross-bred horse which has long ago been bred out, it has no significant part to play in this book.

CHAPTER II

The Origins of the Iberian Horse

Look back at our struggle for freedom,
Trace our present day's strength to its source;
And you'll find that man's pathway to glory
Is strewn with the bones of a horse.

ANONYMOUS

A celebrated account of the Arab horse claims that this breed – as if uniquely – has prehistoric origins, yet it is now quite clear that the Arab is not as old as the Barb. Strabo, the Roman geographer (born approximately 10 AD) writing in the lifetime of Christ, claims that in Arabia at that time there were no horses whatsoever. Such a sweeping generalisation can, however, be misleading; we may yet discover in a future archaeological breakthrough that horses did migrate as far south as Arabia from Turkey and Syria; but as we shall see in Chapter III the Barb horse dates back thousands of years before the Arab, and the Iberian horse several thousand years before the Barb.

The temptation to generalise about the origins of horses is all too easy and the honest chronicler must endeavour to sift through the known facts as revealed by his research. Where he has to form an opinion through lack of written records, visual evidence such as cave paintings or ancient artefacts, and rely on careful supposition, he must make this clear; the reader is then at liberty to make up his or her own mind.

Throughout this chapter we shall trace how invading forces and new civilisations spreading into Spain and Portugal from the south and north were to affect the evolution of the early indigenous horse and encourage its final emergence as one of the most beautiful and influential breeds of all time.

The story of warfare and the techniques of combat offer the equine researcher an opportunity to follow more accurately the development of a particular breed and proves particularly helpful in establishing salient dates. The use or non-use of cavalry has always been a powerful indication of what type of horse was available at specific times and it is little known, for example, that in the days of Mohammed, in the early seventh century – around the same time that St Augustine was bringing Christianity to southern England – warfare in Arabia was conducted mainly from the backs of camels. Yet in the Iberian Peninsula, for some *four thousand* years previous to this, Neolithic warriors were fighting on horseback and had long ago established themselves as a race of superior horsemen.

Before we go on to explore the various invasions and influences that were to affect the Iberian horse throughout his early history, there is one further observation to make. We often tend to forget that despite the lack of the mechanised communication systems which we enjoy today, the early civilisations of the world possessed almost uncanny powers of endurance and enterprise. With no known source of power other than their own hard labour and determination, whole continents were crossed and thousands of men and horses were transported across mountains, oceans and desert plains to new lands separated by formidable distances. The passage of Hannibal's elephants over the Alps is one of the best-known examples of this, and an appreciation of the audacity and ingenuity of these people may help us to visualise better how horses were spread from one country to another.

Also, we should not forget that the world map has changed considerably from those ancient days. Countries once linked by landbridges and now separated by channels and seas could be traversed more easily by wandering herds of horses as well as organised cavalry. It is ironic that in North America (where some of the earliest fossils of *equus* yet discovered exist) horses were to disappear completely at the end of the Ice Age, leaving that great continent apparently horseless for the thousands of intervening years up until the time of the Spanish Conquistadores, who introduced their foundation Iberian stock in the fifteenth and sixteenth centuries.

With every passing year, exciting discoveries are made about a particular species as new evidence is uncovered, and this often leads to the dismissal of an established theory. For this reason, books written at the turn of the century may contain theories which by the 1980s have been proven incorrect, and no doubt books published in the near future will put forward ideas which may well be in dispute by the turn of this century as a result of new archaeological finds.

As regards the Iberian horse, we are blessed with a great deal of historical evidence, not only from the study of warfare, but also from cave paintings, pottery, traditional artefacts, ancient writing, and remains of early saddlery, bits and shoes. By perusing the illustrations in this book, the reader may develop his eye and will be surprised how the early (prehistoric) Iberian characteristics can still be visually recognised in today's breeds.

The Very Earliest European Saddle Horse

When, in 1879, magnificent cave paintings were discovered in Altamira in northern Spain, and these and others were linked with previous discoveries in the Dordogne in France, historians and archaeologists alike were astounded by the indication of a prehistoric horse hitherto unrecorded.

The results of tests later conducted on these murals eclipsed all previous theories and seemed to point to an earlier contact with or domestication of the horse in the Iberian Peninsula and south of France than we have so far been able to discover in any other part of the world.

Cave paintings dated at approximately 5,000 BC in Canforos de Penarubia in the north-east of Spain, portray Mesolithic horses being led by men; but Magdalenian horses dated at around 15,000 BC are shown with rope halters on their heads which suggests an even earlier domestication.

In 1905 a Spanish farmer discovered huge caves on his land at La Pileta, near Ronda, in the rugged hinterland which lies behind Malaga and is named Sierra

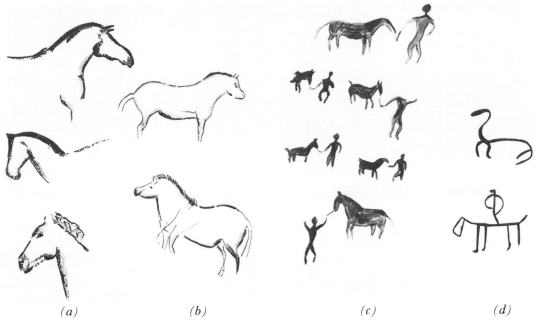

(a) Palaeolithic horses display sub-convex or straight profile and long necks.
(b) Palaeolithic ponies display concave profile and short necks.
(c) Domesticated horses led by Mesolithic man.
(d) Neolithic horses and mounted warrior.

de Yeguas – which, literally translated, means Mountains of the Mares. These craggy peaks run as an offshoot of the Sierra Nevada high above the river basin of the River Guadalquivir. Exploration of the caves revealed murals of horses so impressive in quantity, colour and clarity that, gradually, archaeologists from all over Europe were attracted to this remote area. In 1909 Willoughby Verner, an Englishman, came and spent the next two years there studying and researching the paintings. Then came an expedition from France. Finally, in 1924 the Spanish government was spurred into taking steps to declare La Pileta a protected area, and today the caves, with their wealth of prehistoric equestrian art, are open to the public. The horses portrayed are very similar to the Sorraia. Those murals painted in colour, mainly red and ochre, have been officially dated at a period between 30,000–20,000 BC. Those painted in black are dated at 20,000–10,000 BC.

Portugal and Spain's leading equine historian, the late Dr Ruy d'Andrade, avers that the horse became domesticated within the Iberian Peninsula as early as 25,000 BC, a theory supported by the discovery of small tools made of bone and dating from that period, which were used to make rope from the hair of horses' manes. Other chroniclers are more conservative and although they accept that horses were hunted for meat in the Palaeolithic age, they will not commit themselves to a firm acceptance of the horse's domesticity before the Neolithic period.

Comprehensive, up-to-date coverage of the earliest types of horses and their evolution is provided by Daphne Machin Goodall in her book, *A History of Horse Breeding*. She maintains that the early Iberian ancestor of today's Andalusian and Lusitano is a cross between the Tarpan and the Przevalski Asiatic horse represented by *Equus stenonius*. This theory is also supported by Dr d'Andrade who points

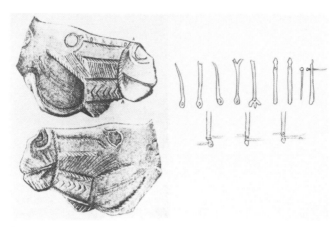

Left: *Magdalenian horses from the Dordogne wearing rope halters.* Right: *Bone artefacts found in the Iberian Peninsula, dated at approx. 25,000 BC. These are almost exact replicas of instruments used today in Portugal and Spain by the* campinos *and* vaqueros *to fashion rope out of horsehair. This would point to an even earlier domestication of the horse.*

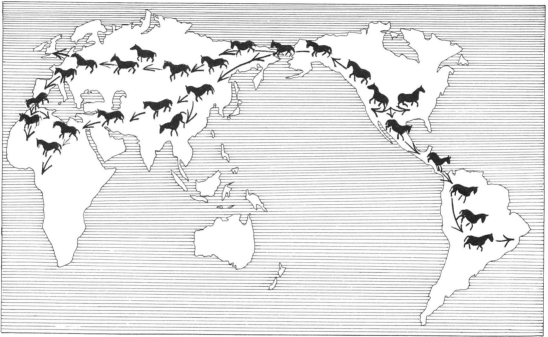

The migration of the prehistoric horse. Millions of years ago the ancestor of equus *migrated from the Americas as the continents separated, and crossed the Bering Strait into Euroasia. Climatic and geographic upheavals caused the prehistoric horse to become encapsulated in a number of natural zones, and thus emerged certain distinct types of primitive horse such as the Sorraia of Spain and Portugal.*

out that such a cross would result in a bigger animal than either the early Tarpan or Przevalski progenitors. With this advantage *Equus stenonius* rapidly spread across the Peninsula becoming big enough to carry a male adult, and through selective breeding it reached suitable proportions and conformation where it could be used for cavalry, unlike the early Assyrian horses which, because of their weak backs, were only suitable for chariot racing.

Fortunately, a last-remaining herd of *Equus stenonius* still exists in the Portuguese Alentejo. This is, of course, the primitive Sorraia which is described in Chapter I, and like the primitive Tarpan (now only to be found in Poland) and the Asiatic wild horse, the breed has survived, as if encapsulated by its habitat, in its original prehistoric state. Another example of a breed becoming isolated as an ancient type is the Exmoor pony in Britain. This occurred in approximately 6,000 BC when the land route joining Britain to the Continent was flooded over by melting glacial ice from the North Sea, creating the waterway known as the English Channel.

In the case of the Sorraia it was the nature of its steppe-pampas habitat enclosed by rugged hills which protected this horse and prevented the last few Portuguese strains from crossing with oriental blood which began to be introduced into the Peninsula in the last two millenniums BC.

With the advantage of having the primitive Sorraia to study before our very eyes, the task of following the future Iberian horse's development from thereon is made very much simpler. Today's elegant, more refined Andalusian and Lusitano breeds still bear many of the characteristics of the primitive Sorraia, and without this inherent toughness would probably not have survived in such a distinctive form.

Long before any refinement had taken place, the Sorraia was already beginning to display the characteristics of temperament for which his descendants are famed. Although measuring little more than 13 h.h., he was strong and wiry. His methods of grazing and the hilly terrain over which he travelled had led to the evolvement of a thick, arched neck and strong, short-coupled body. By Neolithic times it would appear that he was already being used for skilled warfare. Sr d'Andrade claims the proof of his existence as a functional war-horse during this period lies in the appearance of a weapon – the halberd made from a large piece of flint and said to be contemporary with the megalithic monuments which can be found in the west of the Peninsula and which date back to 4,000 BC. He makes the assumption from subsequent research that Neolithic warriors were fighting on horseback all over the Iberian Peninsula. The halberd, which continued to appear in the Copper, Bronze and Iron Ages, is a long lance-like weapon used against cavalry to unseat another rider, as later employed in the Middle Ages. As cavalry tactics were being used by these ancient tribes, a suitable horse must have already evolved for this practice which was then to be pursued for many future generations. This theory adds weight to the possibility that the horse could have already been domesticated in this part of the world as early as the Palaeolithic Age.

From this knowledge it seems probable to suggest that the expansion of the civilisation known as the Vaso Campaniforme, which started in the Iberian Peninsula during the Bronze Age in 3,000 BC and which spread to north and central Europe, was due to the success of this type of warfare and this type of horse.

Invaders and Traders

Modern horse books frequently refer to the Moorish invasion of Spain, which took place in 711 AD, as being the most influential period in the formation of today's modern Iberian breed. This may not, however, reveal the whole truth and the Spanish and Portuguese themselves become so frustrated by the assumptions proffered by the pens of foreign writers that they will sometimes deny that there has ever been *any* oriental blood present in today's Andalusian and Lusitano. 'Pura raza espanola' is the name on the Spanish Stud Book, and purity of blood is taken so seriously that the mere suggestion of foreign influences at any time will be coldly received and hotly rejected.

The truth is that a generous quantity of oriental blood from Libya, Egypt and Syria was inevitably introduced into Spain and Portugal, but crossings resulting from these invasions happened several hundred years before the birth of Christ.

As for the Moorish invasion, which took place centuries later, the introduction of new equine blood into the Peninsula obviously took place during that period but it should not be given too much significance. Contemporary evidence shows that more horses went *out* of the Peninsula during the first century of occupation than were ever introduced at that point by the Moors, as we shall read later on.

The early influential periods of civilisation which left their mark on the indigenous horse are as follows: Ligurian, Iberian, Phoenician, Celtic, Greek, Carthaginian, Roman. Originally Ligurian, the Peninsula was inhabited by tribes which had dwelt there since Palaeolithic times, and the first of the southern and eastern people to discover it from afar were the Iberians, a fierce war-like tribe from North Africa who arrived in approximately 3,000 BC to be closely followed by the Phoenician sea traders in around 2,000 BC. By 1,100 BC the Phoenicians had also colonised Cyprus, Rhodes, Sicily, Malta and Sardinia and for a time they also dominated the Iberians. They did much to establish sea trade along the Mediterranean, venturing also into the Atlantic as far north as Cornwall, Ireland and Brittany. In his *Book of the Horse*, published in 1947, Brian Vesey-Fitzgerald suggested that not only did horses progress from east to west under the Phoenicians but from west to east. Symachus, a writer of the second century AD, states that Spanish horses were famed because of their speed and were exported to Syria.

Many historians believe that there is a possible connection between the high-stepping Iberian horse and the equally high-stepping 'bloodsweating horses' of China. Certainly trade existed between Portugal, Spain, Italy and China in the last two centuries BC but unfortunately we do not yet have any direct evidence of an interchange of horses between China and the Peninsula although wherever trade took place it is likely that horses were included.

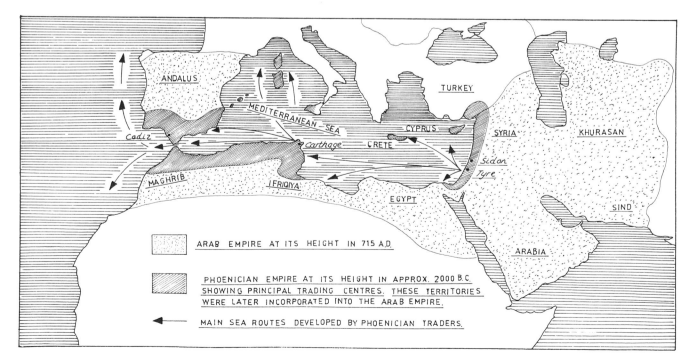

The Greeks

The next civilisation to set up settlements in the south of Spain and Portugal were the Greeks. By 700 BC they had become well established along the coast and Greek culture was to play an important part in art and architecture. The Greeks introduced two important plants, the olive and the vine. Round about the same time, the Celts were thrusting into Spain and Portugal from the North, and by this time there must have been an interesting mixture of horses when the native Sorraia began to breed with other bloods. By 300 BC the Ligurians had been pushed northwards towards Germany, and the Phoenicians retreated back along their sea routes to Tyre. As the other races lost their stronghold and more land became available to them the Celts and Iberians began to intermingle, becoming known as the Celtiberians, with a stronger Iberian influence on the people of Spain, and a Celtic prevalence in Portugal.

The Celtiberians

It was the horses of the Celtiberians that were to become famous throughout the civilised world. By this time there is little doubt that finer, oriental blood had lightened, heightened and refined the native Sorraia, and there is a striking similarity between the Dongola[1] of the east and the Iberian war-horse. From this period onwards we find many references to the Iberian or Celtiberian horses of the Peninsula by Greek and Roman chroniclers.

Homer refers to them in his *Iliad* around 1,100 BC, and the celebrated Greek cavalry officer Xenophon[2] had nothing but praise for the 'gifted Iberian horses' and horsemen who travelled by sea to help the Spartans in their war against the Athenians in the Peloponnesian Wars of 457 and 431 BC. The outcome of the Iberian cavalry tactics was to disorganise and finally defeat the enemy forces from Athens, and this form of combat became highly admired. Xenophon's description of these tactics runs thus:

> 'then Dionesian's fifty Iberian horsemen spread out across the plain and galloping full tilt, hurled their javelins; if they were counter-attacked they retreated, turned and hurled their javelins again. During this manoeuvre they dismounted and rested. If they were about to be attacked they quickly remounted and withdrew; and if any was unwise enough to separate himself from the rest of the army and follow them, they would close in on him and wound him with their lances; and in this way they obliged all the troops to alternate between advance and retreat.'

On another occasion, Iberian cavalry, in the pay of the Carthaginians who had hired them as mercenaries, fought in Sicily against the Greeks in the fifth century

1. The Dongola is described in detail in *The World Atlas of Horses and Ponies* (see References). Today it is concentrated in the Sudan, but is thought to have crossed and recrossed into North-West Africa and the Iberian Peninsula in prehistoric times. Dr d'Andrade explores evidence of a close association between the Dongola and the Iberian horse in *O Cavalo Andaluz de Perfil Convexo*.
2. Xenophon (approx. 445–355 BC), the Athenian writer, philosopher and great cavalry leader was a disciple of Socrates. His famous treatise on equitation, *Hippike*, which has been translated and retranslated over the past five centuries into almost every language in the world is as applicable today in its content as it was over two thousand years ago.

Celtiberian horsemen of the fourth century BC, photographed from an ancient vase discovered in Liria, near Valencia. Note the highly crested neck of these chargers, their proportions compared to man, and the shape of the head.

BC and a contemporary writer, Diodoro of Sicily, remarks, 'It is recognised that not only their cavalry [Celtiberians] is excellent, but also their infantry which distinguished itself for its courage and daring.'

As the Iberians and Celtiberians were achieving fame abroad as being a fearless, effective race of horsemen, another race of people was encroaching into Iberian territory. The Carthaginians quickly took hold and exploited the colonies of their Phoenician and Greek predecessors but their main achievement seems to have been to induce the conquering Romans to come in as well. With Greek predominance broken, the Iberian penetration of the interior gathered great headway, and by 300 BC the most flourishing Iberian centre in Spain was in the valley of the River Ebro.

The Carthaginians, Iberians and Celtiberians appear to have dealt well together and again Carthage seconded the services of their hosts' cavalry in the battles which were to ensue against the Romans. Some attractive painted pottery of the period shows Celtiberian warriors mounted on highly crested, comparatively large war-horses of imposing appearance. (It has been suggested that these soldiers rode side-saddle, but it is more likely that the sideways appearance of these figures is nothing more than a highly stylised art form as was similarly developed by the Egyptians.) What is of more interest is that in these visual relics we see a striking resemblance of the horse of that period to the Iberian war-horse of some two thousand years later. In particular we note the pronounced arched muscular neck, and the fine elegant limbs which are synonymous with the blood horse. The reader's attention is drawn to the fact that this established appearance is present several centuries before the Moorish invasion. This helps to authenticate the theory that oriental blood had already been present for a number of centuries, brought in by the successive civilisations we have traced in the preceding paragraphs.

Under their great campaigning general, Hannibal (247–182 BC), the Carthaginians almost defeated the Roman usurpers who spread into the Peninsula to Latinise the West. The Romans had never until now been great horsemen, having relied predominantly on their highly trained armies of infantry. It is almost certain that because they had never really mastered the full use of cavalry and because their earliest campaigns were fought in hilly country where Iberian and Celtiberian horses were at their best, the Romans lost battles which might have ended in victory for them.

In the Second Punic War (218–201 BC) Hannibal scored against the Romans time and time again because he handled his cavalry with genius. His heavy cavalry had been drawn from northern Europe, but his light cavalry was not only from Spain but also was comprised of Berber horses from Numidia (see map on page 44). Hannibal's brother, Hasdrubal, is reputed to have introduced as many as 20,000 Libyan horses into the Peninsula during the period, which would have had an important effect on breeding. This points again to the significant periods in the establishment of oriental blood in the Peninsula being *prior* to the birth of Christ and not as is so often suggested being fixed at the time of the Moorish invasion in 711 AD.

Whilst the Celtiberians had developed the bit and the art of handling the reins, so that their horses were referred to as *frenati*, the Numidians guided their horses without bits. An African writer, Nemesianus, writing in approximately 300 AD, stated that the North African horse wore no bridle but was controlled by light taps with a stick which caused him 'to start, to turn, to run directly on'. It was the agility of these Spanish and Berber horses, coupled with the ability of the horsemen to handle the javelin and lance with such deftness, that scored victory after victory for the Carthaginians.

Iberia Under the Romans

During these wars, the Romans came to fear and respect the 'barbarians' of Spain and Portugal. According to the Roman historian Tacitus, all the cavalry of Europe was mounted on Spanish horses; and Oppian, another writer of that time, is quoted as stating that the Spanish were the fastest horses then known, but that for long distances 'the dappled Moorish are best'.

Lucius Junius Moderatus, the wisest of the agronomists of ancient Rome, recognised only three breeds of horse in Europe – the Persian, used by the Parthians; the Sicilian, used by the Greeks; and the Spaniard of Berber type.

This excerpt from the Roman Appian on the Iberian War illustrates the point that the Iberian method of warfare daunted the Roman mounted soldier so much that he was prepared to sacrifice his honour, a rare occurrence in the proud Roman army.

> 'Once, one of the barbarians [i.e. Iberians] mounted on a horse, presented himself before the two armies, dressed in shining armour, and challenged any of the Romans to single combat. When none accepted, he turned his back on them, mocking as he did so.'

Eventually Scipio, a young man of great courage who was later to lead the Romans in Africa, went forward – the only Roman, the passage relates, prepared to tackle the Iberian horseman.

One of the very few descriptions of a war-horse which has been handed down to us by Virgil (70–19 BC) in the Latin *Georgics*, could have well been written for the Iberian horse of that period.

'His neck is carried erect; his head is small; his belly short; his back broad. Brawny muscles swell upon his noble chest. A bright bay or a good grey is the best colour; the worst is white or chestnut. If from afar the clash of arms be heard, he knows not how to stand still; his ears prick up, his limbs quiver; and snorting, he rolls the collected fire under his nostrils. And his mane is thick and reposes tossed back on his right shoulder.'

The Roman philosopher Strabo also gives us an interesting reference which to this day holds good: 'In Spain, the horses are born chestnut and turn grey or dappled at once.'

Hispania (the Iberian Peninsula) and North West Africa under the Romans.

After their war against the Iberians, the Romans adopted new weapons using the short, strong lance with its two iron points, as well as a sturdier, inflexible shield better able to resist the blows of the rigid lance. As well as adopting Iberian weaponry, the Romans took up the Iberian form of single combat on horseback, and for this practice Iberian horses were then used to improve their own breeds.

Roman stud farms were set up and soon government remount depots were being proficiently organised and run for the exclusive use of the Roman cavalry as the Empire spread northwards, increasing in dimension and power. Remounts for all the western provinces, including Britannica, were drawn from Hispania, and as we may see from the map above, these were centred specifically around Baetica, which corresponds roughly to today's Andalusia.

The excavation of Roman remains in Portugal has also exposed a wealth of ancient stud farms and estates centred round the Tagus valley. One of these has yielded spectacular mosaics portraying favourite horses reared there, with their different names captioned alongside. The Tagus valley was particularly famous for its brood mares at this time. During the Roman occupation of the Peninsula we find many written references to the native horse. Elder Pliny, a Roman cavalry officer (who was later to die at Pompeii after the eruption of Vesuvius in AD 79), describes the horses of Portugal as being 'a fine docile type' and later he states that the mares were 'impregnated with the west wind, and brought forth an offspring of surprising fleetness'. Posidonius, the Stoic philosopher who visited Spain in 90 BC, records that the Iberians and Celtiberians had horses of excellent quality. An interesting passage runs as follows:

'the Iberians used cavalry interspersed with their footmen. Their horses were trained to traverse the mountains, and to sink down on their knees at a word from the rider, when necessary. They also had a practice of mounting two men on one horse, so that in the event of an engagement, one might be at hand to fight on foot.'

Top: *Roman coins from the Iberian Peninsula depict a distinctive horse of the same type. All have a highly arched, powerful neck, high wither and short-coupled body.* Far left: *Marcus Aurelius (121–180 AD). This statue, c.170 AD, is of significance since it portrays an Iberian charger remarkably similar to those painted by Velasquez, Van Dyck, Goya etc., thus proving that the indigenous horse changed very little.* Left: *Head of a Neolithic flint halberd.*

This would seem to indicate a horse of fair proportions, for with rough armour and weaponry and two able-bodied men on his back, an animal greater than the small Sorraia would be required. Posidonius also notices that the 'Celtiberian horses were rather starling coloured', which one presumes to mean flea-bitten or dark grey flecked with white, colours which still dominate to this day. All these references to speed, to size and to colour indicate a horse which had received a strong complement of Libyan and possibly Persian blood at various stages throughout its evolution.

Whilst the Romans looked on the Iberian horse primarily as a vehicle for war, there is one interesting reference to Spanish horses being taken back to Rome for charioteering. Major Lamb reports in *The Story of the Horse*, that a famous charioteer, Avilius Teres of the first century AD, left a list of the horses he drove to victory inscribed in Latin which was recently revealed in the wall of the Castle of St Angelo in Rome. These were: thirty-seven Libyan, two Spanish, two Greek horses and one horse from Gaul. It is perhaps significant that no Arab horses feature in the list.

The third and fourth centuries saw a decline in Roman influence and prosperity within the Peninsula, and the seven centuries of Roman domination ended with the Barbarian invasion of 404–406 AD. The Iberians themselves were no longer 'barbarians'. Christianity had come to the Peninsula during the strongest period of the Roman occupation, the seeds of faith having been sown by St Paul in a country thirsty for mystic ideals.

Roman culture had certainly had its effect on the central provinces of Spain and Portugal, and Roman habits, social behaviour and privileges became widely accepted. Great country estates had been cultivated which triggered off a system of feudal landowning which only in recent years has dramatically changed, and although the Romans contributed magnificent roads, aqueducts and bridges[3] to the Peninsula, they exploited its resources prodigiously. With regard to the horse

3. Famous Roman aqueducts include that of Tarragona and Segovia in Spain, and of Elvas and Lisbon in Portugal. The finest of the large Roman bridges still remaining in Europe is the one across the River Tagus at Alcantara in Spain.

population, the Romans, unlike the previous invaders, contributed little (it would seem) in the way of new blood, but they were the first to set up breeding in an organised way, something for which Spain and Portugal would later be grateful.

With the irruption of the Vandals, the Suevia or Swabians and the Alans into the Peninsula at the beginning of the fifth century AD, a long history of division and confusion begins, with Portugal achieving some form of national autonomy under the Swabian kingdom, and Spain remaining with deep divisions under the Visigoths. There is remarkably little evidence of horses being brought into the Iberian Peninsula by these northern invaders, and the only void in my researches into this history of the Iberian horse, yawns over the next three hundred years. We do know that southern Spain was badly plundered by the Vandals on their route southwards to Africa, and horses from Baetica were swept along in the wake of these departing peoples. It seems logical, however, that the horses they took were Iberian, and if any northern blood was introduced, it probably remained to the north-east of the Peninsula and did not affect the established breeding centres of the Tagus and Guadalquivir valleys.

Perhaps the greatest clue as to whether or not the indigenous horse vastly changed after the arrival of the Visigoths is to study the many examples of Roman equestrian art from the Peninsula, and compare them with the horses of later years. We have some excellent pictorial evidence of the Iberian horse on Spanish coins and pottery at this time, and the high-stepping, muscular body of the Hispanic-Roman horse is truly remarkable in its similarity to today's parade or driving horse. The equestrian statue of Marcus Aurelius (121–180 AD), the first Roman emperor to fight the Barbarian invaders, again shows a horse so similar to the Spanish combat horses of seventeenth-century Europe and to the bullfighting horses of Portugal in the twentieth century, that perhaps, for once, without back-up research, we may accept the word of the Iberian horse breeders themselves, who without exception deny that the horses from the north had any influence whatsoever on today's Andalusian and Lusitano.

It would seem, therefore, that by the end of the Roman Empire the Iberian breed was firmly established, and whatever changes were to take place during the Moorish Conquest, the inherent genetic constitution of the Iberian horse would continue to manifest itself.

Table II.1: The Development of the Horse Throughout the Iberian Peninsula

(as indicated by prehistoric discoveries and recorded ancient invasions from approximately 30,000 BC–200 BC)

PALAEOLITHIC AGE	Cave paintings discovered at La Pileta, Ronda, southern Spain, portray horses of convex profile, radiocarbon-dated from 20,000 BC to 30,000 BC. Similar cave paintings discovered at Altamira, Santander, northern Spain, demonstrate a horse of concave and straight profile.
	During the Palaeolithic period it is thought that horses from south of the Iberian Peninsula crossed and recrossed into North West Africa, and began to breed in the area of the Atlas mountains particularly round the Rivers Mouloya and Loukos.

MESOLITHIC AGE	As horses became domesticated throughout the Peninsula during this period it is likely that crossings took place between the two indigenous types; although in the extreme north and south (i.e. around Andalusia, Alentejo, etc.) the two distinct types remained well-defined, those latter horses being represented by *equus stenonius* – the Sorraia.
NEOLITHIC AGE (including the Bronze Age)	With the infiltration of ancient Iberian tribes from the north African coast into the Peninsula, subsequently followed by Phoenician sea traders from Tyre and Sidon (see map) horses of oriental blood from the east were gradually introduced into the Peninsula. These were not Arab (see text) but of a type similar to the ancient Persian and Chinese horses, and subsequently developed by the Assyrians. They became concentrated around Libya, and later, moving westward began to cross with the Sorraia type horse of the Barbary Coast. Brought by sea to the Iberian Peninsula in approximately 2,000 BC they began to cross with the indigenous horse of the south, resulting in a fine-limbed, taller horse of 'blood'. (In fact, it is possible that oriental horses from the east were introduced to the Peninsula at an even earlier date – but we have no direct evidence of this.)
IBERIAN-CELTIC PERIOD (including the Iron Age)	In the north of the Iberian Peninsula trading of horses developed between the Celtic tribes of northern Spain and Portugal, France, Belgium, Britain and Ireland from approximately 500 BC onwards. As horses from the south interbred with the Celtic pony types of the north, some warm-blood crosses were achieved and subsequently introduced abroad.
	In the south of the Peninsula, more oriental blood was inevitably introduced by the Greeks in approximately 700 BC.
	By the time of the Carthaginian occupation of the Peninsula which reached its climax in the Second Punic War against the Romans (218–201 BC) a well-established breed of horse existed in the southern regions of Spain and Portugal which is hereafter described as the Iberian Saddle Horse.

Table II.2: The Domestication of the Horse Throughout the Iberian Peninsula
(as indicated by prehistoric discoveries from approximately 30,000 BC–200 BC)

PALAEOLITHIC AGE	Cave paintings discovered at La Pileta, Ronda, southern Spain, portray horses of convex profile, radiocarbon-dated from 25,000 BC to 30,000 BC. Similar cave paintings discovered at Altamira, Santander show a horse of concave and straight profile.
	Later Palaeolithic cave drawings at La Pasiega portray a horse with its foot caught in a noose.
	Magdalenian horses are depicted with rope halters.
	Bone artefacts, dated at approx. 25,000 BC, would appear to be instruments used for the making of rope from horsehair and are similar to instruments still used for that purpose today by *campinos* (stock men) in the Iberian Peninsula.
MESOLITHIC AGE	Cave paintings from Canforos de Penarubia, in the east of the Iberian Peninsula, depict horses already domesticated and being led by men. These have been dated at approx. 4,000–5,000 BC.
NEOLITHIC AGE (including the Bronze Age)	Flint halberds, and lances with counterweights (which would indicate that they were used by horsemen designed to be handled with one

hand only) were discovered between 3,000 and 4,000 BC.

Prehistoric drawings in the Tower of Bredos, Coruna, Galicia, depict a mounted horseman from the same period.

IBERIAN-CELTIC AGE (including the Iron Age)

Iberian Celt's weapons, horseshoes, bits and spurs from Aguilar of Anguita, in the period between 500 and 200 BC indicate the establishment of a well-accoutred cavalry which was subsequently enlisted into the Carthaginian cavalry under Hannibal in the Second Punic War (218–201 BC). Bronze statuettes of the 5th century BC depict horsemen carrying lance and shield. Some of these indicate the use of a stirrup which may have been made from rope. The saddle of that period is not unlike the Portuguese bullfighting saddle of today.

CHAPTER III

The Development of the Barb or Berber

Thou shalt be for Man a source of happiness and
wealth; thy back shall be a seat of honour, and thy
belly of riches; every grain of barley given thee shall
purchase indulgence for the sinner.

The Koran

Much has been written about the influence of the Barb[1] or Berber on the horses
of Spain and Portugal. It is therefore important to discuss the state of this little-
understood breed from its ancient beginnings, remembering that it made a considerable impact on the Iberian Peninsula during the time of the Carthaginian
and Roman Punic Wars (in the third century BC) and again during the Moorish
invasion of Christian Spain and Portugal in the eighth century AD.

The Barb reached its zenith of popularity in England and throughout Europe
during the sixteenth and seventeenth centuries. Marcus Fugger,[2] a well-travelled
German banker who was a leading expert on horses and lived from 1529–1597,
has this to say about the breed:

> 'The Berber horses are wonderful noble horses, they are fast and strong
> and can stand great hardship, and if they were as big as European horses,
> there would be no better horses for use in war. The ancients too valued
> these horses a lot and even now they are highly regarded especially
> amongst the Turks.'

The Barb's influence on the Thoroughbred racehorse will be discussed in Chapter
XIII, and it is a tribute to the original sound genetic composition of the breed
that it is mentioned with such noteworthy regularity in the early stud records of
the Royal Mares of England.

Sadly, today, in many parts of North Africa the breed has been allowed to
degenerate, despite the fact that Barb stallions proved invaluable to the mounted
units[3] of the French African Army from 1830 onwards, and were esteemed for

---

1. Although the word Berber is more correctly used to describe the horses of the Barbary Coast, N.W. Africa,
   the author recognises that the majority of the horse-loving public is more familiar with the word Barb,
   and therefore this word will be used to describe the breed in a general sense; and Berber will be used
   in the historical sense.
2. Marcus Fugger wrote about all the breeds of Europe and ran his own stud farm in Hungary.
3. The most famous of these was the Seventh Spahis, an Algerian-based troop formed in 1915. The Spahis
   enjoyed an illustrious career, being renowned all over France for their courage and ability. They fought
   against the Germans in both World Wars and were responsible for defending French colonial power
   throughout the North African territories. They were always mounted on Barb stallions.

their stamina, strength and courage. With the withdrawal of French colonial power, hundreds of Barb horses passed into indifferent hands and in too many cases the Barb of today is a poor specimen, expected to flourish on the meanest of diets, broken in too early and treated with no more respect than the lowliest beast of burden.

Certain excellent private studs still exist, and in many cases, particularly in Morocco, a special strain of Arab-Barb has been developed as opposed to the traditional pure-bred indigenous horse of the river and mountain country. King Hassan II of Morocco still keeps a number of magnificent animals in the royal stables. Recently in France there was a revival of interest in the classic Barb, and L'Association du Cheval Barbe[4] was formed in 1978, which, it is hoped, will promote and protect this ancient breed.

Traditionally, the Barb has been confused with the Arab horse because many old-time writers, particularly those who did not travel, described the inhabitants of north-west Africa as 'Arabs'. This was a result of the Arab invasion of the Barbary Coast when the Berber tribes were defeated and converted to Islam by invading Arab and Egyptian forces in 702 AD. Consequently, many English and French writers then referred to these independent peoples and their horses by the all-embracing term Arab instead of Berber or Moor.

But the Barb's place in history commences long before 702 AD. It is now almost conclusively established that the Barb developed as a breed from primitive Sorraia (*Equus stenonius*) stock which gradually migrated from Spain and Portugal into North Africa in prehistoric times. Contrary to popular opinion, therefore, the Iberian horse was the likely forefather to the Barb and not vice versa. This is not so controversial as it may sound. The difference between this author's account of the Barb and several others which exist indicating a contrary conclusion, is simply that many recorders omit the foundation period and only start their research at the time of the Moorish Conquest of Spain when indeed fresh Barb blood was brought into the Peninsula. What is not explained is that this Barb blood had probably come from the Peninsula in the first place. It would be more accurate to say that at the time of the Moorish Conquest, Barb blood was *re-introduced* to the Iberian Peninsula.

There is much evidence to underline the prevalence of early Iberian blood in the Barb which can be divided into the following categories:

    (i) geographical;
    (ii) environmental;
    (iii) visual, i.e. the observation of certain genetic characteristics;
    (iv) recorded and written (by modern and contemporary researchers).

Let us first turn to the geographical evidence.
(i)   Until recently, many historians thought that there were no horses at all in North Africa prior to 1,500 BC. Now, with the discovery of the Palaeolithic cave paintings in Ronda (described in Chapter II) in southern Spain, and the recognised existence of an ancient landbridge between the continents of Africa and Europe, filling in what is now the Strait of Gibraltar, it seems more than likely that pen-

---

4. L'Association du Cheval Barbe, 15 rue du Parc, 77950 Moisenay, France.

Roman mosaic from Volubilis, Morocco. The horse depicted is almost identical to those on similar Roman mosaics found near Lisbon and in Palma de Mallorca. Note the long face and typical powerful neck set on the short-coupled body of the Iberian Barb.

etration into Northern Africa by horses from Spain occurred as early or even earlier than 10,000 BC. Dr d'Andrade points out from his intensive researches into the two areas that climatically and geographically the continual movement of horses was inevitable.

The fact that much of the Barbary Coast, and what now constitutes Morocco, Algeria and Tunisia was not a desert region but a comparatively fertile haven, well-watered by the great rivers of the Moulouya and Loukos and many smaller rivers on the west coast, is often ignored. In the north, the Berbers were a distinctively 'white' race with dark hair and brown or hazel eyes. In some cases, there were blue-eyed blonds but their frequency has been considerably overstated. Also known in Roman times as Numidia and Mauretania, these lands supported a river and mountain people as well as a river and mountain breed of horse. The conformation of the Barb therefore developed in the same way that the Sorraia evolved in Iberia. He had to be wiry, stocky and short-coupled to cope with this rugged landscape, and because he was nearer the Equator often experiencing sharp rises in temperature, he toughened into an animal of incredible endurance though smaller than his European counterpart.

How different was this horse from the Arab? The environmental argument can be determined by the answer to this question.

(ii)   Up until the eighth century the two types, Berber and Arab, could not have been more dissimilar. The former, though fleet and hardy was built for handiness and agility; he was selected over the centuries as he became domesticated by the indigenous tribespeople for his high-stepping, careful action and short-backed conformation enabling him to collect and balance himself over difficult terrain. The latter, also fleet and hardy, was a miracle of sustained forward energy, his body engineered in such a way that the predominance of his weight was thrown onto the forehand, ideal for prolonged cantering without tiring over the endless flat plains of the desert. Two different types, two very distinct horses; one from the mountains, one from the desert.

(iii) Visually the Barb horse, even today, displays so many Iberian features that we are left in no doubt that the strong genetic dominance of Sorraia blood became fixed within the breed at its most formative time. During the Barb's evolution, in the same way that Iberian horses developed, other breeds came from the east and the oriental blood of the Libyan horse in particular heightened and refined the original primitive horse. Nevertheless, the Barb still displays a number of characteristics which are symptomatic of that early foundation blood. These are:

> the same convex face which we see displayed in the early cave paintings at Ronda;
>
> the characteristic high wither, short back and deeply sloping croup, with low-set tail;
>
> a rib cage which is somewhat flat at the sides and a flat shoulder (the latter characteristic has been bred out of the more refined Iberian horse but is typical of the Sorraia);
>
> rather upright, small, hard hooves;
>
> and finally, the non-visual but equally important characteristic of the Sorraia temperament: kind, docile and full of courage.

(iv) From a recorded viewpoint there is a shortage of very early writings concerning the horses of North Africa but the Romans have left us with two important references.

Publius Vegetius Renatus, a celebrated authority on species of horses, wrote a book on veterinary medicine in 400 AD which states quite categorically that the Spanish horse was the ancestor of the African horse. Also, there is a revealing reference by Marcus Aurelius to the 'ugly heads of the African horses', for it was well known that the Romans were used to the concave head of the Tarpan and took some time to become accustomed to the horses of Spain and the Barbary Coast which they were later so much to admire.

Claudius Adelianus, a Greek writer of the second and third centuries AD, wrote a book entitled *On The Nature of Animals* in which he describes the Berber horses thus: 'They are small and not very beautiful, but extraordinarily fast and strong withal so that they can be ridden without a bit or reins and can be guided simply by a cane, so that only a lead rope is necessary on the halter.' This again exemplifies the parallel dislike of the facial profile; the apparent ease with which those horses were ridden is again characteristic of the docility that had been passed on from the Sorraia. This report of horses being used without bridles is supported by an earlier description in Chapter II of Hannibal's seconded army of Berber mercenaries.

Marcus Fugger, of the sixteenth century, whom we have mentioned before, also disclaims the presence of Arab blood in the Berber. In comparing the two breeds, he says:

> 'and I mention this particularly since I know well, that generally no dif-
> ference is made and they are held to be the same. But if anyone looks
> at the countries he will see that there are many hundreds of miles between

The Barb and Arab horse compared. The 1778 German engraving (left) by Johan Meno Haas, of a Moroccan soldier riding his Barb, contrasts noticeably with the lithograph (right) by Victor Adam (1860), depicting an Arab horse being ridden by a Bedouin warrior. Note the dished face, longer back and horizontal croup of the Arab.

Arabia and Barbary, and that Arabia lies in oriental Asia and Barbary in meridional Africa. This is where the Moorish or Berber horses come from.'

In the same passage he goes on to give us an unusual and vivid description of the Barb's courage, '. . . and they are the only horses that are not frightened by lions; other horses are terrified.'

More modern research carried out by O. Antonius in North Africa is particularly interesting in the light that he appears to have had no idea that the Sorraia still existed when he wrote on the subject in 1912; neither did he have the pictorial evidence which we enjoy today, of the Ronda cave paintings. His statement strongly supports that of Publius Vegetius Renatus.

'We can accept, without the slightest doubt, that a more or less uniform strain strongly inclined to the ram-nose was spread from the Spanish Peninsula to the Atlas mountains.'

Let us now turn from that summation of evidence to the use of the word Barb. It is perhaps understandable that people often speak of the Spanish or Portuguese horse as having Barb characteristics instead of the more accurate description of the Barb having Iberian characteristics. What they are really implying is an Iberian horse with all the original characteristics which were discussed in Chapter I, so many of which were incorporated into the Berber horses of North Africa when migratory herds progressed southwards into that great continent during the Ice Age.

As some of these characteristics, particularly the distinctive convex or sub-convex profile, have gradually been bred out of some Spanish studs in recent years, it is not surprising that *aficionados* of the classic Iberian horse nostalgically fasten on to the word Barb which has a romantic ring to it and then use it to imply a horse of the old war-horse type.

Berber, in fact, is a more accurate term for the Barb horse, but as the shorter version was used extensively by Shakespeare and great equestrian writers such as the Duke of Newcastle in the seventeenth century, the name has caught the imagination in a way that the term Berber will never supplant, linked as it is to a byegone age of daring and chivalry.

In *Othello*, Iago speaks of 'a Barbary horse'; Osric in *Hamlet* tells the Prince that 'the King hath wagered six Barbary horses', and much controversy surrounds the famous 'roan Barbary' ridden by Bolingbroke in *Richard II*, which, having belonged to the King might just have easily been a horse from the Court of Cordoba.

M. M. Reese quotes a passage in *The Royal Office of Master of the Horse*, about Prince Rupert who fought on the Royalist side in the English Civil War and always rode a Barb.

> 'He took pride in his dress; a gentleman who served under him during the Civil War said "He was always very sparkish in his dress," and was a magnificent sight riding into battle "clad in scarlet, very richly laid in silver lace, and mounted on a very gallant Barbary horse."'

There is no doubt that poets and writers the world over prefer the term Barb or Barbary and quite justly; it will always be synonymous with the Iberian horse, both breeds bearing the aspect of courage and nobility.

Although we must now progress several centuries ahead of this early foundation period, it would be misleading to leave the Barb at this juncture, for when the Arabs invaded North Africa in 702 AD and conquered the Berber people for Islam, the Barb horse inevitably underwent certain changes.

The Arab Horse and His Influence on the Barb

As we have seen, the original Berber horse had no Arab blood whatsoever as the Arab horse simply did not exist as a race before the birth of Christ. By 700 AD, however, when the Arabs invaded Numidia and Mauretania, it is likely that most Berber horses received some Arab blood and consequently the breed was refined to display, in many cases, all that was best in the foundation Spanish stock and the 'pure blood' of the Arab race.

Despite claims to 'prehistoric ancestors' by Lady Wentworth, England's leading Arab expert, no one really knows about the early forerunner to the Arab horse. In *The Noble Horse*, a magnificently illustrated book recently translated into English from the original German, the opening paragraph on the Arab states: 'Although geographically close to where the first advanced civilisations developed, for millennia the Arabian Peninsula remained untouched by historical events. The Bedouins of the wild barren deserts bred sheep and used camels as riding and draught animals.'

Archaeologists agree that horses did not exist in central Arabia before the

Christian era began. Professor Hitti in his *History of the Arab* refutes all claims to an ancient strain existing in the Arabian Peninsula and sums up: 'Renowned as it has become in Moslem literature, the horse was, nevertheless, a late importation into ancient Arabia.' Whether the breed is descended from a race distinct from the ancient Euro-Asian strains of wild horse is still not clear. Professor Ridgeway writing in 1905 believes they are direct descendants of the 'Libyan horse', but other historians are less specific and will only subscribe to the view that they were probably derived from Tarpan stock of central Asia and Siberia. Sir Richard Glyn expounds the theory that they were introduced into the Arabian Peninsula by the Persians, who brought a large cavalry into the Yemen which was formerly a fertile area, approximately three hundred years before Mohammed.

In *A History of Horse Breeding*, the author suggests that 'the likely source would be the descendants of the ancient Syrian and Assyrian chariot horses, whose ancestors, as we have seen, originated in the steppes of inner Asia.'[5]

There is a legend that all pure-bred Arabs are descended from Mohammed's five special mares, and such was the value and rarity of the Arab horse in the Prophet's day that rules for breeding and preserving horses were incorporated into the *Koran*. We do know that the Arab horse finally came to live in Nejd in central Arabia and by the fifth century – contrary to the Mohammed legend – had become the special breed of certain Bedouin tribes with Saracen links, who regarded them as ancestral possessions.

The Arab is classified as *Equus orientalis*, but the term 'oriental' can be misleading for it does not necessarily signify Arabic blood exclusively, and can equally be applied to the blood horses of Iran, Turkestan, Egypt, Syria and Libya.

When comparing the Arab horse to the Barb, we should remember that the Arab horse arose out of hostile conditions: burning sun in the day and freezing temperatures at night. Often fed on camel milk and dried meat in the dry season, they recovered in springtime when their travelling owners took them to the fertile springs of Syria and Mesopotamia. The Arab horse was spared as much as possible in those early times, and whenever a journey of more than three days was foreseen the camel would be used rather than a precious, less replaceable horse. Mares were preferred because they were quieter. Unlike the stallions they did not give away the presence of a raiding party, and secondly, and more importantly in those early days when the Bedouins struggled to rear horses in the desert, they fretted less and were better doers. As Colonel Juan Llamas points out in his book, *Caballo Espanol – Caballo de Reyes*,[6] the Arab was a horse of pure luxury in the time of Mohammed: difficult to maintain and breed and not for use in battle. Camels were used for transport and for the wars of the Arabs, and it was by camel and not on horseback that the Arabs first crossed frontiers to open the way of Muslim to the world.

In William Youat's book, *The Horse*, it is recorded that when Mecca finally

5. Lady Wentworth takes a contrasting view from the evidence offered by historians, archaeologists and zoologists with regard to the likely ancestors of the Arab horse and quotes the views of Lady Anne (Blunt) which state: 'The term Arabian is limited to *truly* such, and not to all those outlying rejected Mesopotamian, Syrian and borderland mixtures . . . the Arabian of Arabia is the only Arabian.'
6. In the same book, Colonel Llamas points out how as late as 1878 Lady Anne Blunt only found three hundred Arab horses in Arabia.

Pure-bred Barb stallion from the Atlas mountains. Note the similarity to the Iberian horse. (Photo by Sally Anne Thompson)

fell, Mohammed's gains were '24,000 camels, 40,000 sheep, 20,000 silver weights and not one single horse'. In the whole of Mohammed's invading army, which consisted of 10,000 soldiers, only 200 of them were mounted.

The object of drawing attention to the Arabian horse's rarity at this point of the narrative is not to detract in any way from the excellence of the breed, but to question the likelihood of the invading Arab forces bringing as many Arab horses into North Africa in their sweeping campaign for Islam as might be assumed. Mohammed died in 632; the defeat of the Berbers occurred in 702; and the entry of the Moors and Arabs into the Iberian Peninsula began in 710 AD.

These dates are highly significant. Much can happen in four score years, but it is perhaps over-optimistic to suppose that the horse from Arabia had multiplied to the extent that is sometimes implied. It is far more probable that the initial conquest of the Berbers took place with a mixed complement of camels (the traditional vehicle of war), some Arab horses, and a considerable quantity of cavalry horses from Egypt and Libya, belonging to the Islamic forces which combined to help the Arabs secure their hold on the conquered territories. Consequently, the Barb horse at that stage would have had less than a decade to change very much from its existing state, and therefore the horses that were introduced into the Iberian Peninsula in 710–711 AD would still have been made up of a predominance of Spanish blood.

Even today, most Barb horses as we have seen retain largely Spanish characteristics, particularly in the countryside where function necessitates adaptability. The face has tended to straighten in some strains where cross-breeding has occurred, but the body conformation and action of the pure Barb is to this day distinctively different to that of the Arab horse and remains primarily Hispanic. In *The World Atlas of Horses and Ponies*, Peter Churchill supports this view, and has made the following contemporary comments on the Barb breed:

'In Libya the purest Barbs occur in the most inaccessible mountains. In Morocco, Algeria and Tunisia too the Barb is dominant in the mountain regions of the interior. The Berbers preserved their own horses. In the west of Morocco, which was reached by only a small number of Arab invaders, the Barbs are purer than in the east; the western Barbs have little or no trace of Arabian blood in their appearance or general characteristics.'

It is fascinating, therefore, to realise that as the Muslim forces were preparing in Tangier to invade Spain, the horses that they would bring with them were the very horses which traced their early bloodlines back to the country they were now about to attack.

It was as if Nature had run full circle.

The Moorish Invasion of the Iberian Peninsula

So many conflicting stories exist about the numbers of horses brought into Spain by the invading Moors who first landed near the Algeciras of today in 710 and 711 AD, that it is important to examine the situation in more detail.

The first landing, when four small ships set forth from Ceuta on the coast of North Africa to make the short crossing to Hispania, was never intended as an act of invasion. Rather, it was a mission of reconnaissance, and the man who gave the Moors an excuse to instigate this was in fact a Christian, a rather shadowy figure, sometimes referred to as Count Julian or Count Urban. Greedy for power in the south, and peeved because he had lost his daughter to the licentious court at Toledo, he chose to quarrel with his Visigoth overlord, Rodrigo, King of Spain, and he called upon the Moors to assist him.

There are many legends and accounts of how events escalated from thereon, but the outcome was that a second invasion took place in 711 and at the Battle of Guadalete, King Rodrigo was killed by a combined force of Moors and Christians. The rapid way in which the Muslim forces, aided and abetted at first by rival Christian factions, then took hold of the Peninsula, merely demonstrates the structural weakness of the Visigothic state as it crumbled away. Resistance continued in the north west, principally in the Asturias, but within seven years the Moors had gained control of almost the entire Peninsula which they renamed Al-Andalus. Thus, they transformed themselves from the role of allies to conquerors.

We have already remarked that certain names conjure up romantic ideas from the past. One popular conception of the invasion by the Moors and their Barbs is of black hawk-faced warriors dashing across the Spanish mainland on white desert-bred chargers from the east, slashing with their curving scimitars at honest Christian men, women and children who dared to venture in their way. Fortunately (or unfortunately perhaps for the film-makers), all these images are unfounded, as we shall see.

In the first landing, we know from contemporary chroniclers of both Arab and Christian denomination, that the initial mission was led by Tarif ibn-Malik, a young Berber officer who brought only one hundred Berber horsemen. (As we have already discussed the Berbers were not a black race.)

A second landing took place in 711, this time a serious act of aggression against the Visigoths and led by the governor of Tangier, Tariq ibn-Ziyad, also a Berber, after whom Gibraltar[7] was named. According to Jan Read (see References): 'Of the seven thousand men who sailed with him, almost all were Berbers and themselves only recent converts to Islam.' We have no figures of how many horses were brought into Spain by this army, but again it is logical to assume that they were mounted on mainly Barb horses.

In 712 another invasion took place consisting of more Arabs than Berbers but these seem to have been mostly infantry. From the battles that followed against the Visigoths, the equestrian picture becomes more and more confused. One chronicler reports a figure of up to 300,000 horsemen, which Colonel Llamas puts down to 'pure fantasy'. A concise account of the years of invasion found in the writings of Tarif Aben Taric, a Moorish chronicler of the time, states that the Moors found the Spanish Christians' horses to be bigger and better than their own as well as more numerous. According to Tarif the Moors requisitioned or captured the Christians' horses and used them in their ensuing battles rapidly converting their infantry into cavalry.[8] This procedure would seem reasonable especially in view of the fact that several Christian groups had sided with the Moors initially.

Perhaps we shall never know how much equine Arab blood was introduced to Spain and Portugal during that century of penetration and the several centuries of occupation that followed. The Spanish and Portuguese themselves insist that little Arab blood was introduced and certainly this seems logical in view of the facts we have discovered so far. Neil Dougall,[9] an Australian publisher who has spent years in Spain writing about and breeding Andalusian horses, is emphatic in his dismissal of Arab blood being present in the pure-bred Iberian horse. In an article published in *Riding Magazine*, entitled 'The Mount of Kings', he states,

> 'Impressed by the influence that the Arab has had on so many of the light horse breeds of the world, horse historians mistakenly assume that the original ancestry of the Andalusian was Arab. But, in fact, there is absolutely no evidence whatsoever of Arab influence in the Andalusian; neither historically nor in the horse's physical make-up.'

Undoubtedly, however, a generous quantity of Barb blood was introduced, but as this was largely Spanish dominated already, as discussed, the evolutionary pattern of the Iberian horse would not significantly change from where we left Marcus Aurelius. We do know that the Spanish horses were so esteemed by the Moors that many were sent back as gifts to the Arab rulers in Constantinople and Damascus. As well as 'fair-haired slave girls, rich weapons, silks, embroideries and jewellery' we read that 'one hundred African horses' were despatched by the Caliph Omiadas of Cordoba to his superior in Constantinople in approximately 800 AD together with 'ten lovely Spanish horses richly harnessed', as though these

---

7. The name Gibraltar comes from the Arabic Jabal Tariq (the Mountain of Tariq).
8. This view is also supported in the writings of Ben Adhary, Al Makkari, El Doby, El Silense, etc., who were all contemporary chroniclers of the Moorish Invasion.
9. Neil Dougall was the founding president of the American Andalusian Association (now the AAHA) in 1966, and was the first chairman of the British Andalusian Horse Society.

St James of Compostela. The shrine of St James attracted pilgrims in their thousands, not only from all over Spain, but particularly from England and France in the Middle Ages. Santiago, as he is known in Spain, is invariably portrayed mounted on a white Andalusian charger leading the Christians into battle against the Moors. This engraving by A. Guerro shows the saint on the battlefield of Simancas in 919 AD.

ten were the *pièce de résistance*.

The great Al-Mansur, who was to become one of the most powerful Moorish rulers of Spain, came from a noble Berber family and was the only Moor known to have set up organised stud farms in Spain. This he did near Cordoba using his own strain of Berber war-horse.

Despite the requisitioning of their horses by the Moors, the Christian knights had the advantage of thousands of years' cavalry experience bred into them, and the people of the north assumed the role of defender of Christian civilisation within the Peninsula, with resistance continuing throughout these lands until the Reconquest. After the reported discovery of the body of St James the Apostle at Compostela in the ninth century, the Christian Galicians erected a shrine, and St James, or Santiago de Compostela, inspired the people of the north to fight back for their lands. Many claimed to have seen a vision of the Saint riding before them to victory on a white charger. This became the subject of many famous pictures, now scattered throughout Spain.

The same method of mounted combat that had once thrust fear into the hearts of the proud Romans was also to daunt the Moorish troops, as we learn from the writings of Abu Bakr al Tartusi at the end of the eleventh century in the *Sirag al Muluk*. It is worth quoting a few sentences translated from this book:

'During one of Al Mansur Ibn Amir's expeditions, a Christian, dressed in armour from head to foot, advanced ahead of his army and, galloping and turning in front of his adversaries, shouted:
   '"Will no one come and fight me in single combat?"
'A Moor went out to meet him and after a brief fight was killed by the Christian, causing cries of delight from the enemy and filling the Moors with grief. The Christian, riding back and forth, threw out another challenge, "I challenge two to one!" [presumed to mean a second time]
   'A Moor stepped forward and after a short struggle was also killed.
   'Once again the Christian challenged: "Three to one!"
   'A third Moor advanced and met the same fate.

'The Christians shouted victoriously and the Moors were humiliated and almost beaten.

'Then someone said to Al Mansur: "Only Ibn Al Mushafi can redeem our shame."

'"Did you see that Christian's work?"

'"Certainly. I saw it with my own eyes," he replied. "What do you want?"

'"That you finish it!"

'"All right. It shall be so if Allah will!"

'The story goes on to relate how a man from the frontier was eventually found after much searching, and he alone was prepared to take the Christian on. He did so, and at length flung the Christian's head at the feet of Al Mansur.

'Then said Ibn Al Mushafi: "These are the men you need!" pointing at the Christian's head. "But in your army you have not one thousand, nor five hundred, nor one hundred, nor fifty nor even ten of them!"'

This account, similar to some of those related by the Romans, portrays the admiration the Moors had for the horsemen and horsemanship of the Iberian peoples.

Moorish Civilisation and Culture

Despite fighting in the north, and the overthrow of the Moors by the Portuguese in 1249, the Moorish invaders had enjoyed at least three centuries of comparative peace and prosperity within Southern Hispania which was to give this country a unique character all of its own.

After the initial period of trauma, more and more of the Arab peoples came to the Peninsula, although they were always outnumbered by the Berbers. Many of these were from proud Arab 'royal' families and as they integrated with the Spanish, and even in the beginning shared their places of worship, the Moorish invasion began to take on all the appearances of a peaceful occupation. Arabic culture, particularly architecture, poetry and art, flowered into Hispano-Islamic art, and agrarian reform which reached its height when Christian and Muslim co-habited peacefully together, particularly in the south of Spain, brought a high degree of civilisation to a country which under the Visigoths had been essentially unruly. The Moors brought many new words to the vocabulary – algebra, alcohol, alchemist, aubergine and orange passed into English use – and in the Spanish language we find many more. *Alcazar* (castle), *arroz* (rice), *aduana* (customs house) are used daily, and proper names abound – Algarve, Almodover Algeçiras, Almeria are only a few examples among countless others.

The Reconquest of Spain under the Christian kings started peaceably enough and during the Moors' years of decline and withdrawal, some of the latter's greatest monuments were completed. Most striking perhaps is the great Mosque at Cordoba, the Giralda at Seville and the magnificent Alhambra of Granada where all the brilliance of Moorish architecture and design is embodied in a legacy of rich colour and intricate pattern.

In terminating this chapter, it is perhaps a little ironic to conclude that while every facet and feature of Spanish life was touched by the Moorish occupation, the influence thereof growing stronger as one progresses southwards, the one element which remained remarkably intact was that of equestrianism. It was not the Moors who taught the Iberians to ride their horses with light switches, but the Iberians who impressed their methods of highly disciplined equitation with the use of a bit and a bridle on the Arabs. We know from the Roman philosopher Claudius Ptolemy, who flourished about 140 AD and wrote a famous *Geography* of the known world, that the horsemen of the Iberian Peninsula had developed a distinctive riding style. He says: 'Spain has always been noted for the swiftness of its horses, ridden beautifully by lightly armed horsemen who grip with their knees.' This observation makes nonsense of the claims by certain writers that the art of horsemanship was brought to the Peninsula with the Moorish invasion of 711.

We have seen how the Barb horse originated in the Peninsula, and how it was reintroduced, thus bringing back the old Iberian blood. We have also examined the state of the pure-bred Arab horse in all his rarity at the time of the early invasions, and noted the admiration displayed by leading figures such as Al Mansur and the Caliph Omiadas towards the Christians' horses. We read of horses being taken from Spain to improve breeds in Syria, from whence we understand the Arab may in part have originated. All this we know as fact.

What is mere supposition is how many Spanish horses were taken back by the Moors during their long retreat from the Peninsula. Presumably, the departing people who had given so much to Spain and enjoyed its mild climate and fertile valleys, did not return home on a camel. A very natural means of transport back to north-west Africa would be on a ship with a fine mare from Al-Andalus ready to take up the journey on the other side. Could *this* explain the continued strength of Spanish features in the Barb horse of later years? Sadly, we shall probably never know.

We do know, however, that after the Arab invasions of the eighth century and subsequently the eleventh century, the Barbary Coast was temporarily occupied by several successive foreign powers. These included the Normans, the Portuguese, the Spanish and later the Turks, all of whom would have to some extent influenced horse breeding, particularly for cavalry at that time.

In Chapters VII and VIII we shall discuss Spain and Portugal's modern history and check the progress of the great Iberian war-horse through the troubled times that were to follow in the Peninsula. Somewhere at the back of our mind may lurk that picture of Marcus Aurelius or St James of Compostela, mounted on a Spanish Great Horse. But now the time has come to cross the Bay of Biscay and discover what has been happening to the equine population of England, and how the Great Horse was to develop there, which we shall endeavour to discover in the next chapter.

CHAPTER IV

The Great Horse
and the Age of Chivalry

Hast Thou given the horse strength?
Hast Thou clothed his neck with thunder?
Canst Thou make him afraid as a grasshopper?
The glory of his nostrils is terrible,
He paweth in the valley, and rejoiceth in his
    strength;
He goeth on to meet the armed men . . .

JOB 39, VERSE 19

The role of the Iberian horse as the Royal Horse of Europe in the sixteenth and seventeenth centuries and his significance in the military history of England in particular at the time, will be better understood if we consider his predecessors.

Horses in Ancient Britain

Iberian blood was first introduced into Great Britain as early as the Iron Age. This commenced around 500 BC and during the latter part of this era a powerful tribe known as the Brigantes began to import a small breed of horse or pony from the north-west of Spain for the purpose of chariot driving. The territory of the Brigantes was split between County Waterford in Ireland, and the lands now known as the North Riding of Yorkshire, County Durham, the plain of the Humber and the Yorkshire wolds, bordering onto Northumberland. Another branch of the tribe had become established in the extreme north-west corner of Spain round the port known then as the Groyne, and now called Coruna. In Roman times, this was referred to as Brigantium, the harbour of the Brigante tribe.

Trading between these Celtic tribespeople was well established long before the Romans came to Britain. This was to set a precedent for later generations living on the English and Irish coasts as well as for those on the Atlantic seaboard of Spain and Portugal, which would last well into the Middle Ages. From Santander to Wexford is only 700 miles, and the Phoenicians had long ago mastered these sea routes and led the way for the ancient Britons.

Another tribe of Celts which came to Britain around the first century AD were the Belgae, and they in their turn had established trading links with North Africa and southern Spain, bringing in Barb and Iberian horses. In *The Book of the Horse*, Major A.J.R. Lamb suggests that the Belgae were breeding bigger and better horses than had ever been seen before in ancient Britain, and that they were able to use their horses as chargers in battle thus becoming a tribe of real horsemen like their cousins in the Low Countries. Anthony Dent, the historian, would appear to confirm this view when he states that the Brigantes of Yorkshire needed good horses all the time to maintain their security from the Belgic Parisii, whom he describes as 'pushful newcomers'. While the Brigantes continued to control the network of estuaries on the west coast of Yorkshire and Lancashire, the Belgae settled in East Anglia, particularly round the Fens – areas famed forevermore for the breeding of a superior type of horse, as of course is Ireland.

When Julius Caesar invaded Britain in 55 BC, he encountered wild and furious hordes of the yellow-haired leaders of Celtic Britain. The Celts used pan chariots which they appear to have driven with great skill, and a vivid description is given of their tactics by Caesar himself:

> 'At the first onset, they drove their cars in all directions, hurled their javelins, and by the din and clatter of the horses and wheels commonly threw the ranks of the enemy into disorder, and making their way amongst the squadrons of the enemy cavalry, they leapt down from their chariots and fought on foot.'

Although the Romans were defeated in their first round of battles against the British Celts, it was not long before the disciplined legions of Rome withstood the courage and determination of the island people. This led to the Roman occupation of the British Isles which lasted until the beginning of the fifth century AD.

So impressed were the Romans by the islanders' ponies, that they exported many home to Italy, but more importantly they introduced into England fine cavalry blood direct from Andalusia. We read in Chapter II how the Romans had set up an organised system of remount depots in Baetica, Hispania, and we can only guess at the numbers of Iberian war-horses which were shipped into ancient Britain by the numbers of Roman cavalry units stationed there. By the end of the second century there were twenty-eight of these altogether and we know that two Spanish units, the First and Second Asturians were stationed at Hadrian's Wall. In East Anglia, near Colchester, was another Spanish legion, the First Vettones, which were, in all probability, mounted on Iberian horses.

Major Lamb maintains that the Crispinian Legion, stationed in Yorkshire, was mounted on North African stallions. Thus Iberian and Barb blood crossed with the native Celtic pony may have produced a really useful English breed of some quality and speed. It is thought that this cross-breed would have measured approximately 13 h.h., although Roman remains of a horse's skeleton near Colchester have indicated that a horse existed at that time of almost 15 h.h. This, however, was probably a pure-bred Spanish or Barb.

Some sources believe that the Galloway pony,[1] a cross-bred developed for chariot racing by the Romans in the north of England and borders of Scotland, contributed through the early English female line to the development of the English Thoroughbred. This, however, has never been substantiated.

Despite these early infusions of southern, or even oriental blood, horse breeding appears to have been at a rather low ebb in the intervening centuries leading up

1. Daniel Defoe in his *Tour Through Scotland* (Letter XXI) describes the Galloway in approximately 1720 thus: 'these horses are remarkable for being good pacers, strong easy goers, hardy, gentle, well-broken and above all they never tire, and are very much bought up in England on that account.'

to the Norman Conquest of 1066. The Anglo-Saxons were peace-loving people and saw no reason to develop a blood horse. More cold-blooded strains were introduced to England during the Dark Ages from Iceland and Scandinavia. Whilst these were highly useful for working the land, they were no more suited to dashing into bloody battle than a pack mule.

By sheer contrast, William the Conqueror's army was mounted on wiry, forward-going, active war-horses which would appear to have had a generous complement of warm-blood. These were known as 'destriers' or 'grete' horses – although we know they were not very large.

The Emergence of the Destrier or Great Horse of War

Before we go on to examine the Battle of Hastings in more detail, let us discuss the somewhat misleading term 'destrier' or Great Horse. It is apparent from the many books which abound on the subject of horsemanship through the ages, that contrasting views are held, and whilst some authorities, particularly influenced by the film industry, maintain that all destriers looked like Shires or Clydesdales, others disagree. Taking a balanced view, it would appear that there were three types of destrier or Great Horse during the period of his existence from 1066 to the end of the seventeenth century. Using significant dates to highlight the differences, these may be divided into the following categories, all of which were accorded the name 'grete' in ancient English to imply excellence or suitability for their task as a cavalry horse. There were, of course, many intervening stages during which these types overlapped one another and one type did not abruptly die out to give way to another. The examples given below merely list the type of destrier to be found in England over that period and serve to illustrate when each of those types was at its height of usefulness and popularity within the cavalry. The Spanish horse, for example, was already being used in the Norman army by William the Conqueror in 1066, and this trend for kings and emperors to lead their knights into battle seated on such a horse was to increase throughout the following centuries. Only, however, in the sixteenth and seventeenth centuries did this vogue explode into the situation which was fired by the Renaissance when every cavalry officer of good birth rode into battle on a Spanish or Barb charger. Owing to the varying sizes of the horses concerned, 'grete' would not appear to indicate height.

> 1066 – The destriers of the Norman Invasion. These were cob size, between 13.2 and 14.3 h.h. Clean-limbed, forward-going and strong enough to carry a man in chain-mail into battle at the gallop, they were probably at least in part warm-blooded as France had always imported horses from Spain and crossed them with her own local breeds.
> 1505 – Durer's Great Horse (see photograph). This was the type of horse being imported by Henry VIII from the Netherlands to upgrade the cavalry horse of that time for height and weight-carrying ability; he averaged between 14.2 and 15.2 h.h. He had a hairy fetlock and round, heavier feet. This horse was able to support his own weighty plate armour and that of his knight (who would weigh around thirty stone, including

Left: *Detail from the Bayeux tapestry. The majority of equine researchers accept that the horses of the Norman knights depicted in the eleventh-century tapestries were sturdy Norman cobs with sufficient blood from Spain and Morocco to give them impulsion and courage in battle.*

Below: *The horses shown in this Gothic altar-piece by O. Galiano from the Episcopal Museum, Palma de Mallorca, are typical of those used by the Spanish crusaders in their struggle against the Moors. Note the distinctive shape of the head of these light-limbed chargers.*

Max Diamond, a twentieth-century jousting expert, mounted on his Lusitano charger Marquesa, at Chilham Castle, Kent. (Photo by the author)

This fifteenth-century engraving from Froissart is one of many which shows royalty and the knights of Britain or France mounted on horses of blood: high-stepping, clean-limbed chargers which appeared on the equestrian scene centuries before the Arab and Turk were imported into either country. These horses were invariably Iberian.

weapons and saddle) but he could manage little more than a slow lumbering trot in the battlefield or at the lists.

1632 – Charles I's destrier or Spanish charger (see front cover). Close-coupled, compact and measuring between 15 and 16 h.h., this imported horse was now being ridden by cavalry officers all over Europe, proving versatile and agile in the battlefield. Full of fire and vigour, his hot blood manifested itself in his courage. Clean-limbed but very powerful in the back and loins, this horse could carry a man in plate armour but he himself did not wear armour.

Thus, the useful cobs of the Norman invaders were as different from the charger pictured on our front cover, as were the lumbering horses of the last days of the joust, but they all came under the heading of Great Horse or destrier which separated them from the palfreys, rouncies,[2] pack-horses, sumpters and capuls.[3]

Artists are often blamed for seeking to flatter the rider by distorting the proportions of the animal on which he is seated, and yet in my research I have not found this to be so. Indeed, visual evidence is extremely useful and the horses faithfully portrayed over the centuries by sculptors, portrait painters, tapestry artists and seamstresses give the observer a very clear picture of what horses looked like in each period and how their size differed in relation to the mounted or standing figure. It must always be remembered, however, that the average man in the Middle Ages was no taller than approximately 5ft 6in.

The translation of the term destrier is altogether simpler. Together with so many other Latinised French words, it was introduced by the Normans into the English language at the time of the Invasion. It implies what it suggests – horses of the

2. Rouncy comes from the Latin *runcinus* and indicates a small cob of no great quality, which in the Middle Ages would have been ridden by an artisan. In Chaucer's *Canterbury Tales*, the Shipman rode a rouncy.
3. A sumpter or capul was a type of pack-horse; ridden by the Miller in the *Canterbury Tales*. If one considers that the knight's destrier came at the top of the scale of horses, followed by the palfreys and hobbies, the capul came virtually at the bottom with the sumpter and other baggage animals.

right hand. These war-horses were extremely valuable, and when not in action, they were spared as much as possible and led by a mounted squire by the right hand from the offside of his rouncy.

The cost of raising a force of heavy cavalry has always been an expensive one but in the Middle Ages it was overcome by the system of feudalism which affected all areas of life. The king granted large tracts of land to his principal followers, and gave them his protection. In return, they owed him their fealty, or loyalty, and were honour-bound to provide him with fighting men whenever he needed them. These lords and barons then granted land to their knights, and at the lower end of the scale were the yeomen, freemen and finally the serfs who actually worked the land and bore the brunt of the cost of equipping their lords and knights in their soldiering career.

One of the first great rulers to make use of an army of destriers with armed knights was Charlemagne, King of the Franks, in the ninth century. His cavalry was equipped with axes and lances. It was the sheer impetus and force of his horses and men which enabled them to smash through enemy ranks and put them to flight.

The Norman Invasion of 1066

'The Battle of Hastings,' wrote A. J. Frost in 1915, 'was waged between Harold's English army of infantrymen and William the Conqueror's army of horsemen, ending in a victory for the latter.' 1066 is indeed a landmark in European history, and thanks to the unstinting efforts of the good wives of Bayeux is well recorded from an equestrian point of view, therefore it is an appropriate place from whence to start in our assessment of cavalry.

Although well established on the Continent by the middle of the eleventh century, the destrier was relatively late coming to England and was clearly never the indigenous horse of Great Britain, probably having his origins in Norman, Flemish and Spanish stock.

Highly favoured by the Normans, who had been responsible for his concentrated breeding at that time, when William the Conqueror set forth to invade England, it is unlikely that Harold and his men possessed more than a handful of such useful fighting animals. As we study the Bayeux Tapestries a little more closely, we soon realise that, with the exception of one or two English horses depicted with hogged manes, every charger shown is a Norman destrier with a Norman cavalryman on its back. What a stomach-churning, sickening, never-ending stream of horseflesh and weaponry they must have presented to Harold and his lines of infantrymen. Until that huge turning point in British history, England had known no organised cavalry since the time of the Romans and was therefore totally unprepared for this type of assault. Sturdy and strong, yet light enough to be able to gallop, the destrier of William's army was an efficient war-horse, although as we have seen he was little more than a cob. Despite the lesser height of the average rider, the lower leg of the cavalryman hangs down well below the horse's belly.

It was not the weight of the horse which procured victory for the French invaders, but rather his weight-carrying ability, and his thrust. Harold and his men fought gallantly with their terrible five-foot Danish axes and sharpened staves, but they were no match for William's knights mounted on their galloping destriers as they swept through the English infantry, raining down vicious, hacking blows with hatchet and sword from their superior height.

Here we find the beginnings of the huge popularity that the Iberian war-horse was destined to enjoy later on in the sixteenth and seventeenth centuries, for the Spanish horse was already considered a status symbol. William had been given two fine Spanish stallions by Duke Alfonso of Spain, to ride into the most important battle of his life. Later, as he and his victorious troops were to bring more Iberian horses to England's shores, they repeated the work of the last invaders under Caesar and eventually helped to contribute, albeit in a small way, to the improvement of Britain's existing native breeds.

The Norman Conquest heralded the introduction of the fully-armoured knight to Britain. Such was the cultural and social impact of the Norman occupation that by the twelfth century the aristocratic order of chivalry was a way of life in England. Mounted knights were everywhere depicted as the epitome of military might and their code of conduct in war and peace came to symbolise the highest ideals of human behaviour. A whole new way of life sprang up which centred round the Crusades, Pilgrimages and tournaments.

The Crusaders

One of the ways in which an adventurous knight from England, Germany or Normandy could be assured of gaining everlasting salvation in an age when such a consideration weighed heavy, and at the same time safely indulge the bellicose and acquisitive sides of his nature, was to set forth to the Holy Land on one of the great Crusades.

From the beginning of the twelfth century until the end of the thirteenth, a stream of adventure seekers set forth for the east – almost in the same manner as, in more modern times, men hurried towards a newly discovered goldfield. Knights with their horses, carried by ships, were followed by a wake of lesser mortals scurrying across Europe on donkeys, mules or on foot in unregulated numbers. Such was the revivalist surge of enthusiasm that fired the genuine Crusader, that he was prepared to put up with any discomfort on the way, in order to ensure a more exalted position in the next world. As with all spontaneous movements conducted on a vast scale, the camp followers included amongst their ranks a less dedicated, motley cross-section of excommunicated or banished monks and friars, criminals, fugitives and hucksters (pedlars). But the idea behind the Crusades was first and foremost a chivalric one, conceived originally in France to retrieve the Holy Sepulchre from the Mohammedan rulers and reclaim Jerusalem for Christianity. This challenge particularly appealed to Normans on both sides of the Channel with their old Norse instinct for adventure.

Out of the Crusades arose chivalric orders of knights, such as the Templars, the Knights of St John of Jerusalem, and so on; but there was little that was chivalric – in our sense of the word – about the wholesale slaughter of Moorish men, women and children, carried out to the cries of 'Deus Vulte', until the blood ran down the streets of Jerusalem and the Crusaders ran 'sobbing for excess of joy' to the Church of the Sepulchre at the end of the first Crusade.

Throughout the Crusades, the Christian knights rode on predominantly cold-blooded destriers in full armour, chain-mail, long shield and heavy casque (helmet) and seemed to make little provision for the fact that they were no longer on native soil and exposed to a very different climate. Whilst returning Crusaders may have brought back some light, eastern horses captured from the Mohammedans, we also know that Iberian horses were being collected from friendlier shores nearer home, particularly from Lisbon where many Crusaders had stopped on the way and eventually decided to settle (see Chapter VIII). It is only towards the end of the Crusades that we read of the Christians being impressed by the swifter, more agile form of riding displayed by the superb cavalry of the infidel on their oriental horses.

Historians usually consider the Crusades a failure, due in part to the lack of suitable cavalry and ill-adapted methods of attack employed by the knights of the west, for they ended not in the occupation of the east by the Christian west, but in the conquest of part of the west by the Mohammedan east, with the Ottoman Turks entrenched round the Danube. But in other respects, success was attained, with the coasts of the eastern Baltic won for Christianity by the Teutonic Order of Knights. Also, the centuries of battles against the Moors by the Spanish crusading knights was to end eventually in the Reconquest of the whole of Spain for Christianity.

We have already seen in Chapter II how the *ginete* horsemanship of the knights of Spain and Portugal had earned them a worldwide reputation of respect. Since their early wars against the Phoenicians, the Greeks and the Romans, they had continued to maintain their bent-legged position in the saddle (in direct contrast to the straight-legged posture of the heavily-armed Norman, English and German knight) and carried a minimum of body armour and weaponry. Their horses too had not changed and were infinitely more suited to scaling the rocky heights of the Peninsula and bounding across arid plains scorched under a hot Andalusian sun, than any cold-blooded destrier from the north with his round, soup-plate feet, designed to carry him through soft-going marsh and woodland, in a landscape so contrasting to that of the Holy Land. In consideration of these important factors, it is perhaps not surprising, in hindsight, that the thrust of the western Crusaders should fail in the east, and the Reconquest by the southern Crusaders of their own land should succeed. The Moor, with his swift, streamlined horse was a slippery adversary, and, at times, the Christian knight, perspiring under his shining armour beneath a Galilean sun, must have felt as vulnerable as a beached whale, whereas his counterpart in Spain[4] and Portugal possessed the means to cope.

One Spanish horse which earned a place in history was Babieca. This horse, reputed by all Spanish historians to be a pure-bred Andalusian, was the destrier or charger of El Cid, the Castilian knight whose bold exploits and heroic deeds are celebrated in the great epic *Poema del Cid* of the twelfth century. El Cid, far from being a gentlemanly courtier, was obviously something of a rogue. One

4. After the Crusading spirit had died a natural death amongst the majority of Englishmen, we read about the occasional English knight volunteering to fight with the Spanish against the Moors in the Peninsula. One such was Lord Scales of the Woodville family who was rewarded by Queen Isabella in the 15th century with 'some costly gifts including twelve Andalusian horses and pavilions hung with cloths of gold.'

moment he fought for the Spanish crown, the next he was a hired mercenary on the side of a Moorish prince. The Moors dubbed him *Al Cid* (the Lord) and he is also known in Spanish literature as *El Campeador*, the Warrior.

The traditional story is that as a youth, El Cid (born Rodrigo Diaz) had selected Babieca, a mere scraggy colt not yet weaned. As Babieca developed into a full-blooded charger and his master became famous for his daring skirmishes in the military field, the horse was referred to as 'a steed without equal'. After the capture of Valençia from the Moors by the Christians in 1094, Babieca's fame spread throughout the whole of Spain, and even the

El Cid, grim and uncompromising reigns supreme on his Andalusian charger Babieca over the ancient city of Burgos in Castile.

king, Alfonso of Leon and Castile, respected this noble stallion. When, on one royal occasion, El Cid made a gesture of offering his horse to his monarch, Alfonso exclaimed, 'God forbid that I should take him! A horse like Babieca deserves no other rider than you, my Cid, so that both together you may drive the Moors from the field and go in their pursuit!'

Babieca was to survive his master by two years and is said to have died at the remarkable age of forty. El Cid was buried at a monastery near Burgos (though later his remains were removed into the city itself) and the horse was laid to rest outside the monastery gates, where two elm trees were planted in his memory. As late as 1948, the Duke of Alva erected a monument on the site in dedication to the horse, and wherever one walks in Burgos – one of Spain's most historical and elegant cities – there are constant reminders of the romantic knight and his stallion at every turn, not least in the shape of a dramatic equestrian statue which dominates one of the main avenues. El Cid and Babieca sum up the crusading spirit of the era.

Pilgrimages

The mediaeval Church adopted the practice of pilgrimages from the ancient Church. Just as the Greeks and Romans had made their devotional journeys, undertaken in honour of their gods, for purposes of prayer and in quest of assistance, especially for health reasons, the German, French and English devout entered into the spirit of the pilgrimage with a fervency reminiscent of the Crusaders. Rome and Palestine had always been the prime target for pilgrims, but with the Holy Land no longer held by a Christian power, shrines nearer home became popular.

The most important of these for the English was the shrine of St James of Compostela (Santiago de Compostela) in the Spanish province of Galicia. Here the remains of James, the son of Zebedee, were reputed to lie, and by the twelfth century, so popular had this pilgrimage become, that it ranked amongst the English on a level with one to Rome or the Holy City. It would be churlish to suggest that the easy accessibility by sea for eager British pilgrims may have outweighed St James' miraculous cures, but nevertheless by Chaucer's time pilgrims in their thousands were following the western sea route to land at Corunna or Pontevedra for the easy journey up country to Compostela itself.

During these expeditions a considerable number of Spanish palfreys were bought and shipped home. In order to cover the thirty-five miles or so from the port to Santiago, pilgrims would undertake the journey in two stages by mule or palfrey. Anthony Dent tells us that 'some of these palfreys were so popular that as soon as a pilgrim had landed he would arrange to have it shipped home.' If, however, on his journey he did not like the animal as well as expected, he could always sell it again on the return journey to his ship 'down at port – and one would still be better off than paying the hire fee'.

The Great Tournaments

Originally tournaments were a method of cavalry training, positive proof that a knight had mastered the skills of mounted fighting in close formation. But as tournaments grew in popularity, they became more of a spectacle than a serious military exercise, and the chronicler Geoffrey of Monmouth takes a rather sardonic view when he writes:

> 'Presently, the knights engage in a game on horseback, making a show of fighting a battle, whilst the dames and damsels looking on from the top of the walls, for whose sake the courtly knights make believe to be fighting, do cheer them on for the sake of seeing better sport.'

There were strict rules to abide by, and as early as 1000 AD, a certain Geoffroy

de Preuilly of France had compiled a set of regulations governing the tournament for the French court, although this did not seem to prevent a horrifying amount of serious accidents with large loss of life in both men and horses.

The joust developed into a highly embellished social occasion, much enjoyed by the ladies at court. Although a heavier horse is depicted, note that the lower leg of the knight hangs well below the horse's belly and that the horse is clean-limbed. This contradicts the idea of a Shire-like jousting horse.

Sometimes, however, these dangerous jousts had a happy ending, as we learn from a vivid account by Sir John Froissart in a description of the tilt which took place between Sir John Holland of England and Sir Reginald de Roye of France on the Spanish–Portuguese border, in the presence of the King and Queen of Portugal and the Duke and Duchess of Lancaster. This gives us some idea of the magnificence of these occasions which were as popular abroad as they were in England.

'the King of Portugal, the Queen, the Duchess with her daughter, and the ladies of the court, set out for Etenca, in grand array. The Duke of Lancaster, when they were near at hand, mounted his horse; and attended by a numerous company, went to meet them . . . Three days after the arrival of the King of Portugal, came Sir Reginald de Roye, handsomely accompanied by knights and squires, to the amount of six score horse . . . On the morrow Sir John Holland, and Sir Reginald de Roye armed themselves and rode into a spacious close in Etenca, well sanded where the tilts were to be performed. Scaffolds were erected for the ladies, the King, the Duke and many English lords who had come to witness the combat, for none had stayed at home . . .

Having braced their targets and examined each other through the visors of their helmets, they spurred on their horses, spear in hand. Though they allowed their horses to gallop as they pleased, they advanced on as straight a line as if it had been drawn with a cord and hit each other on the visors . . . the spectators cried out that it was a handsome course. The knights returned to their station . . . when ready they set off full gallop for they had excellent horses under them, which they well knew how to manage and again struck each other on the helmets that sparks of fire came from them, but chiefly from Sir John Holland's . . . Sir John and Sir Reginald eyed each other, to see if any advantage were to be gained, for their horses were so excellent that they could manage them as they pleased . . . and so they tilted again without either man unseating the other.'

In the end the English and the French knight, fighting on Spanish soil and riding Iberian destriers finished their fight on foot and it ended in a draw with everyone happy. This passage sums up the spirit of the age, and is particularly interesting from the equestrian point of view. The horses were obviously full of fire and jousting was conducted at that period at a headlong gallop, so that the sparks literally flew.

Later in history we learn, however, that many kings and leaders began to rebel against the injuries inevitably sustained by their best fighting men, and ways were thought up to radically change the nature of the tournament without banning it altogether. The outcome was that the joust was encouraged to flower into a highly embellished, lavishly social occasion without the danger. Where once knights dashed down the lists on their useful galloping steeds, the emphasis was now for a show of magnificence in armour and horse attire, and with sumptuous banners, cloaks and drapes flowing in a gorgeous profusion of colour, horses now lumbered towards each other at little more than a sedate trot.

By the time of the tournament which continued for two whole weeks at the

Field of the Cloth of Gold in 1520, the military and sporting objects of the tournament had given way to a rich, formalised entertainment with singing, dancing, poetry and artistic pursuits taking over from the athletic nature of the occasion.

The Heavy Horse

This was the heyday of the heavier destrier. The useful, swifter horses of the Norman invaders had given way to an altogether stolider type by the beginning of the fourteenth century. How had this come about?

King Henry II (1154–1189) had imported horses from the Low Countries in an attempt to raise the height of the British horse and he kept these imported stallions at the royal stables in Winchester. King John (1199–1216) imported a hundred large stallions from Flanders and Holland likewise, and with England intermittently at war after the accession of Edward I (1272–1307) with the Scots, Welsh and French, the expansion of the cavalry studs and improvements in breeding became a matter of prime importance. In the thirteenth century we read about Halingrat, a crossbowman, being sent abroad by the keeper of the king's horses to buy 'better and more handsome horses' for the royal household to Gascony or Spain, and under Edward II (1307–1327) there is a record of William de Guernun, merchant, and Dominic de Rouncavales, King's Sargeant, being sent to Spain for war-horses. Therefore, whilst heavy cold-blood horses were being developed for weight-carrying purposes, it is clear that the popularity of the blood horse was also increasing, particularly as a suitable mount for monarchs and leaders.

A new age in the horse began after the victories of Crecy in 1346 and Poitiers in 1356 which brought so much glory to the English crown. These illustrious battles were won by skilled archers whose clothyard shafts penetrated the French knights' chain-mail, making them suddenly vulnerable in battle. Knights on both sides of the Channel now clothed themselves and their horses in heavy plate armour, and Edward III[5] spent enormous sums of money on heavy Great Horses from the Low Countries, with one consignment from the Count of Hainault costing 25,000 florins. This heavier cavalry horse lacked the speed and impulsion of the Norman destriers and the fiery Spanish chargers, but his weight-carrying ability was undeniable and an army of knights thrusting through the thick of battle on these powerful, almost invincible armoured tanks were a formidable foe. Flemish and Friesian blood became very popular in England at this time, and the Flemish horse which was black and hairy-legged may have been an early forefather to the Shire, although he still lacked almost two hands in height. An example of the prolific importation of war-horses during that period is found in the royal archives in the inventory kept by William Farlee who was Keeper of the Wardrobe to the royal household. A list is given detailing the horses shipped to Calais for the King's campaigns abroad (from 1359–1360), and we read that the Black Prince took with him 1,369 horses and returned with 2,114; the Earl of Richmond took 741 horses and returned with 787; and in the same expedition, the Duke of Lancaster, later

---

5. Edward III also imported destriers from Spain and sent his Keeper of the Horse, Arnold Garcy, to the Peninsula for this purpose.

known as John of Gaunt, took out no horses but returned with 1,611. When we take into account that hundreds of horses were maimed or killed in battle, it is clear that the importation of horses from the Continent, particularly Normandy, Gascony, Spain and Portugal, was conducted on a generous scale. This was a natural measure for a small island at war, with no hope of breeding enough horses of the necessary stamp to supply its growing cavalry. In the same inventory there are examples of compensation being paid for 'replacement of horses lost in the war', and one English knight, Sir Edward Courtenay, received £55 for one destrier lost, which gives an idea of the value of these horses.

Under Henry VIII strict laws[6] were introduced to encourage breeding for height, and this unfaithful king's infamous remark about his wife, Anne of Cleves, being similar to a 'Flanders mare' was probably only too apt. Albrecht Durer's copper engraving of a German Great Horse (dated 1505) – see illustration – would seem typical of the weight-carrying horse of that period. Henry VIII himself, however, is always to be seen riding a clean-limbed destrier which looks more Iberian than Flemish or English.

By the time the destrier had reached the proportions required by Henry VIII for his knights, the whole system of maintaining him had become extremely complex and costly.

In theory, for every Great Horse in the mediaeval army, excluding the transport horses, there were several smaller horses. The knight and his destrier as the basic fighting unit of the army needed a *minimum* of three other horses to keep them in action, day in and day out. Preferably, knights had a second destrier in case anything befell the first, for these horses, particularly the heavier types, were not so hardy as the earlier cobs. In any case, the destrier was only to be ridden in action, but a second destrier meant a second squire, which added even more costs to the basic entourage, unless the knight had a second son, old enough to accompany him. Also required was an easy-gaited palfrey for the knight to ride when not in action, and a rouncy for the squire to ride whilst leading the destrier. A pack-horse was also needed, to carry the knight's armour, and when chivalry reached the point where the destrier wore armour too, then a second armour-carrying pack-horse had to be found. The war-horse would travel at a trot, and the accompanying rouncy trotted too, but the palfrey would be encouraged to amble. As we have seen, many palfreys had been brought into England in the past by pilgrims and in the earlier days of trade between northern Spain and certain English and Irish sea ports, and these willing horses of Iberian descent were easily trained to pace. Palfreys were similar to the post horses maintained by the Romans to convey the Imperial messengers from one end of the empire to another, and as the Romans rode without stirrups, they were the most comfortable to sit to. No doubt too, the knight on his long journey over the dusty miles of mediaeval England was grateful for this soft-backed steed with his smooth, ambling gait.

6. One of these royal decrees governing the maintenance of stallions on common land ran as follows: 'Therefore for the increase of stronger horses hereafter be it enacted that no commoner or commoners within any forest, chase, moor, marsh, heath, common or waste ground at any time after the 31st March 1543 shall have or put forth to pasture in any such ground etc., any stoned horse or horses being above the age of two years and being of the altitude and height of 15 handfulls.'

Far right: *Albrecht Durer's copper engraving 'The Great Horse' (1505), is as dissimilar to that of Stradanus' Spanish destrier (1570) (below) as is possible to conceive. Note in particular the soup-plate feet and hairy fetlocks of the German war-horse, and the neat, upright feet and clean fetlocks of the Spanish horse.*

Right: *Henry VIII's plate armour.*

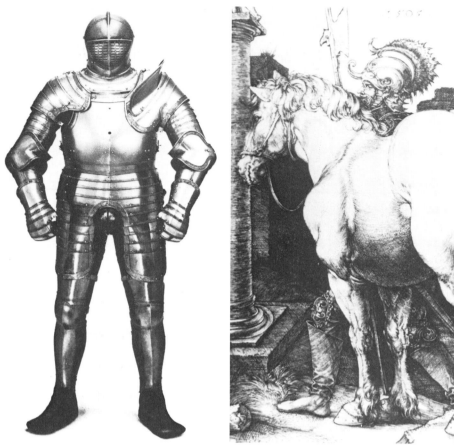

EQVVS HISPANVS.

The Demise of the Weight-carrying Cavalry Horse

It is certain that economics played a large part in hastening the downfall of the knight's solid horse. We have already seen how progress in the invention of weapons – notably at the Battle of Crécy – showed up a vulnerable side to an army of destriers when the powerful French cavalry charge was repeatedly cut down by the English longbowmen. The longbow had at least double the range of the crossbow and could be fired at six times the speed, thus wreaking havoc among enemy lines; but it was the invention of small firearms that really struck the death knell for the heavy destrier. It was almost as though warfare had turned full circle, for all at once mobility was required again in the war-horse. Only, this time, mere impetus and impulsion were not sufficient. Now military leaders were looking for a horse which was full of fire as well as courage, a horse which had the blood to anticipate and quiver under saddle, a horse which could wheel and turn and pirouette at a moment's notice. Suddenly, attention was focusing on the Spanish destrier, once the prerogative of the king and of the Iberian knights; the only horse to outwit the Moors in mediaeval history; and a horse admired for so many centuries by the likes of Xenophon, Hannibal and other great cavalry leaders.

For the first time in England, France, Germany and Holland, there was a very real demand for a hot-blood war-horse. The Andalusian horse was the natural choice and the way now lay clear for a charger blessed with manoeuvrability and agility as well as courage. Spanish blood had already been introduced at court, as we have seen. Thomas Blundeville was to summarise the Iberian charger admirably when he wrote:

> 'The horse of Spayne is finelie made, both head, bodie and legs, and very seemlie to the eie, saving that his buttocks be somewhat slender, and for his making lightnesse and swiftness withall, he is very much esteemed, and especiallie of noble men.'

Of course, nothing in history is cut and dried, as we were swift to remind ourselves in Chapter II. As with all evolutionary processes, there were intermediate phases. One of these worth noting is that in 1600 a Neapolitan named Juan Jeronimo Tinti[7] was placed in charge of the royal stud at Cordoba, in Spain. Possibly to deal with the ever-growing demand for Spanish war-horses flooding in from abroad, he decided to breed the perfect war-horse by crossing Norman, Italian, German, Danish and Flemish stallions with the light-limbed Andalusian royal mares. According to Spanish historians, the cross was disastrous. The Duke of Newcastle might have told him to do things the other way round and use hot-blooded stallions with cold-blooded mares as was successfully being carried out at Welbeck, as we shall read in Chapter XIII, and the so-called disaster might have been a roaring success.

Suffice to say that it is always easier to be wise in hindsight. As we leave the age of chivalry and the heavily-armed knight with his predominantly cold-blooded

---

7. Tinti (sometimes Tiutti) is mentioned with pronounced regularity in all literature published over the past thirty years by the Directorate of Horse Breeding and Cavalry Remounts in Spain. The author's views on the constant reference to Tinti are discussed in Chapter XI.

destrier, we glimpse before us a period of passion and romance where the dancing horses of the Baroque school seem to match the intense temperaments of their largely Catholic owners, setting the scene in England for a king to lose his head.

Table IV.1: Significant Dates Relating to the Iberian Horse and its Gradual Introduction into Great Britain (500 BC to 1547)

Iron Age from approx. 500 BC onwards	Celtic tribes using ancient Phoenician sea routes begin to trade between Britain, Belgium, France, N.W. Spain and N. Portugal. Asturian horses and horses already showing Iberian traits introduced into S.E. Ireland, N.W. England and S.E. England. Crossings with local stock inevitably took place.
Roman Period, 55 BC to approx. 410 AD	During Roman occupation of Great Britain, Iberian horses drawn from Roman remount depots in Baetica (Andalusia and Alentejo) and imported to serve mounted legions of Roman army stationed in Yorkshire and East Anglia. Subsequent crossings resulted in swift running horses, e.g. Galloways, used for Roman racing in north of England.
Dark Ages 5th–10th century	Active trade between Ireland and Iberian Peninsula. During latter half of this period, introduction of warm-blooded palfreys to Ireland (later known as Irish hobbies), subsequently imported by England. This trend continued into the Middle Ages.
11th century	1066 Norman Conquest. William the Conqueror given two Spanish stallions by Duke Alfonso of Spain. From this period onwards, Spanish destriers would become the natural mount of kings and leaders all over Europe.
12th century	Spanish destriers introduced to Wales by Earl of Shrewsbury. Introduction of imported stallions (almost certainly Spanish Jennets) during King Stephen's reign (1135–54). First mention of formal race meeting with hot-blood war-horses during reign of Richard I (1189–99). Returning Crusaders from Siege of Lisbon (when Portuguese overthrew the Moors in 1147) brought back Portuguese war-horses.

13th, 14th and 15th centuries	Pilgrims from Santiago de Compostela in N. Spain brought back Spanish palfreys.
	
	    Edward I (1272–1307), Edward II (1307–27) and Edward III (1327–77) sent agents abroad to Spain to procure war-horses.
	
	    Marriage of Philippa of Lancaster, daughter of John of Gaunt, to King D. João I of Portugal. Usual exchange of gifts included horses.
	
	    English volunteers fighting the Moors in Spain were rewarded with gifts of horses by Castilian kings, e.g. Lord Scales of the Woodville family was rewarded by Queen Isabella of Spain (1479–1504) with twelve Andalusian stallions which he imported to England.

16th century	Large and frequent importations of Spanish horses arrived during the reign of Henry VIII (1509–47). Gifts of horses from Emperor Charles V, Ferdinand of Aragon, and the Duke of Savoy. The King sent his agents throughout Spain to bring back war-horses and running horses, and his marriage to Katherine of Aragon brought the customary wedding gifts of horses.

CHAPTER V

The Age of Revival
and the Baroque Horse

The back of thy horse subjects the world to thee,
I will fashion it into a throne for thee,
Whence thou shalt wield a sceptre of power, of joy,
And of Freedom, such as is beyond thy expectation.

RUDOLF G. BINDING

A Change in the Role of Cavalry

The invention of small firearms brought about a huge revival in equitation. They first appeared at the end of the fourteenth century and by the time they were firmly established in the middle of the fifteenth century, their effect had radically changed the whole style of warfare.

In England, under Elizabeth I, tilting had declined, and the somewhat crude methods of charging together at little more than a trot in a lumbering mass of armour and horseflesh employed by the heavier cavalry of the Middle Ages, no longer made sense in the face of cannon and gunfire. From now on a cavalry horse with natural agility would have to be developed and tactics of attack and evasion practised and understood. Above all the new destrier must now be versed in all gaits and turns if his rider was to be able to load and fire unhindered. Precision and balance were suddenly of prime importance and a horse which could pull up dead from the gallop and wheel away from the line of enemy fire could save a man's life.

Once the dreadful realisation had sunk in that gunpowder had come to stay and firearms were the weapons of the future, even the most diehard military commanders were forced to rethink completely their methods of warfare. It was no longer sufficient to equip a knight with a weight-carrying horse, well-made armour, sturdy weapons and a saddle designed to keep him firmly in place. (In the previously good old days an armoured knight was almost invincible provided he was not lanced out of the saddle into a crashing fall, but even if his horse was injured, he still had a fair chance of restoring his honour by fighting on foot with shield and sword.) In this new, changing age of gunpowder, a good cavalryman had to be acquainted with riding techniques which hitherto had never been required in the field, not only for defence purposes but to complement the various firing positions he was compelled to take up if an attack was to be efficient.

The Renaissance had heralded the age of cultural rebirth, and its effects were now to penetrate beyond the established routine into the realm of horsemanship and self-defence as a highly polished technical art. King James I, the first of the

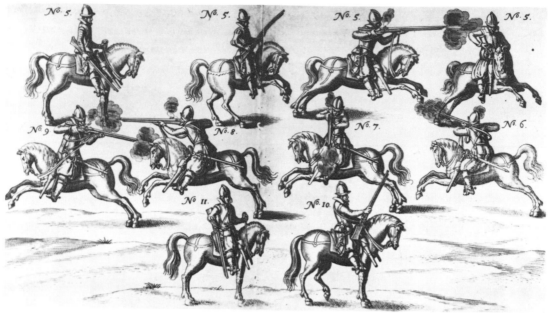

After the invention of small firearms, various positions for aiming on horseback came to be taught, as shown in these two illustrations. Above: Engraving from Wallhausen's *Art of Military Riding (1616).* Left: *Later engraving from the Portuguese* Luz da Liberal e Nobre Arte da Cavallaria *(1790), which not only illustrates work with the pistol but also 'Moor baiting' with the lance and sword.*

Stuart kings, was to set the scene for equestrian thought and attitude at the beginning of his reign in 1603 when he observed, 'the honourablest and most commendable games that ye can use are on horseback; for it becometh a Prince better than any other man to be a fair and good horseman.'

With encouragement of this nature from the courts of Europe, together with lavish spending on the purchase of horses from abroad, it was hardly surprising that the royal mood should catch the imagination of great cavalry leaders throughout England, France, Italy and Germany. The Great Horse was no longer a mere vehicle for war; he had to be carefully selected, schooled and edified to reflect the military might of the country he represented. Leaders very naturally preferred a beautiful and impressive horse, and suddenly, with the monarch leading the way, fortunes were being spent on building up resplendent stables and studs to furnish the court and cavalry with hot-blood chargers. With the rediscovery of antiquity and ancient writings, tacticians of this time found themselves turning back to the theories of classical riding as once presented by the Greeks of long ago. New rule books were now being written to explain the ancient art of horsemanship and the principles of Xenophon and his followers were cribbed and repeated word for word by military commanders all over Europe.

The Development of Riding Academies

Throughout the civilised world, military riding academies were set up for the practical purpose of training horse and rider for warfare with firearms. Schooled movements such as the capriole were to be used for evasion; whereas the levade enabled the rider to take careful aim from a position of vantage. Piaffe was to keep the horse in a constant state of anticipation – literally on his toes – prior to a sortie or attack. As these exercises developed, the discipline became so exacting that *haute école* as a sport and pastime in its own right came to be revered and extolled by its eager participants. Young men of noble birth flocked to learn the *rigueur* of the manège and soon the various schools and methods currently in fashion had become the talking point of the courts and *salons* of post-Renaissance Europe.

At around this time, under the colonial rule of Philip II in the mid-sixteenth century, Spain had become the most dominant power in Europe boasting as she did the finest fighting force in the world, comprised of a superb cavalry built up over centuries of dependence on a fiery, combat horse – particularly in the rout of the Moors. Within her empire therefore, there was much movement of troops and horses, and Spanish horses were appearing in the Netherlands, Germany, Austria, Italy and Sicily – in fact wherever this great Catholic power supported her people. As well as excelling on the battlefield, it soon became obvious that these horses were the ideal mount for the manège. Short-coupled and strong, with the type of compact, united conformation to which collection and turning comes easily, the Spanish destrier was both courageous in the field and docile and obedient in the manège. With his highly crested neck and long noble face, the most insignificant ensign looked impressive on his back; and pupils who might have exasperated their riding masters through lack of ability, were able to sit with ease to the soft, elevated movements of these Spanish war-horses. As the revival of scientific equitation took hold, and the military aspect of horsemanship blossomed into equestrianism in the cultural and artistic sense, highly technical battle manoeuvres took on a new significance and the horses which responded best to these movements became greatly in demand.

Naples and the Neapolitan Horse

The first civilian riding academy of importance was started by Frederigo Grisone, a Neapolitan nobleman, in 1532. As Naples established itself as the first centre of the rebirth of cultural equitation, it should be remembered that southern Italy had been annexed by Spain in 1502. Therefore the Italian School might be more accurately named the Neapolitan/Spanish School for all political and military events in that small kingdom were greatly influenced and manipulated by Spain. Spanish rule continued in Naples until 1707, which covers most of the period when Neapolitan horses were being exported in large numbers to England, Germany,

Austria and other European countries. The fortunes of the island of Sicily were also inextricably bound up with those of the kingdom of Naples, and even after 1707, Spanish princes were to play a part in the affairs of 'the Two Sicilies', as Naples and Sicily were known by the Spanish. Sardinia also formed part of the Spanish–Hapsburg empire.

When Gonzalo of Cordoba drove the occupying French troops out of Italy in the late fifteenth century and claimed Naples for the Spanish crown, a deciding factor was the brilliant use of Spanish cavalry. Great numbers of Spanish horses remained on Italian soil. These war-horses or *ginetes* were to contribute greatly to Naples' reputation as one of the finest centres of horse breeding in Europe. Thus, from approximately 1510 onwards, the Neapolitan charger or courser[1] (from the old Italian *corseiro* meaning a battle horse) was as likely to be a Spanish *ginete* or a direct descendant of a Spanish charger crossed with an Italian mare, as a pure-bred Italian.

Those Neapolitan horses from the court were known as *Veneten del regno* and certain strains were almost indistinguishable from the Iberian *ginetes* of the time. It was these horses which were to prove so suitable for work in the manège under Grisone and his disciples.

The horses of Sardinia are described by Blundeville in the following terms, 'they have short bodies and be verie bold and couragious', which sounds typically Spanish; and to the south of the kingdom, in Calabria, a famous type of carriage horse was bred, but they all conformed to a remarkably similar stamp.

Further north lay the famous Italian breeding grounds of Mantua. Situated 88 feet above the lagoon and marshland of the lake of Mincio, excellent horses had been bred here for generations. Francesco Gonzaga, Marquis of Mantua, had a knack for successful experimental breeding. With his famous imported Barbs from North Africa, he founded the Marmolata Stud and some portraits of these Mantuan mares by Giulio Romano are to be found in the Palazzo del Té there. A large consignment of these horses were offered as a gift to Henry VIII in 1514 shortly before the Marquis's death.

Francesco's son Frederigo continued the family tradition of horse breeding and Spanish and Turkish blood[2] was also introduced to produce light, running horses.

Hore's *Annals of the Turf* records that in 1520 Sir Gregory de Cassalis acquired the best horses in Italy for Henry VIII, and there were frequent gifts not only from Frederigo of Mantua, who was created a duke by Emperor Charles V[3] in 1530, but also from the Dukes of Urbino and Ferrara as well as the Emperor himself. A consignment of mares which arrived in England in 1533 was termed by Henry's Keeper of the Horse, 'a gift most agreeable not merely because he [the King] delights in horses of that breed but also because they were sent by his Excellency' [i.e. Frederigo, Duke of Mantua].

1. In the Middle Ages, a run at the tilt was described as a 'course' (see Froissart's description of jousting in Chapter IV), hence 'courser' or *corseiro*. Only since the eighteenth century has the word 'courser' become fashionable to imply a racehorse.
2. Blundeville says of the Turkish horse, which was also imported into England long before Arab blood was introduced: 'These horses which come from Turkey as well into Italy as hither to England, be indifferent faire to the eie, though not verie great, nor strong made, yet verie light and swift in their running, and of great courage.'
3. Emperor Charles V, Holy Roman Emperor of the Hapsburg dynasty, was also King Charles I of Spain.

Queen Isabel of France by Velasquez, Prado Museum, Madrid

La Caza de Meleagro by Nicolas Poussin, Prado Museum, Madrid

Cavalcata by B. Gozzoli (1420–1497). The Neapolitan parade horse of the fifteenth century was an altogether heavier type prior to the influence of Spanish blood after 1502. Note in particular the sturdy limbs and shorter neck, which in later pictures gave way to the Iberian characteristics of fine limbs and longer neck.

Those Neapolitans and Mantuan horses which were imported so steadily into England during this period for the royal studs at Hampton Court and Tutbury (see Chapter XIII) bore a strong preponderance of Spanish blood. Letters still exist in the archives of Mantua which refer to the dealings between Henry VIII and Duchess Catherine, daughter of Philip II of Spain, who owned yet another famous stud farm in the region, and at the same time her uncle Ferdinand of Aragon was also exporting Spanish horses to England.

Before the Spanish annexed Naples pictorial evidence suggests that an altogether heavier, more massive horse existed in this part of Italy – similar to those portrayed by Ucello in *The Rout of San Romano* and in *Cavalcata* by B. Gozzoli. Richard Glyn, in *The World's Finest Horses and Ponies*, states that in early times the Italian horse was crossed with the weight-carrying charger of the Lombard cavaliers, a horse whose origin was purely Teutonic. These weight-carriers enabled the Lombard to 'wield a huge lance called the *contus* . . . The Lombards eventually rode south into Italy, where their massive stallions gave substance to the local horses.'

In the *Book of the Horse*, Brian Vesey-Fitzgerald suggests that the Mantuan chargers were heavy horses[4] for armour carrying, and are typified by the horses of the Plaza San Marco, and in Donatello's famous statues. The Italians at that time preferred a bigger horse for carriage driving, but one understands that these horses were less kind and their appearance somewhat ungainly compared to the more compact *ginete*. The Duke of Newcastle has this to say about them: 'I have often heard Neapolitan horses commended, which I think they justly deserve; but those I have seen were ill-shaped though strong and vigorous.' However, in another passage he appears to like them better, and perhaps here is referring to the *ginete* type: 'In the choice of breeding mares, I would advise you to take either a well-shaped Spanish one, or a Neapolitan.'

Another indication of dominant Spanish blood being introduced comes in the writing of Thomas Blundeville. He describes the Neapolitan as 'being both comelie and stronglie made, and of so much goodnesse, of so gentle a nature, and of so high a courage as anie Horse is.'

According to Blundeville his physical characteristics particularly include 'a long slender head, the nether part whereof, that is to say, from the eies downward, for the most part is also somewhat bending like a Hawke's beak, which maketh him to rein with better grace.'

Therefore, by the time Grisone opened the first riding academy of sixteenth-century Naples, many Spanish and Spanish Neapolitan horses would have filled his manège as the ideal mounts for those young exponents of courtly equestrian discipline. As Diogo de Braganza points out in his book *L'Equitation de Tradition Française*:

> 'It was then that the Renaissance Italians discovered the horses come from the Iberian Peninsula. Unable to obtain from theirs what they saw done with seemingly great ease by the Spaniard, they were led to invent rules bringing their mounts up to the degree of concentration observed

---

4. In this context 'heavy horses' should not be interpreted in the way that we think of heavy horses today, i.e. draught horses, but rather as weight-carrying horses of substance, well-muscled up and round and with clean legs.

in the Peninsular horses which, in that balance, handled themselves with the greatest of ease.'

Grisone had studied the recently unearthed works of Xenophon with great care, adopting without deviation the ancient Greek's rules. Unfortunately, he insisted on applying these rules to the letter by force. When we observe the many bridles and bits invented by him and illustrated in his book *Ordini de Cavalcare* published in 1550, it is all too obvious that Grisone believed in breaking his horses with a view to the end justifying the means.

Another famous Italian school was opened in Rome, and with the publication of a second famous book on equitation entitled *Il Cavallerizzo*[5] in 1573 by Claudio Corte and the emergence of important figures such as Giovanni Pignatelli[6] and Prospero d'Osma (see Chapter XIII) Naples had proved an important springboard for equestrian revival.

Fortunately, the harsh methods of the Neapolitan School were to give way to an altogether kinder, more artistic approach by the French.

The Age of Splendour in France

Antoine Pluvinel, born in Crest in 1555, was a pupil of Pignatelli's. Instead of resorting to the Neapolitan's cruel methods with hedgehog skins and hot branding irons placed on strategic points of the horse's anatomy to force it into a leap or back onto its hocks, together with the use of wicked bits to obtain collection, he initiated the golden age in France's equestrian history. His book *Le Maniege Royal*, published in 1623, expounds theories of achieving obedience in the horse through praise and reward and brings a breath of fresh air to the discipline of the manège. Pluvinel reintroduced the use of the pillars, and sought to eliminate all violent treatment of horses. In his book, there is a wealth of beautiful copper engravings by Crispian de Pas which clearly show Spanish horses.

The kings of France had always had a preference for the Spanish horse, and in 1600, Salomon de la Broue, head groom of Henri IV, said, 'Comparing the best horses, I give the Spanish horse first place for its perfection, because it is the most beautiful, noble, graceful and courageous.'

Louis XIII favoured the Spanish horse above all others, and Garzal, head groom to Louis XIV, in setting forth the necessary qualifications of a horse for the manège, said: 'It must have an excellent mouth, be lively and graceful without rigidity, light and strong, it must have strong cannon bones and very good loins.' He then adds, 'The Spanish are the best that are known for these uses.'

Jaques de Solleysel, Master of the Horse to the Sun King who kept 5,000 horses at the royal household of Versailles alone, wrote in *Le Parfait Mareschal* in 1664:

> 'The Genettes have a wonderful active walk, a high trot, an admirable canter and an exceptionally fast racing gallop. In general they are not very big but there are nowhere better bred horses. I have heard extraordi-

---

5. This was dedicated to the Earl of Leicester in 1573 by Claudio Corte on a visit made to England.
6. Pignatelli was a student of Grisone, and later became director of the Neapolitan academy. He was the inventor of the curb bit.

Louis XIII was a pupil of Antoine Pluvinel. In this contemporary engraving by Crispian de Pas, the young king demonstrates the correct riding posture.

nary tales of their courage . . . the best horses are bred in Andalusia and especially in the royal Cordoba stud.'

One of the greatest European horsemen of all time was the celebrated Francois Robichon, Sieur de la Guerinière, who founded his Academy in 1717 having been granted the right to form his own school by the French court. This gave him the title of Ecuyer Academiste. It is thought that he served as a cavalry officer in the War of the Spanish Succession (1701–1713) when France supported Philip V of Spain, and it is certain that Spanish horses were brought back to France during this period as so many French illustrations of the war-horse of this time depict a Spanish type. Engravings from La Guerinière's book, *École de Cavalerie*, printed in 1729, show Spanish or part-Spanish horses being used for all the work of the manège. Invariably, these horses have a sub-convex head, and strong neck and shoulder; the fine, high-stepping legs portray Iberian blood. La Guerinière was to invent *l'épaule en dedans* (shoulder-in), a very important exercise which has remained popular in dressage to this day, and with his kind, artistic approach, he was to revolutionise riding all over Europe.

La Guerinière had combined theory with practice, thus elevating the art of riding onto a modern scientific plane. He wrote that 'it is my conviction that without theory such an art [i.e. riding] cannot be carried to perfection at all.'

The Classical School in Germany

Germany's first major literary work on the subject of the High School was written in 1588 by the equerry at Wolfenbüttel in Brunswick, one Georg Engelhard von Löhneyssen and called *A Thorough Guide to Bridling and the Correct Use of Mouthpieces and Bits*. This was later expanded into a work of scholarship, *Della Cavalleria sive de arte equitandi, exercitiis equestribus et torneamentis*, which showed a strong influence from the Neapolitan School although the methods advocated were less harsh than those of Grisone. In a later edition of the same work it is clear that Spanish horses were being used prolifically in the manège at that time in Germany, and von Löhneyssen remarks: 'It ought to be recognised, moreover, that of all the horses on earth the Spaniards are the most intelligent, the most likeable, and most gentle.'

The influence of the Spanish horse on modern German breeds of horses is indisputable. Both the Hanoverian and Holstein, and other warm-bloods such as the East Friesian and the Oldenburg horse, had Spanish ancestors which were brought in mostly during the seventeenth century at the height of the Iberian horse's popularity on the Continent. The strong hock action and excellent high-trotting ability of the Spanish horse contributed towards breeding distinguished coach horses in Germany, and some remaining dominant influence has without doubt contributed to the jumping ability of several of these breeds. Whilst many other breeds of horses, such as Neapolitan and Barb, were introduced at the same time and then later English Thoroughbred and oriental blood, it is surprising how, for example, the Holstein horse, which was originally promoted by the monasteries, still shows a tendency to the sub convex profile, at least in the old-fashioned types of which sadly nowadays we see less. The introduction at a later date also of Yorkshire coach horse blood also brought back a modicum of the original Spanish hock action. The Holstein licensing regulations were laid down as early as 1719 whilst the breeding of the Hanoverian, always the prerogative of the ducal and later royal families of Hanover, dates back even earlier.

The Foundation of the Spanish Riding School of Vienna

Archduke Charles II, son of Ferdinand I, Holy Roman Emperor from 1556–1564, inherited as part of the Spanish–Hapsburg empire the crown lands round Lipizza in the Karst, which now constitutes the north-western part of modern Yugoslavia. In July 1580, some of the best horses in Spain were sent to his newly formed stud in this relatively unimportant part of the world. These, comprising of twenty-four mares, three stallions and six colts, were to provide the foundation stock for the Imperial Stud. At the time of the founding of the stud, an area which had been favoured by the Romans for the breeding of horses, and obviously carefully sought out by Charles for his precious Spanish horses, there had already existed a riding school in Vienna for eight years. This had been an open wooden structure, close to the palace, but it was replaced 150 years later by a splendid building traditionally known as the Winter Riding School and created by Emperor Charles VI who assured the future of the Spanish Riding School as an Imperial institution.

From 1600 until well into the eighteenth century, the stud at Karst was carefully and studiously expanded by frequent importations of more Iberian horses, and breeding was undertaken on a prolific but deliberately planned scale. From about 1700, other breeds were introduced including Italian, German and Danish horses, but as the majority of these came from the royal stables of Naples, Fredericksborg and Lippe-Bückeburg, where there already existed a considerable preponderance of Spanish blood, the breed was not significantly changed except to expand the chest and create a horse of generally stockier type. Among a number of famous Spanish stallions still being imported direct from Spain during the eighteenth century were Cordova (imported in 1701) from whom come many of today's valuable brood mares; also Montorodo, a dun, and Toscanella, a piebald, the two last mentioned being imported in 1749. The Lipizzaner horse was therefore well established as a breed long before oriental blood was introduced with the famous Siglavy in the early nineteenth century. Indeed this measure was only taken when in the words of former Director of the Spanish Riding School, Colonel Hans Handler, 'there were no more ancient Spanish stallions that could be used' – no doubt as a result of the shortage of good horses left in Spain after the Napoleonic Wars (see Chapters I and VII).

The development of classical riding in Austria is naturally inseparable from the progress of the Imperial Spanish Riding School of Vienna. Unfortunately, none of the original books exist which laid down the various disciplines of the early Viennese school. It is almost certain, however, that an established form of classical training had started at the time of the first wooden manège, and this was then handed down from noble-bred rider to rider.

By the time the new Imperial Riding Hall was completed, the casual observer was left in no doubt as to its purpose and the Latin inscription immortalised in stone above the proscenium states: 'This Imperial Riding School was constructed in the year 1735 to be used for the instruction and training of the youth of the nobility and for the schooling of horses in riding for art and war.'

His Imperial Highness Emperor Charles VI, who had instigated this mammoth work, was not only devoted to the artistic pursuit of the High School, but he was also deeply interested in breeding. He had inherited three principal studs which were in full operation within the Austro–Hungarian empire and these he treasured and developed further. Lipizza had to produce manège and carriage horses; the Imperial Stud at Halbthurn was to provide royal parade horses, and the Imperial Kladruby Stud (now in Czechoslovakia) near Pardubice on the Labe, and said to be the oldest operative stud farm in the world, was responsible for the heavier coach horse.

These Kladrubers, as the breed came to be called in more modern times, were systematically bred and selected for their height and strength. The Stud had been founded in 1572 by Emperor Rudolph II with horses imported directly from Spain. Stallions were often interchanged within the three studs and in those early days Spanish blood was kept pure. At Kladruby, only jet black and snow white horses were bred: black for solemnity and funerals, white for festive processions when the Emperor himself was present. In those exotic days, coaches and phaetons were heavily plated with silver and gold and lavish displays and entertainments were given. One of the most famous of these was the coach quadrille included in the programme of the *Damenkarussel* or Ladies' Carousel which was presented in the hall of the Winter Riding School by Maria Theresa in 1743. Despite their great height, the Kladruby horses used to pull the heavy state coaches were also popular as riding horses amongst the court. Another of the Emperor's favourite mounts was a dark dun Andalusian stallion from the Halbthurn Stud which measured over 17 h.h.

As with Lipizza and Halbthurn, it appears that Spanish stock at Kladruby was kept pure until the end of the seventeenth century, but thereafter some Neapolitan blood was introduced. L. Simoff, a contemporary writer of the nineteenth century, remarked, however, about the breeding stock at Kladruby: 'the ancient Spanish breed is preserved in all its purity,' which would indicate that Spanish Neapolitans were in all probability introduced.

Empress Maria Theresa, a dashing horsewoman who loved brilliant displays and elaborate pageantry, encouraged the use of the Riding Hall at Vienna to the full, and 'Moor baiting', recalling the time of the battles against the Turks, became a popular way of demonstrating equestrian skill. Dark Turkish heads were fashioned in wood and mounted on posts from which then had to be struck off with the pistol or lance at full gallop. This sport was echoed all over Europe as may be seen from the many engravings which have been handed down illustrating the various exercises of the manège. The Empress also concentrated on breeding according to Gassebner, who reports that planned breeding for the army began in 1763, and Maria Theresa founded the army studs of Waschkouz, Mesohegyes and Babolna-Kisber.

Now that colour has become more regimented in modern times (the modern Spanish Stud Book will no longer allow chestnut although the Portuguese does) we tend to forget that in the fifteenth, sixteenth and seventeenth centuries, unusual colour met instead with royal favour. There are instances of favourite spotted horses and J. G. von Hamilton, who painted prolifically for the Emperor Charles VI, portrays a number of coloured horses, including a spotted stallion painted in 1704 from the Schwanberg Stud at Murau. The celebrated 'springer' or jumper, Cerbero, from the Bohemian Stud was a Spanish skewbald. Most of Hamilton's equestrian portraits hang in the Rössel room at the Schönbrunn Palace, Vienna.

The fabulous Wilton House Riding School collection, commissioned by the 10th Earl of Pembroke and painted by Baron Reis d'Eisenberg, a Riding Master attached to the Hapsburg court, also features many pure-bred coloured horses from Spain. There is one unusual portrait of a grey Spanish horse with deep black spots shown in 'full gallop, off fore leading', and Number 33 in the collection shows a 'burnt chestnut' (what we now call liver chestnut) in a demi-pirouette to the right; he is also described as Spanish. This would seem to disprove the theory held by some today in Spain that chestnut indicates a recent addition of Arab blood. One of the original Spanish Riding School horses was Joya, a 'golden brown' chestnut. He was sent to Halbthurn in 1719 and was a very successful sire there. All horses carried the brand of the stud where they had foaled and some in addition bore the royal 'C' with a crown. To remind themselves of the old colours of the Riding School horses, it is still the practice at Vienna to include one brown stallion in the displays carried out by today's white Lipizzaners.

It is indeed a pity that despite the name 'Spanish Riding School' being religiously adhered to for over five centuries, and despite the existence of records and stud books all over Europe which catalogue quite clearly the introduction of pure Iberian blood which founded so many of today's magnificent breeds, there is still a general ignorance on the part of the riding public about these horses. Genuine surprise is invariably expressed when one points out that the world-famous Lipizzaner would simply not exist as a breed had it not been for those early Spanish foundation mares and stallions.

Fortunately, however, the Spanish link is not forgotten by the authorities on breeding at Vienna. Emissaries from the Spanish Riding School still visit Portugal and Spain with the intention of buying stock to refresh the bloodlines at Piber. In 1968 Dr Lehrner was presented by the Spanish breeders with one of the famous Terry stallions, Honroso VI, from the stables of Dona Isabel Merello, and this horse has been used for breeding at Piber and a number of his progeny were seen at the School's fourth centennial celebrations held in Vienna.

Other Famous Breeds within Europe

During this period of the schooled cavalry charger, Spanish horses travelled within the Empire as far afield as the Netherlands and Denmark. King Frederick II of Denmark founded one of the most successful studs of the sixteenth century when in 1562 he imported Spanish and Neapolitan stallions to produce a more active horse than had ever before been seen in that country. Riding-school airs had also become popular at the Danish court, and horses bred at the Fredericksborg Stud began to acquire an excellent reputation abroad for their obedience and courage not only in the manège but as chargers for troopers and officers alike. A magnificent collection of equestrian portraits depicting the Danish Royal Family riding Fredericksborg stallions in the various High School airs, hangs today at the Castle of Rosenborg.

Later, oriental and English blood was introduced and the Fredericksborg became so popular that it was over-exported in the nineteenth century, by which time it had become one of the most elegant carriage horses in Europe. Sadly, in 1839 the Stud was wound up for lack of suitable brood mares and stallions, and those Fredericksborgs which are bred privately today have changed considerably from the original Spanish type of the sixteenth and seventeenth centuries. One of the great contributions made by the foundation Fredericksborg horse was to help create the famous Hanoverian Cream coach horses, which were forerunners in turn to the Windsor Greys. In *A History of Horse Breeding* we read how

> 'the King of Denmark, Frederick IV, stayed at the Court of August the Strong at Dresden on his return from a visit to Italy and he probably presented the King with horses from his own stud. This is confirmed by another painting of a white or cream horse, held by a groom carrying a pair of pistols which belonged only to the more opulent and ornamental tack of the Fredericksborg Stud.'

Another Danish horse of Spanish descent dating back to later times, but worth mentioning as it is also descended from the royal stock of the Fredericksborg Stud, is the Knapstrup. This spotted horse is traced directly to Spanish horses which were left by Spanish troops stationed in Denmark, who had escaped from the

Crown Prince Frederick IV depicted on his High School Fredericksborg stallion,
a direct descendant of the Spanish horse. (Courtesy of Bent Branderup).

French during the Napoleonic Wars. One particular mare, Flaebehoppen, was purchased by a Major Villars Lunn who took her back to his own stud of mainly Fredericksborg horses. The resulting progeny from this mare, crossed with a 'yellow' Fredericksborg stallion, retained the spotted appearance of the mother and constitutes the foundation line for the now popular breed of Knapstrup which is greatly in demand for driving and High School work.

Many of the Dutch warm-bloods of today were influenced by Spanish foundation stallions and mares at the royal studs of Europe. The Netherlands were under direct Spanish rule for the major part of the sixteenth century and during the early days of peace under Charles V, the breeding of cavalry and High School horses flourished with imported stallions from the royal studs in Spain. Halfway through the century, William of Orange tried to free Holland from her Spanish overlords and during this period of bitter conflict (most concentrated between 1559–1579) Spanish troops were stationed throughout the land.

The Dutch Hardraver, in particular, is thought to trace its origins back to those early Spanish horses; so too is the Friesian and the Gelderland with its brilliant forward-going action helped by Norfolk Roadster blood (which also had Spanish characteristics). From thence comes the Dutch warm-blood which still shows some traces of those dominant genes.

The Royal Horse of England

In Chapter XIII we shall discover the enormous influence the arrival of Spanish and Portuguese horses exerted on the future of the blood horse in England, particularly from the reign of Henry VIII to that of Charles II; but again, as in the rest of Europe, as well as contributing towards racing stock, these high-stepping chargers were extremely popular as riding horses and for the cavalry.

The heyday of the art of classical riding was enjoyed in England a little later[7] than it was within the Austrian empire for example, but nonetheless 'the noble art' was to catch the imagination of not only the aristocracy but also the wealthy, landed families. Suitable horses from Spain or the Barbary Coast were in hot demand by every horseman, young or old. Successive ambassadors from London to the court of Madrid, namely Cottingdon, Doncaster and Rich, appear to have been assiduous in arranging almost unlimited shipments of these sought-after animals, and as we shall see again in a later chapter, there were the inevitable royal gifts which also followed. When James I wrote to his Master of the Horse, the Duke of Buckingham, to remark on a fresh arrival of Spanish stallions that had just been achieved by the English ambassador, he enthused, 'God thank the Master of the Horse for providing me with such a number of fair useful horses, fit for my hand; in a word I protest I never was master of such horses.'

The Duke of Newcastle

Still regarded today as England's greatest-ever exponent of dressage, William Cavendish, Duke of Newcastle (1592–1676), was chosen by Charles I to be tutor to the young Prince of Wales. Newcastle held the Spanish horse in the highest esteem, and the first chapters of his book, *A General System of Horsemanship*, applauds the virtues of these horses of which he obviously had many. Newcastle was highly regarded in his day, and Von Solleysel the translator of his book into French, describes him in the introduction thus:

> 'The Duke of Newcastle was such a world-famous man that nothing I could dream of saying about him could begin to add to the exalted reputation he enjoys . . . What I have found most astonishing in one of his nobility is simply that he may quite justly be called the pre-eminent horseman of his time.'

Having schooled the young future king in the art of horsemanship, Newcastle fought[8] on the Royalist side when Civil War broke out in England, but like his protegé he was forced to flee the country when Cromwell came to power. In exile in Antwerp, he opened his famous riding academy and proceeded to school many exiled Englishmen of Royalist persuasion in Belgium as well as his Flemish and

---

7. We do read of one early mention of the art of the manège being conducted near London. The historian, Stow, in his *Annales of the 16th Century*, writes: 'this art is taught also upon Clarkenwell Greene, and was not long since at Mile End, by Signor Prospero.' Prospero, as we have already seen, was a Neapolitan.
8. An illuminating glimpse of new cavalry methods is given in Wilkinson's book, *Prince Rupert, the Cavalier*. Prince Rupert was a somewhat controversial cavalry leader on the Royalist side. 'What he did for the cavalry was to give them increased *mobility* . . . he insisted that it was their duty to get to close quarters with the enemy.' This was the type of action where a horse of Iberian descent was so useful.

The Duke of Newcastle preferred the Spanish horse above all others, particularly for work in the manège. We know that in the sixteenth and seventeenth centuries the Spanish horse had reached up to 16 h.h. and over. (Note the almost straight leg of the rider and compare the proportions of rider to horse with the illustration of the Bayeux tapestry in the colour plates.)

Dutch pupils. 'A short horse seems to be the proper mount for the manège,' he advised his students, and in his book we are told that the Spanish Jennet is 'the lovingest and gentlest horse . . . much more intelligent than even the best Italian horses, and for that reason the easiest dressed.'

Despite the ineffable but rather likable conceit of the man, which the reader of his book cannot fail to notice as he delves into its contents, Newcastle's methods were not unkind and he, like La Guerinière believed in affection and reward to encourage the horse on the path of learning. What lowers his standing in more enlightened times, is his fondness for artificial gadgets such as the draw-rein which caused many of his horses to become overbent and lacking in impulsion.

For all his faults, Newcastle certainly left his mark on the young Stuart prince, later to become Charles II, and perhaps it was with his royal master in mind that he wrote the following description of the Spanish horse: 'The Spanish horse is the noblest in the world . . . and the most beautiful . . . and the fittingest of all for a king in the day of triumph.'

Certainly, when he was crowned King of England after Cromwell's death in 1660, Charles II did appear to acquire a number of Iberian chargers, sharing his father and grandfather's love of a spectacular stallion, but by then many of the royal court's original Spanish stallions and mares had been sold off in the dispersal of the royal studs of Tutbury and Malmesbury (see Chapter XIII). To his faithful mentor, Charles gave a dukedom; and marriage to the Portuguese princess, Catherine of Braganza, ensured a magnificent royal dowry which included not only half a million pounds, but also the Portuguese ports of Bombay and Tangier. Portuguese horses stationed at Tangier were swallowed into the British cavalry and fought in engagements against the Moors between 1662 and 1684. Originally called the Tangier Horse, the regiment which arose from this later became the King's Own Regiment of Dragoons (the Royals) which, when they returned to England, were embodied into the main army.

Another great exponent of the High School was Henry Herbert, 10th Earl of

These four illustrations from engravings in A General System of Horsemanship *(1658) show the Spanish horse (*top left*), the Barb (*top right*), the Turk (*above left*) and the Neapolitan (*above right*) of the Duke of Newcastle's time, all pictured at the ducal home.*

Pembroke. In 1761 he published *A Method of Breaking Horses and Teaching Soldiers to Ride*, designed for the use of the army, in which he encouraged the use of athletic manège exercises to improve the flexibility and manoeuvrability of the military horse. A rich collection of David Morier pictures hangs at Wilton House, Salisbury. These depict the 10th Earl of Pembroke as Colonel of the Royals, and he and his contemporaries are mounted in the manège on horses of Spanish or Barb appearance. This give us a rare glimpse of English army officers working their horses through all the more advanced movements such as capriole and levade. Pembroke states in his book: 'This lesson of reining back and piaffing is excellent to conclude with and puts a horse well and properly on the haunches.'

Even as late as 1771 when Richard Berenger, Gentleman of the Horse to His Majesty, wrote his book *History and Art of Horsemanship* and dedicated it to George III, he unremittingly heaped praise on the Spanish horse as the unrivalled horse for war and the manège in the same way as his predecessors, Gervase Markham, Newcastle, Cox, Barret and many others of the older school who had also named the Spanish horse as the stallion to be employed for improving the English breeds.

Renaissance and Post-Renaissance Horsemanship in Spain and Portugal

At a later stage in this book we shall be exploring the equitation of the Portuguese *corrida* (bullfight) which must have been so similar to the horsemanship of the great sixteenth and seventeenth-century academies. Although the fashion in the rest of Europe was for the straight-legged, highly collected seat, with more emphasis placed on the handling of the reins and the influence of the direct and indirect rein, which led to equitation in the French or Italian manner becoming known as *à la bride*, horsemanship in the Peninsula at that time was forward-going as well as collected, and a bent leg in a comparatively shorter stirrup was often employed. This method obviously stemmed from the days of the lightly-armed knights who guided their cavalry horses over the rough and often treacherous terrain of Iberia as they routed out the Moors.

French and Italian influence, however, was strong, and pressure was put on the Spanish school to conform to the new methods of riding. For a time *à la bride* was adopted at court, and we can see pictures of Spanish dukes and infantas in the seventeenth century riding their steeds in such a way that their mouths are half-open in protest, and the overbending of the neck is ugly and contorted.

The Benedictine monks in Spain, full of Gallic tradition, advocated the French style, but the Catholic monasteries of southern Spain upheld the *ginete* style of old (see Chapter I), proclaiming it to be the only true form of horsemanship and regarded by the devout as a glorification to God himself – just as the noble Spanish horse which had vanquished the Muslim was a living proof of God's smiling favour on His people.

Two names stand out in Spanish history as exponents of classical dressage. Pedro Aguilar who wrote *Tratado de la Cavalleria de la Gineta* in 1570, and Vargas de Machuca whose book *Teoria y Ejercicios de la Gineta* (1600) is still widely quoted in Spain today. These two noblemen are thought to have studied under Grisone at Naples.

Portugal, however, had become enlightened in the art of classical equitation at an even earlier date. King Duarte of Portugal (1401–1438) well ahead of his time, had written *Da Arte de Domar[9] os Cavallos* and *O Livro da Ensynança de Bem Cavalgar — Toda a Sella*, training treatises which were to compare most favourably in their lightness of aids to what was to follow in Naples. A succession of comprehensive books followed throughout the next century and a half, until the 4th Marquis of Marialva and 6th Earl of Cantahede, who was Master of the Horse to King Dom José I, emerged as one of the most influential horsemen of post-Renaissance Europe. Marialva's methods were similar to those of La Guerinière, and horsemanship in Portugal today is still based on his principles of softness and lightness in the manège. It was he who laid down the modern-day rules for chivalric mounted bullfighting. His *ecuyer*, Manuel Carlos Andrade, wrote the important

---

9. *Domar* meaning 'to dress' – from whence comes the word 'dressage'.

Luz da Liberal e Nobre Arte da Cavallaria which not only expounds the theories
of classical horsemanship, but discusses the etiquette of conducting oneself in the
royal manège with great emphasis on the servilities and privileges of this position.
Several engravings from this book have been reproduced within these pages, and
it is still used and referred to by the great equestrian families of both Spain and
Portugal alike, and within the Peninsula is still the classical horseman's Bible.

A Horse Fit for a King

Thus, as the seventeenth century drew to its close, the Iberian horse had become
so important, not only on the battle front, not merely in the great riding academies,
not simply as a graceful pleasure mount, or a carriage horse fit to be driven by
an emperor, but it had also established itself as the active progenitor for all future
blood horses within the royal studs of Europe. It was only to be expected therefore
that no self-respecting officer of rank, wealthy landowner, baron, princeling or
king, would dream of having his portrait painted astride any other breed of horse.

Today, a wealth of richly coloured equestrian portraits constantly reminds us
of the important part the Iberian horse played at that time. Van Dyck, Velasquez
and later Goya are the artists whose household names are synonymous with producing this array of aristocratic pictorial history. There were, however, many excellent lesser-known artists who faithfully reproduced these great horses, and their
works are to be found in the private homes of many families all over Europe as
well as in public galleries and huge stately collections. We are fortunate also to
succeed to an ample heritage of monuments and statues struck in bronze of these
royal animals standing sentinel in our parks, squares and parades all over the world.
The Iberian look is unmistakeable, the slightly Roman head, the upright, thick
and powerful neck, the well-muscled shoulder and the fine-boned, elegant legs.
Those people who do not recognise this breed sometimes talk of 'old-fashioned'
horses, and it would intrigue them perhaps to take a step back through history
and discover this very popular modern-day horse in a thoroughly modern stable
in Spain or Portugal. How exciting that could prove.

TABLE V.1: Significant Dates Relating to the Iberian Horse and its Gradual Introduction into Great Britain (Mid-16th century onwards)

16th century	Mary I of England (daughter of Henry VIII) married Philip II of Spain (son of Emperor Charles V) and in the customary fashion, more Spanish horses brought to England. In the reign of Elizabeth I (1558–1603), as Royal Master of the Horse, the Earl of Leicester imported horses from Spain and Italy. Detailed inventory made by Prospero d'Osma of in-mates of the royal studs shows Spanish Jennets and mares. Spanish Armada defeated in 1588. Possibility (not proven) of Spanish horses swimming ashore from wrecks off the Irish coast.
17th century	The heyday of the Spanish horse in Great Britain. Under James I (1603–25), the Duke of Buckingham, Master of the Horse and Lord High Admiral, freely imported horses from Spain with the assistance of British Ambassadors at the court of Madrid. Betrothal of marriage

between the Prince of Wales and Spanish Infanta led to generous gifts of horses sent to England. Spanish horses filled the royal studs of Tutbury, Hampton Court and Malmesbury; they were also spread throughout the country in private estates owned by friends or relations of the Duke of Buckingham, including that of Helmsley in Yorkshire.

Duke of Newcastle (1592–1676) England's leading exponent of equestrian art helped to popularise the Spanish Jennet as being the most suitable for war, the manège, racing and breeding.

Charles I and Charles II always rode Spanish horses on parade as did all European monarchs, princes, military commanders and gentlemen of fashion at the time.

Charles II married Catherine of Braganza of Portugal in 1662 and as part of the royal dowry Portugal ceded the garrison of Tangier. A major part of the Portuguese cavalry was embodied into the English army.

18th century onwards	With the concentrated development of the Thoroughbred horse from the mid-18th century onwards, the Iberian horse gradually faded from the equestrian scene, although it was still the popular mount of leaders until and throughout the Peninsular Wars of the late 18th and early 19th centuries.

TABLE V.2: European Breeds Most Deeply Influenced by the Horses of Spain (from 1500 to approx. 1800)

Although it is generally accepted that the majority of today's European warm-bloods have all at one time or another been influenced by Spanish blood derived from their ancestors of the sixteenth and seventeenth centuries, this table clarifies the point.

Date from which breed developed	Country, kingdom or empire	Historical event	Type or Breed	Today's collective type or breed
1502	Naples	French driven out of Naples by the Spanish. Spain annexes southern Italy.	Neapolitan Calabrese	Salerno Calabrese
1519	Netherlands	Charles I of Castile became Charles V of the Holy Roman Empire, and the Netherlands passed under Spanish rule.	Friesian, Dutch Hardraver, Gelderland	Dutch warm-bloods
1562	Denmark	King Frederick II founded the royal stud and royal manège from Spanish stock.	Fredericks-borg	Danish warm-bloods
1808		During Napoleonic Wars in Denmark, Spanish troops which had been held under the command of Marshal Bernadette, escaped by ship leaving many Spanish horses.	Knapstrup	
1580	Austro/ Hungarian Empire	Archduke Charles II inherited the crown lands round Lipizza. Emperor Charles VI expanded Spanish Stud and built the Winter Riding School at Vienna in 1735.	Lipizzaner	Lipizzaner
		Carriage horses developed at Kladruby, Halbthurn, Bohemia, etc. from Spanish stock.	Kladruber	Kladruber
1620 (approx.)	Germany	No specific historical event caused a sudden infusion of Spanish blood into the native stock of Germany but the Spanish horse had been popular in the manège since the time of von Löhneyssen and increased as breeds developed, as may be seen from the early stud books.	Hanoverian (Hanoverian Creams) Oldenburg Holstein	German warm-bloods

TABLE V.3: Classical Equitation 550 BC–1800 AD

Approximate Period and Countries	Type of Equitation	Horsemen who Influenced the Course of Equitation
550–350 BC	Outdoor-ring (school) riding and cross-country riding.	Plinious, Simon of Athens and Xenophon. Almost 2500 years after it was written, Xenophon's classic *The Art of Horsemanship* still stands up extremely well when compared to modern works on the same subject.
350 BC–1400 AD	Wars, hunting, equestrian games and tournaments.	Saddles and stirrups were developed from the beginning of this period onwards, and horses were shod with iron. This period was unenlightened and probably the most cruel.
1400–1500 Portugal	Earliest development of indoor-school riding since Xenophon.	Mestre Giraldo and King Duarte of Portugal, both ahead of their time, wrote training treatises for working a horse in the school.
1500–1600 (Renaissance Period) Predominantly Italy, where the Spanish influence was very strong	Development of indoor-school riding.	Leonardo da Vinci, Grisone, Pignatelli, d'Osma, Corte, De La Broue, Fiaschi, Antoine, Löhneyssen, Aguilar and Vargas. This century saw the end of total brute force, and the beginning of artistry in riding although many cruel methods were still employed. Neapolitan School founded. Spanish Riding School founded in 1572.
1600–1700 Italy, Austria, France, Germany, England, Denmark, Belgium and Spain	Further development of indoor-school riding displaying valuable attributes for cavalry.	Pluvinel, Newcastle, De La Broue, d'Au, Antoine, Adlersflugel and Geissert. This century saw a new and enlightened approach to the schooling of horse and rider expanding on Xenophon's techniques. Founding of the Versailles School.
1700–1800 France, Austria, Germany and Portugal	Indoor-school riding becomes a sophisticated art displaying highly polished technique and detailed theory.	Guerinière, Du Paty de Clam, Eisenberg, Seidlitz, Huhnersdorf, Sind, Seidler, Galego, Pacheco, Andrade and Marialva. The basis of modern classical riding is developed, still carried out today by the Spanish Riding School, the Cadre Noir, the Portuguese School of Equestrian Art, and the Andalusian School of Equestrian Art. A glorious century of classicism.

(The author acknowledges the research of Charles Harris in the compilation of the above table.)

Family Hunting Party, one of a pair by Judith Lewis, signed and dated 1755/56. This early English hunting scene illustrates the type of hunter still used in England by many aristocratic families whose blood horses had been developed from early Iberian stock. Hunting scenes only became widely popular subjects for painting in the latter part of the century by which time the Baroque horse was giving way to a more streamlined horse (see over). (*Courtesy of Arthur Ackermann & Son Ltd*)

Richard Simpson on Struggles with the Puckeridge Hounds, signed by R. B. Davis, 1841. A typical old-fashioned hunter – note the shape of the head. (Courtesy of Arthur Ackermann & Son Ltd)

CHAPTER VI

The Cavalry Horse and the Sporting Horse

Far back, far back in our dark soul the horse prances . . .
The horse, the horse! The symbol of surging potency
and power of movement, of action . . .

D. H. LAWRENCE

The Tudor and Stuart periods demonstrated how extensively Iberian blood was used in England and abroad to improve the predominantly cold-blood breeds and produce a war-horse of distinction. In a later chapter, we will trace the influence of the Iberian during the foundation era of one of the finest breeds of horse ever to grace the face of the earth, the English Thoroughbred.

Up until this moment during our adventures through history, we have observed time and time again how the very nature and constitution of war was to influence the development and selection of horses throughout the centuries. Now, with the dawning of the eighteenth century glimmering on the horizon, a new sense of direction was to pervade the countryside and the expanding, prosperous cities. It was as though the interregnum had stopped the English nation in its tracks, and whilst the sobering period of Oliver Cromwell's rule was rapidly replaced by the jubilation and optimism of the Restoration, a growing sophistication had taken root thus enabling a solid, dependable middle class to emerge at last, fully-fledged and efficient. This would create a new factor in the ever-changing pattern of horse breeding: the use of the horse not only in battle but also in sport.

This consideration alone, unleashed from any military or chivalric influence, made the advent of the Thoroughbred, which was to take the equestrian world almost unawares, hardly surprising.

But before leaving the war-horse for good, one last glimpse of the style of battle on Europe's divers fields will prove enlightening. Yet again cavalry tactics were changing drastically as 1714 proclaimed the first German king to ascend the English throne, and these modifications were to prove as influential in the evolution of the horse as in the past. Happily for England, the direction this would take would also complement the new sporting aspect of horse breeding.

Under George I of Hanover, the temper of the British people strikingly changed. The strife and striving for high ideals which had caused so much bloodshed quietly disintegrated. Church and Parliament had been seen to come out together on the side of the people, and a period of calm replaced a period of passion. Ambitions which once had blazed so fiercely for noble causes now channelled themselves into peaceful and practical directions – trade, national welfare and expansion overseas.

Somehow it comes as no surprise that the pride of the Stuart kings' stables, and the star of the great academies of scientific equitation, the Iberian horse, was already giving way to a more modest, more practical cavalry horse. In England at any rate, the day of the Great Horse was over.

A Forward-going Horse for the Professional Soldier

The Seven Years' War in 1756 when Britain under William Pitt, sided with Prussia against France, Austria and Russia, could not have prepared Britain better for what was to come less than fifty years on at the hand of Napoleon. Pitt was ambitious for overseas territories, and as conquests were made and trading bases established in the West Indies, Canada and in India (under Clive), the army had to become highly organised to establish and maintain English supremacy overseas and in Europe.

John Churchill, 1st Duke of Marlborough (1650–1722), had already begun to reorganise British cavalry during the Wars of the Spanish Succession earlier in the century, and with the formation of light dragoon regiments, moving in flying columns over the countryside and presenting a united front combined with well-armed infantry on the battlefield, there was no longer any real place for individual acts of courage and chivalry in a close-encountered skirmish. The whole concept of warfare was changing from one of honour and nobility to one of hard-headed professionalism, and suddenly those gallant knights who had first led the field with their sturdy cobs, then with their armoured destriers and finally with their prancing chargers had become obsolete and out of place. The invention of more sophisticated firearms in the form of the flintlock and field gun had hastened the demise of the aristocratic cavalryman as surely as if he had been ordered from the field.

In the same way that Marlborough had reshaped the British cavalry, Napoleon, as he set out on the road of European conquest, was to reorganise the French cavalry into fifteen crack regiments of Hussars, which were to play an enormous part in the little Corsican's ensuing victories. These highly drilled, mounted regiments were to form an important and integral part of his impressive war machine. The French had always had excellent horses, their own Norman breeds liberally interspersed with Spanish and Barb blood, and more recently the newly accessible and highly prized Arab blood. Mounted units were made to work together and at all times in harmony with infantry and artillery. The way to the top in Napoleon's army was through sheer ability. The son of a peasant could become a captain on merit. The days when countless officers of distinguished lineage led the field with elegant style on their Spanish chargers were gone for ever.

Napoleon had set up a system of horse spies comprising of sinister men who rode at night on black horses with muffled hooves. Their long, crow-like habits shrouded them in the dark and enabled them to penetrate deep into enemy camps and thus pass back information. This was to prove a superb system of communication, and in this way the Emperor always appeared to be one jump ahead of his adversaries, as light cavalrymen streamed between the vanguard of the advancing army and the Imperial headquarters, constantly keeping him informed and up to date.

The Demise of the Iberian Horse

Thus, with Europe's huge armies continually on the move, transporting their daunting armouries of sophisticated weapons and vast stocks of supplies attended by a multitude of camp followers, a more streamlined, swifter horse had emerged on all fronts. Iberian, Barb or Neapolitan horses might still be seen ridden by the monarch, or by great leaders such as Wellington or Napoleon[1] on parade; but they were now no more than a symbol of prestige, and it was clear that the royal horse of the days of the Renaissance and Post-Renaissance had become an anachronism, even as his blood flowed through the veins of the modern horse which had replaced him.

This oil painting by George Garrard, A.R.A (1760–1826), demonstrates the type of horse which was emerging all over England during the eighteenth century. Certain Iberian characteristics are still in evidence, ie. the shape of the head and a powerful, more upright neck. (Courtesy of Arthur Ackermann & Son Ltd).

Equestrian Sport in the Field

Whilst battles were won and lost in Europe, whilst the South Sea Bubble of the South Americas burst in the City of London, and whilst the East India Company swelled in the sub-continent, a strong middle class was growing up at home in England. The breakdown of the last vestiges of the old feudal system had led to a new class of prosperous farmers and landowners, and the spirit of adventure

---

1. Napoleon rode Spanish, Barb and Arab stallions into battle. One Spanish horse named Montevideo carried him from Valladolid to Burgos (a distance of approximately 75 miles) in three and a quarter hours.

which took men overseas to make their fortune and return to invest in mills, mines and factories at home had given the ordinary man financial independence and the freedom to use his money as he wished.

In the past, equestrian pastimes had been enjoyed as recreation by the aristocracy alone, often integrated with their military aspirations; but now the middle classes were determined to enjoy horses with equal gusto.

Perhaps the halls of scientific equitation smacked too much of Stuart extravagance, for they – the last stronghold of the Iberian-type charger – were quick to disappear from the English equestrian scene (although they were retained in Germany, France, Austria and other countries on the Continent). It was as if High School might be wrapped in the popish cloak of High Church for by the time the House of Hanover was firmly ensconced on the English throne, the people themselves had lost interest in studying equitation as an art and thrown themselves wholeheartedly into the thrilling sports of racing and hunting.

The Growth of Hunting Amongst the Middle Classes

Until 1800 there had been more deer hunts than fox hunts, but with enthusiasm growing for hound work, particularly now that fields were becoming fully enclosed again and the observer had to move in closely to watch a pack of foxhounds or harriers at work, before sprinting away across country, a swift jumping horse was required. Just as after-dinner conversation had once centred around caprioles and leaps in the manège, the talk was now – as it is still today amongst many country people – how a neighbour's new horse had jumped a five-foot stone wall.

In the old days the royal pastime of the stag hunt had been undertaken by the king and his retinue on their war-horses or coursers. Hunting had almost been regarded as a pleasant duty by some barons, in order to keep their destriers fit and hard. The thick forests which covered England in the Middle Ages and provided excellent cover for the red and fallow deer necessitated a fairly collected form of riding, so whilst Giraldus Cambrensis, a prolific English writer from the twelfth century, points out the 'magnificent proportions' of the destrier were inclined to be a liability in the hunting field, it would seem that as there was little open country to gallop across, and jumping was almost unheard of in those days, the Iberian horse of the sixteenth and seventeenth centuries was not so unsuitable for the royal sport as might be assumed. His natural balance and high-stepping agility would have made him a safe and dextrous mount, and it was not until England's great southern forests began to be heavily culled to provide timber for Nelson's warships[2] that a more forward-going hunter was required. With the advent of jumping at about the same time, the English began to adopt not only a forward-going horse but also a forward-going seat.

A New Style of Riding

As we observe the old-fashioned charger which could pick its way carefully through the hazardous forests, avoiding roots, rabbit warrens and unexpected boulders

2. It took 4000 mature oak trees to build one of Nelson's ships-of-the-line.

while its rider kept it constantly collected beneath him, giving way to a bigger, rangier hunter which could extend its lean body and fly across the Shires, we may marvel how events on both the battlefront and in the peace of the English countryside dovetailed together. Such a fusion of equestrian ideals was to bring about a momentous change in breeding and selection procedures which resulted in a modern horse to complement both environments. This is the horse we have inherited today. A horse full of natural sporting instincts and a horse which excels in all cross-country pursuits.

Delight in the chase paved the way for an altogether new approach to riding, and again, through pictures, prints and portraits of the period we notice that the ancient classical seat was relinquished in favour of the new trend to shorten the stirrup. This had the effect of pushing the rider towards the cantle, but as new hunting saddles were designed, the rider had the freedom to rise up out of the stirrup and lean forward as the action of the extended horse threw him towards the withers and a new point of balance was established with more weight on the horse's forehand.

There is an amusing reference to the 'new posture' in a book by John Adams published in 1805 which recommends the 'relieving of the bottom from the friction and heat it would sustain from a strong and continued gallop'. Many new books were to be written on the subject, and it seemed that the bourgeois purse, so quick to embrace the delights of the turf and the hunting field, was proving insatiable for any modern idea which expounded and unfolded the mysteries and virtues of a sport which for so long had been denied it. An Oxford don, William Somerville, who wrote four books of blank verse entitled *The Chase*, describes hunting as 'the magic of war without its guilt,' and this attitude was reflected up and down the country. The fox was suddenly almost exalted, and the foxhunter represented the epitome of English respectability and worthiness.

The Rejection of High School

Looking back over the last three centuries, it is sad to reflect that while other European countries were able to maintain their academies of classical equitation, with the teaching of the classical seat, England was to dismiss totally the principles of the manège. The reasons are understandable: the opening up of the English countryside; the growth of the middle classes, the upper echelons of which were becoming landed; the change in military riding – all these were bound to attract the large majority away from the confines of the school and its disciplines within a restricted area.

And yet other countries had undergone social and political change, so was there something more fundamental at root here, perhaps bound up with the English love of freedom and the national temperament itself?

It was as though with the renunciation of the Stuart kings, and the acceptance of a more down-to-earth style of monarchy and a quieter, less regimented form of worship, the English had found their true element. And having found it and discovered that it was comfortable and acceptable, anything which could be associated with past pomp or over-disciplined artistry was to be sharply resisted, even when it came to riding. People took a pride in adopting a Corinthian attitude in their love of the great outdoors. Purpose and practicality was the new order of the day. 'What damn good was a piaffe on a stomping horse in the middle of a ploughed field, by Jove?...No need for *that* sort of fancy stuff any more!' became the popular attitude.

Surprisingly, such an old-fashioned approach has lingered amongst a few of the more venerable members of the riding fraternity even up until the present day. At one time, not so long ago, popular contempt for manège work except in certain military sectors, was undoubtedly responsible for the lack of understanding and enthusiasm for dressage which we as a nation faced in the field of modern competition. Thus, despite our unequalled supremacy across country, other European competitors were stealing an advantage over us when it came to the dressage marks. Thankfully, however, balance is now being restored due to the perseverance of a number of dedicated trainers – many of whom have come from abroad – and competitors with the guts and determination to remain loyal to the one discipline which has never attracted public support.

It is hardly surprising, therefore, to find that by the mid-seventeenth century the Iberian charger had quietly retired from England's shores, and whilst he lingered here and there on the Continent, his heyday abroad was over. Again, through art we may follow in his wake and it is not difficult to observe the full-crested, wavy-maned Great Horse standing sentinel in our squares and parks, gradually giving way to a more streamlined, horizontal horse, a useful type with excellent proportions and a beauty all his own. The cavalry horses of around 1800 would grace both the hunting field and a regimental stable, and yet here and there, through this transitional period, we still glimpse that old Iberian blood. Even today, we find in some of our best hunter chasers, a slight convexity of the head, an extra deep chest with a more upright neck, and that unmistakeable presence, so often belied by the term 'an old-fashioned look' but so easily accounted for by those dominant Spanish genes.

The Survival Against All Odds of the Iberian Horse

By the middle of the nineteenth century, the Iberian horse was in such short supply, particularly in Spain, that he was threatened with extinction. Successive Spanish kings,[3] alarmed by the huge demand for their prized horses abroad, had placed restrictive measures punishable by death on the export of breeding stock. A number of royal decrees had ordered that all pure-bred Andalusian mares were to be clipped on the ear so that, easily recognisable, they might be prevented from slipping out of the ports or crossing the frontier. Despite this, it is clear, looking back with the hindsight of history, that the Spanish horse was heavily over-exported in the sixteenth and seventeenth centuries. Just as the demand abated and stock might have had the opportunity to recover, Napoleon and his Revolutionary Army burst upon the European scene and, as we shall read in Chapter VII, the already depleted Spanish studs were ravaged and pillaged through war.

It is, therefore, little short of a miracle that the Iberian horse in his original

3. Bans on the exportation of Andalusian mares were placed by King Henry II and Henry III in the fourteenth and fifteenth centuries, and in 1695 by King Carlos II, and in 1712 by King Philip V.

form has survived to this day. Had it not been for the dedication of a handful of Spanish and Portuguese breeders, who somehow eluded the destructive forces of political factions bent on eliminating anything and everything which represented established tradition – and that included horses – the great fighting horse which had borne the history of two great nations on his back would have been lost for all time even in the home of his birth.

Fortunately, the practical work of the countryside of Andalusia and the Portuguese Ribatejo and Alentejo districts, dominated by the breeding of bulls, has continued to save this horse from extinction.

Iberian Equestrian Sport

We have seen how in England the horse changed and developed to suit not only the new style of cavalry charge, but also to adapt to the chase in open countryside which was conducted against a destructive, but defenceless animal, the fox. In neither pursuit was a close-encountered skirmish likely to occur and therefore the days of riding a horse in collection where total precision could be constantly obtained, were allowed to disappear.

The chase in the Iberian Peninsula, however, was a very different matter. This, since before the time of the Carthaginians, had taken the form of hunting savage bulls which ran wild in the thick forests of the mountains of Extremadura and Andalusia and was a highly dangerous sport invariably resulting in grievous injury or the death of one of the hunting party. The idea was to pursue the bull over difficult terrain, and having once got close enough, bowl him over with a *garrocha*, or long blunt pike. The horseman then leapt off his horse and, providing the bull did not turn on him first, something which happened all too often with an enraged animal of such proportions, slew him with his sword. The carcass was then taken back to the local village for meat.

For this sport, the war-horse whose courage and obedience had so inspired the Christian knights to reconquer the Peninsula against their Moorish oppressors, was ideal. All the same characteristics were required, so too was the same style of riding. As we read in Chapters I and V, the *ginete* style of riding had never been so straight-legged as that of the Norman, Flemish and English knights and this undoubtedly gave the rider greater mobility. On the other hand, despite the bent knee (which was no more excessive than in the average dressage seat today) the *ginete* rider developed a deep effective seat, but to assist in keeping the horse constantly in collection, the Spanish introduced a spiked noseband, the *cerreta*, to encourage the horse to flex from the poll without excessive use of the curb.

This is still used in some parts of Spain today, particularly in the preparation of horses (*jacas*) for the *Doma Vaquera*[4] (see Chapter X) and the *Acoso y Derribo*, sports which provide one of the great traditional attractions at the Jerez and Seville fairs. The latter goes back to the days of bowling wild bulls over in the forest, and now consists of the tamer, but no less skilled practice of herding, separating and finally turning over a singled-out wild steer in front of a thousand cheering and excited onlookers.

---

4. *Doma Vaquera*, literally translated, means dressage for the *vaquero* or cattle horse.

Whilst many people may recoil in horror at the use of a noseband reminiscent of Grisone's day, the Spanish will argue with some justification that it is considerably less unpleasant for the horse than the current fashion in many countries of placing thin, jointed snaffles in ponies' and horses' mouths, which in young inexperienced or heavy hands may not only bruise and deaden the bars of the mouth, but also in some cases cause laceration and bleeding. The *jaca*'s mouth, they are proud to demonstrate, remains as soft as butter. Gadgets such as martingales and running reins are almost unheard of, and from an early age horses are made to use their backs, never becoming heavy on the forehand or developing hollow backs.

From the bull hunt, developed other sports, sometimes more associated with war than the chase, but inevitably interwoven and equally requiring a combat horse of agility and courage.

Throwing the javelin, an ancient military sport again dating back to pre-Roman times, was popular as a game of skill on horseback and was practised wherever horses were bred. Participation was encouraged for everyone, not only the *grand señors*, but the farmworkers and the men who worked with the bulls and horses. For this manoeuvre, tremendous acceleration over a short distance was required to aid the impulse of the throw. As the javelin left the rider's hands, just as he came within range of a real (or imaginary enemy), the horse had to have the ability to stop dead, and wheel round with the same agility – lest he be spiked himself. This game has scarcely changed since the days of Xenophon when that great horseman had so admired the aptitude of the Iberian horse for light cavalry skirmishes (see Chapter II).

Another sport which was practised and again has continued right up until the present day, was a fencing match on horseback. This is not dissimilar to what we now see demonstrated by jousting teams in mediaeval re-enactments, today a popular spectator sport all over Europe.[5] In this, the rider is equipped with a long lance. In turning again and again for the attack and defence, the horse has to build up a remarkable sense of anticipation and reaction, and this has given birth over the centuries to complete subjection, obedience and a sense of oneness between horse and rider. Halting from a canter, cantering from halt, cantering in place, reining back and even cantering backwards,[6] the half-turn, side-step and the varying control of each gait, all of which the good fencing horse will undertake with enthusiasm, builds up into a crescendo of quivering expectation and what the Iberians call *alegria* (an overwhelming sense of happiness and joyousness) in the horse.

From this tense, excited state, the progression to the movements required in the manège or in the bullring, came easily to the Iberian horse. The piaffe, passage and high-stepping collected exercises began to be offered naturally as an expression of his anticipation. Collecting himself in this way and remaining in constant balance by keeping up the momentum, provided an in-built launching pad from which

---

5. The 1985 Jousting Championship of Europe was held in France and won by Englishman Max Diamond who runs the British Jousting School at Chilham Castle, Kent. He won the Championship with his purebred Lusitano mare Marquesa. This proves the continued suitability of the Iberian horse for this form of work.
6. Cantering backwards is not an impossible feat. It is frequently performed in the bullring, and Nuno Oliveira cantered backwards at Wembley after a recent exhibition of High School. He was riding a Lusitano stallion.

to make a sudden advance or *sorte*.

Historically, therefore, through all its intermediary phases, the bullfight became the end product of the chase through the forests.

The Development of Bullfighting

As more and more people moved to live in the city, so the *corrida* moved to the artificial confines of the bullring. In Chapter IX, which describes the mounted bullfight in detail – for to understand this is the only means we have at our disposal today to fully appreciate the special attributes of the true Iberian horse – I point out that I have no desire either to support or to denigrate the raison d'être of this peculiarly Iberian sport. The fact is *it exists*, and should it cease to exist, as with bloodsports in our own country, thousands of jobs would be lost, tens of thousands of horses and bulls would become obsolete, and a whole way of traditional country life which for years has protected the environment and stopped the spread of indifferent urbanisation would come to an end.

What is very often not understood is that bullfighting was not always the sole provenance of the Iberian Peninsula. As an organised sport, it originated in Crete in 3000 BC, and in Italy the Romans used Thessalonian bulls before coming to the Peninsula, after which Iberian bulls were taken back to Italy. In the Middle Ages bullfighting took place in both France and Italy, and still in the south of France today, a lighthearted skirmish with bulls takes place in the ring, particularly in the Camargue district. The Camargue had always bred a particularly famous type of bull, and in 1551 a gentleman of Arles, Pierre Quiqueran de Beaujeu, wrote an important chronicle of everyday life in Provence, entitled *Provence Louee*. In this he wrote of the fury of the bulls and mentions that there were 16,000 of them in the Camargue, adding 'Just as their number is large, so is their temper.'

In 1622 Louis XIII of France went especially to Arles to see the Camargue bulls in the arena, and the sport of bullfighting was not finally banned in France until the late eighteenth century, five hundred years or more after the first recorded mention of the practice, in 1222.

In Italy, where the sport had existed in one form or another at intermittent intervals since the Romans, when lions and other animals were used too, the fashion for bullfighting escalated in deadly earnest when it was reintroduced in the sixteenth century by Cesare Borgia, the son of the Spanish pope, Alexander I. Borgia was a remarkable horseman, and bullfighting soon became the rage in Naples, which by this time was a possession of the Spanish crown. Such was the popularity of this arena sport, and so anxious were the Neapolitan nobles to establish an image for themselves of chivalry and daring, that despite lack of training and expertise, large numbers of young men were going forward to fight and dying in the attempt. In 1558 the Church had had enough, and Pope Paul IV banned the practice of mounted bullfighting.

This was to strike a blow for riding *à la gineta*, and after this temporary ban, equestrianism *à la bride* became more accepted, even amongst the very religious, despite the fact that it had once been labelled '*bastarda*'. Riding *à la bride* was never fully adopted, however, in the rural districts of the Iberian Peninsula where traditional methods of working the bulls in the open still demanded a shortened

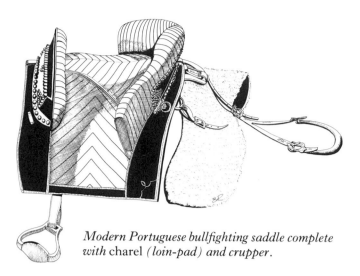

*Modern Portuguese bullfighting saddle complete
with* charel *(loin-pad) and crupper.*

stirrup for practicality. Therefore, while interest in the arena sport waned in Italy, life in central Spain and Portugal continued to revolve around the bull, and mounted bullfighting soon crept back to the courts of Madrid and Lisbon as the principal test of manhood amongst the sons of the nobility.

The battle in the ring was still in many ways associated with the rout of the Moor and the courage of the Christian knight and his horse. It was the ultimate proof of valour and as such was actively encouraged by the powerful factions behind the Inquisition.

Then came a set-back in 1700 when the childless Charles II willed the Spanish throne to Philip, Duke of Anjou, grandson of Louis XIV of France. It soon became clear that the young French king disliked his gentlemen attendants to enter the dangerous rough and tumble of the *corrida*. Spanish courtiers were encouraged to emulate their French counterparts, and gradually the more leisurely, elegant pastimes of the court of Versailles spread to Spain. The young Philip V was to build several new palaces in Castile in the French style, and no doubt court life at *La Granja*, his 'little Versailles', diverted his nobles' attention with licentious amusements of another nature which soon quenched their fiery preoccupation with the bullring.

Those Spanish *hidalgos* who were not prepared to give up their national sport, removed themselves and the contents of their stables across the border to Portugal, which was fast becoming the popular retreat of a number of foreign exiles of noble birth. These latter were not only to make up a formidable elitist society of great horsemen, but were also to bring into that small country some of the finest Spanish horses from Castile, Cordoba and Naples. Thus, whilst mounted bullfighting in Portugal entered a new age of chivalry as the principal amateur sport of the sons of the nobility, Spain entered into a new cultural era under the French influence.

Not until the middle of the twentieth century was the mounted fight of the *rejoneo* horseman revived in Spain. To this day it is still not practised in every Spanish bullring, as the pedestrian fight with the cape which took over from the mounted fight in the seventeenth century remains the most popular sport. However, with every year the *rejoneo* fight becomes increasingly in demand, especially in Andalusia, centre of the Spanish horse. Many Spanish *rejoneadors* cross the border to Portugal to seek the old bloodlines of the best fighting horses which were lost during two and a half centuries of non-participation. Some Spanish bullfighters today tend to place less importance on the High School aspect of the *corrida* (with perhaps a natural aversion to schooling *à la bride* which took hold in Portugal with Marialva – see Chapter V) and concentrate more on speed and dash, which has led to the popularity of the Hispano–Anglo–Arab and even to Thoroughbred horses being used. Classical *rejoneadors*, however, in the mould of Alvaro Domecq Senior and his son, Alvaro, still prefer the Iberian horse, and Spain's most successful bullfighting horse, Opus, at the time this book was written, is a pure-bred Lusitano of the ancient war-horse type and we shall read more of him later.

Thus this ancient sport, which for all its critics and antagonists, continues to flourish not only in Europe but increasingly in Mexico and South America, has without doubt helped to maintain the strict breeding standards and selection procedures within Spain and Portugal, so preserving the Iberian saddle horse. Today he appears in as pure, proud and resplendent a state, it would seem, as when Marcus Aurelius Antoninus mounted the horse which was considered fitting for an Emperor of Rome to ride before the whole Roman army.

CHAPTER VII

Spain – An Insight into Her History and Culture

Sometimes he trots, as if he told the steps,
With gentle majesty and modest pride;
Anon, he rears upright, curvets and leaps,
As who should say 'Lo, thus my strength is tried;'

WILLIAM SHAKESPEARE
(*Venus & Adonis*)

The Essential Differences within Iberia

No two adjacent countries could be much more dissimilar than Spain and Portugal; yet the cult of the horse and the bull in the southern climes of both countries is inextricably tied up in the national character, lifestyle and traditions of each in an equal but varying intensity. One country is fierce, passionate and bold, flamboyantly flaunting its culture and daring its opponents to challenge its singularity and its unique customs with open arrogance. The other, small, less powerful, is soft, romantic and even a little self-effacing in outlook, but beneath the facade of being the poorer neighbour, its people are resilient and intensely proud.

For me, personally, both countries hold greater charm than anywhere else in the world. My love for Iberia is of a deep, unparalleled nature. Something quite passionate, rather disturbing and impossible to quantify or put adequately into words, grips me when I set foot on the hot Iberian soil. Whether it is at the spot near Algeciras where the first Moorish invaders landed, or on the banks of the River Tagus from whence Prince Henry the Navigator sailed forth to make his first momentous voyage of discovery, matters not. The sensation is the same, deeply permeated by the past and threaded with that powerful awareness of history which envelops the landscape and the buildings as one leaves the coast and delves deep into the sun-swept countryside of the Southern Peninsula – something so strongly evocative that one wonders if the bloody imprint of those Catholic offensives against the Infidel, and the ensuing triumphant and traumatic moments in history have indelibly fixed themselves into the atmosphere forever.

The Spaniard and His Horse

In order to understand better the forcefulness and significance of the cult of the horse within Spain, we must try to understand her people. Their close association with *equus* sparks off something deeply romantic within the hearts of all those outside observers who come to Spain. Artists, sculptors, poets, writers, and more latterly photographers and film makers find their creativity touched by it, and there are those individuals who having no love for the horse in their own country, become suddenly bewitched and enchanted by the horsemanship of Spain.

Once the concrete jungle of coastal tourist resorts has been left far behind and one strikes off into the core of unknown Iberia, there are horses to be found unexpectedly at every turn.

Arriving at sunset in the dusty courtyard of a small hostelry or wayside *tapas* bar outside Valencia, one may be greeted by a Don Quixotic figure silhouetted against the gathering dusk, on the back of a magnificent steed which might have sprung from a canvas in the Prado. With studied nonchalance the *caballero* tosses back his tot of fiery local brandy, exchanges a curt word or two with his neighbours and as suddenly as he has arrived, pricks his horse with the spur, so that it executes a perfect pirouette. The glint of the evening sun casts a red glow on the burnished coat of the stallion and highlights the glossy black mane which falls in a thick curling mass to its elbow; as the two set off down the highway there is something about the set of the man's shoulders that shows he is aware every eye is upon him. Cantering in apparent slow motion, this alluring symbiosis of man and beast turn onto a mountain track and soon only the distant hoofbeats, rhythmical as clockwork against the rocks, belie their fading presence. One wonders to which outlying hamlet the pair are bound. Wherever it may be, one thing is certain: the *caballero* is always the most respected man in the community, and when he boasts such a fine horse, he will also be the most envied.

Passing through bull country, the dark, double-than-life-size frame of the Osborne bull – an effective advertisement for this popular brandy and sherry – looms up on the crest of a hill. Far away, across a golden shimmering plain, comes the sound of tinkling cattle-bells, and the jangling of bit and curb or the intermittent harsh cry cutting through the thickly hot air, discloses the presence of *vaqueros* somewhere in the valley. Straining the eyes for a break in the seemingly endless yellow landscape, the heat haze betrays a sudden movement and over the bluff a sight which is ageless meets the gaze. Three horsemen appear as though in a mirage, driving a herd of sleepy steers before them. Tough, rugged and as leather-skinned as their short dusty boots, they ride their *jacas* like princes and take no notice of the car and the foreigner on the lonely road before them. Theirs is a world which has survived revolution and the annihilation of whole families, and riding their cattle horses through the heat of another Andalusian day is as timeless and as natural as it was to their great grandfathers.

Extremadura can be lonely; even on the highway with the car radio blaring for company. The traveller may not pass another vehicle for half an hour, and then suddenly finds himself stuck behind two cement lorries on the crest of a winding hill. All at once he is abreast a smartly trotting stallion. The man on horseback bows his head against the wind; his flat black hat, wedged firmly on top, has seen better days. He sits in his high pommelled saddle with all the ease of a maestro, the still, square body finding no need to rise to the high-stepping action of the gait, one hand holding the reins lightly at the waist, the other on the hip. Where is he going? The last town was twenty miles back, the next – according to the map – is twenty miles on. A narrow sand track runs obligingly alongside the highway for the use of horsemen. It is the same all over Spain. One longs to stop and photograph, but somehow one doesn't. Fiesta is for photographs but these sudden surprise encounters are too private, too Spanish, to take advantage of. But the mind's eye never forgets them.

Spanish History Creating a Special Dependence upon the Horse

Horses have always played an integral part of Spanish life. We have already seen how the Romans set up an organised system of studs and remount depots in the Peninsula before being superseded by the Visigoths and the Vandals. Those early cavalry disciplines must have stood the Spanish in good stead during the long drawn-out years of the Reconquest, when the military war machine of Castile gradually regained Al-Andalus from the Moors and was able to draw from the

Moorish horseshoe arches are to be found all over Spain but are most concentrated in Andalusia. These fine examples come from the facade of the Mezquita in Cordoba.

excellent stud farms round the irrigated valleys of the River Guadalquivir with its famous horses to swell its ranks. Chalkland, because of its mineral content and fine drainage has always produced the best pasture for horses the world over, and the breeding grounds which lay round Cordoba, Arcos de la Frontera, Jerez and Seville had proved over the centuries, from those early Punic Wars, to be the most productive in Spain. The Moors had felt themselves at home in Andalusia, with its scorching, sweeping steppes and its harshly cold sierras. The flowering of Hispano-Islamic culture had not only brought about the most luxuriant art and architecture, but also the practicalities of agrarian reform. Once irrigated, the parched soil yielded up many riches and at a time when the strength of cavalry determined the freedom of a nation, the abundant production of superb fighting horses was valued beyond measure.

Thus, when at last the fortified city of Granada, the Babylon of Andalusia with its hanging gardens, and magnificent Alhambra fell to the Christians in 1492, Hispania had built up one of the greatest cavalries of the world. This was to equip them for the vast empire that was to come and with the ascension of King Ferdinand and Queen Isabella to the Spanish throne which was to bring about the final rout of the Moors, the separate kingdoms of Castile, Aragon, Catalonia and Andalusia unified together to form modern Spain.

The Inquisition, Bloodshed and American Gold

Now that the entire Peninsula with the exception of Portugal was united under one crown, Roman Catholicism reached an unprecedented height of fervour. The expulsion of the Moors who had done so much to cultivate and civilise Spain, was particularly bloody. To protect the faith, the Spanish crown was to institute the Inquisition in order to channel religious thought into one rigid direction. This was to take the form of an horrific persecution of Jews and Protestants, and despite the fact that Jewish gold had contributed handsomely to the wealth of the nation and indirectly to the overthrow of the Moors, thousands of innocent Jews were burned at the stake.

1492 was a remarkable year in Spanish history, for at the same time as Granada fell to the Christians, and Jews and Protestants were being hounded out of the country or executed, Christopher Columbus set foot on the other side of the world, having sailed into the Bahamas with three small ships. The Canary Islands were then ceded to Castile by Portugal which proved a giant stepping-stone towards the colonisation of the West Indies. By the time Cortés was setting off on his Mexico expedition in 1519, Spaniards were already well aware that they were poised on the edge of the most immense wealth from the New World.

The savagery with which Cortés and his Spanish adventurers annihilated the greater part of the native population of the Americas is staggering, particularly in the light that the destruction of these huge civilisations was brought about by comparatively small numbers of men with their even smaller numbers of horses. The Spaniard of that time had a fantastic ability to penetrate, as one writer of the time put it, 'through such rugged lands, such dense forests, such great mountains and deserts, and over such broad rivers.'

For all their cruelty performed in the name of Christianity, the Conquistadores possessed the most enormous courage. It is still almost incomprehensible to realise that Pizarro with only 62 horses and 106 men (see Chapter XV) overthrew one of the world's greatest empires in Peru; and it is feats of this nature which have led to the bravery and ability of the Spanish horse being placed on a pinnacle in the minds of all loyal Spaniards. Within one generation, the whole history of America was utterly changed.

As the noblemen of Spain grew richer from American gold which was being shipped home by the ton-load, bigger and better horses were bred to cope with the demand from abroad and to protect Spain's enlarging frontiers. A whole new class of Spaniard was emerging from the adventurer breed of Conquistador who, with enormous daring, thrust northwards into the United States in search of the 'Cities of Gold', or southward into modern Venezuela in the quest for El Dorado.

Those families left at home began to produce fine horses. Just as today, new-found wealth manifests itself normally in the acquisition of bigger and better cars, so in sixteenth-century Spain, the outward visible sign of established status was magnificent horseflesh.

The word cavalier, in Spanish *caballero*, is still used. Today at home, we speak of cavaliers only in the historical sense, but in Spain a *caballero* is horseman and gentleman rolled into one. Throughout Spanish history a good horse was the symbol of wealth, chivalry and power, and perhaps by the sheer nature of the country, with its special climate, terrain and environment, the dependence on the horse has never died. Whilst English history has been of necessity interwoven by the influence of the sea and ships, Spanish history has without doubt been borne on the back of a horse.

Spanish Wars in Europe and the Steady Drain on Spanish Horses

As fast as Spain was amassing her foreign fortunes, events at home were dispersing them. The marriage of Ferdinand and Isabella's daughter into the House of Hapsburg and the birth of a son in 1500 was to initiate a complicated system of European dynasty. As well as inheriting the Spanish crown, as Charles I of Castile, together with her newly acquired rich foreign dominions, he became Holy Roman Emperor Charles V. This gave him sovereignty of the Netherlands, along with Navarre in France, Naples and Sicily, Luxembourg and Burgundy, all of which had to be protected and maintained for the Spanish crown. This led to a fantastic ebbing away of Spanish resources. The Spanish war machine which had coped so successfully in its contained war against the Moors with its slow and systematic build-up, was now up against a much greater, more formidable problem. The protection of such vast sprawling frontiers was expensive and strategically difficult. Despite the wealth which had poured in from the New World to swell the coffers of the Church and wantonly reveal itself in the treasures of the altar and in the thick gold leaf and silver plate which adorned every church, monastery, castle and palace of the realm, the country began to experience financial difficulties.

The chief drain on men, horses and money was the war against the Dutch rebels in the latter part of the sixteenth century, as they fought to regain independence from the Spanish crown. And there were further commitments which did nothing to assist the weakening financial structure. In 1580 Philip II of Spain had seized the opportunity of bringing Portugal under Spanish rule after the untimely death of King Sebastian of Portugal, and in 1588 the grandiose idea of removing the entire English naval threat with the Spanish Armada ended in disaster. It was becoming very clear that the Spanish crown had committed itself too extensively. As the Dutch war continued into the seventeenth century, leading to German and Swedish involvement in the Thirty Years' War, a senior Spanish minister noted that 'The war in the Netherlands has been the total ruin of this monarchy.'

War is a wasteful occupation, and during this period many of Spain's best horses were lost in battle or at sea or left behind on some far-off lonely frontier. There is a bright side, however, to every melancholy aspect, and as horses disappeared behind enemy lines in Holland, Germany, Navarre and Naples, Spanish blood

Right: *Sr Fernando Palha, one of the most respected breeders of Lusitanos in the Peninsula: 'Iberian horses are noble. They do not bite, they do not kick. Is it not true that aristocrats the world over instinctively know how to behave?'* (Photo by Jane Hodge)

Below: *Waiting for the fiesta.* (Photo by Soskia Mesdag)

Only the kestrels and the vultures disturb the still air round the ancient fortress. In the foreground a Domecq stallion poises himself in pesade – a movement as natural to him as the landscape of Andalusia. (Photo by Arnaiz) (as explained in Chapter V) was being rapidly absorbed into cold-blood native breeds, thus helping to produce the warm-bloods of today in so many European countries.

There was also a steady flow of war-horses between Portugal and Spain as fighting continued at the frontier, and a number of Spanish *hidalgos* (see Chapter VI and VIII) moved with their horses into Portugal. This injection of new and excellent blood from the finest studs of Andalusia contributed much to the strengthening and stimulation of Portugal's own cavalry. Therefore, when independence was regained by Portugal in 1668, at least some of the success of the campaign could be attributed to the acquisition of the cream of Spanish war-horse stock.

From then on, these bloodlines were highly prized by the Portuguese who jealously guarded pure-bred Andalusian mares in their remote stud farms in the Ribatejo and Alentejo, and it is certain that the foundation for many of today's best Lusitano horses was laid down at this time.

The Dispersal of Breeding Stock During the Peninsular Wars

It is ironic that as we progress towards the end of the seventeenth century, when the death-knell begins to toll for the Iberian horse abroad in the face of more sophisticated weapons and methods of warfare, the country which bred the best of these noble animals should have suffered such depletion of her stock. The Napoleonic Wars merely added insult to injury as French soldiers swarmed over the countryside and ravaged the stables of the great Spanish houses as rapaciously as a swarm of locusts in a cornfield. The heart was taken out of the breeding stock as horses disappeared by their hundreds into France. When one considers the excellence of today's modern French breeds, we can rue the fact that the revolutionary army was never to keep records of these actions.

As though Spain had not had enough blood spilt throughout its turbulent history, more troubles were to follow after the expulsion of Napoleon in 1813 when, for once, Spain had allied herself with Britain and Portugal under the leadership of the Duke of Wellington. The Spanish spirit was remarkably brave and indomitable, and despite suffering terrifying atrocities at the hands of the French (which included being burned alive in their houses), the Spaniards never lost sight of their single-minded goal – to drive Napoleon across the Pyrenees. Having endured such great losses in terms of manpower and property, it might have seemed appropriate that a period of peace would follow.

This was not to be. At the end of the War, the Inquisition was still in existence and its cruel and suppressive machinations gave birth to widespread hostility and discontent. Internal political factions, determined for revenge and bitterly opposed to peaceful compromise, ensured that violence became a permanent feature of Spanish life.

Between 1834 and 1835 feelings against the Church ran to blind hatred of the clergy and all that they stood for, and this violent reaction to the effects of the Inquisition brought about the *desamortizacion* or dissolution of Church wealth. Thus, another blow was struck against the Spanish horse when great monasteries such as the Order of the Carthusian monks near Jerez (see Chapter I), were forced to give up their land and their carefully preserved stud farms. Most of these horses passed safely into private hands, but the breakdown of the ecclesiastical breeding tradition was nevertheless a heavy blow for the Spanish horse.

Revolution!

Revolution followed revolution and the misguided religious fervour of the Inquisition gave way to a new, but equally harsh atmosphere of intolerance – political fanaticism. The brutish acts of Cortés and the Conquistadores paled in comparison to the sadistic atrocities witnessed by a startled Europe as Spain turned in upon herself during the Civil War of 1936. The war which was to last three bloody years, became a great ideological issue. Leftist sympathisers on the side of the Republicans came from all over Europe and the United States, and financial and arms support poured in from Communist Russia. On the Franco side, the stalwarts of the Church ranged themselves with Catholic sympathisers from all over the world who joined the cause. Particular support came from the Fascist parties of Germany and Italy.

As with all wars, there was much suffering amongst all the social classes of Spain, and whilst the landed classes had more to lose, the poor suffered tremendous loss of life and many homes were razed to the ground. During this destructive period, whole stud farms were again broken up, and in a number of cases, horses slaughtered. Republicans and anti-clerics embarked on an orgy of despoilment against the Church and the establishment, and those upper-classes who had traditionally always bred the finest horses, were badly hit. Andalusia was one of the worst affected regions in the whole war, and people who lived through that period still shudder at the memory of acts of terror which are impossible to obliterate.

The Modern Church and the Role Played by the Horse

It is a credit to the Church of Rome that religion seems as solid again in Spain as it ever was before the Revolution. Franco did much to restore the credibility of the Church and every Spanish church today appears remarkably prosperous, thriving and active.

The people of Spain have always demanded an outward show of material well-being and ceremony in their religion. Each church boasts its own madonna, and however poor the penitents who come to worship at her feet, she will be endowed with riches beyond the dreams of a lifetime for many of her loyal subjects. Through her sweet smile, and outstretched bejewelled hand, the worshipper is brought closer to God, and often the candles lit at her feet will have been purchased at the expense of a loaf of much needed bread. For these people, the quiet faith of the non-conformist whose only material link with heaven is his well-handled bible, is incomprehensible. They need to be vividly reassured; the processions and pageantry of Holy Week are as life-giving to them as water itself. Each village and fraternity within the great cities takes a pride in its madonna and saints, and the more exotic the clothes, crowns and jewels worn by these alabaster and plaster figures which guard over each chapel and altar great and small, the more confident and fulfilled become the faithful.

Holy Week in Seville with its shoulder-borne processions of a hundred or more madonnas, its floats telling the anguished story of Christ's painful journey to Calvary, and its hooded figures, with the wailing, impassioned *saetas* (incantations) echoing against the castellated buildings and through the narrow alleyways, merges in some miraculous way into all the colour and gaiety of the Seville Horse Fair which starts as Holy Week ends. Harsh gypsy voices take up the notes of the penitents, and the people who jostled and thronged behind *La Macarena*, the most popular madonna in Seville, now run and push to get a better glimpse of the carriages and the glossy horses as they parade to the Fair. Some say that the thousands who flood into Seville from the outlying country districts would not attend Holy Week at all were it not for the promise of the gypsies, the fair and the horses in the days to follow.

But for those who love horses, the *Rocío* is the highlight of the Church's year. El Rocío is the shrine of the Virgin of the Marshes which lies deep within Las Marismas, the wild delta swamplands which stretch over thousands of acres under a wild empty sky. This unclaimed remote Atlantic wasteland of south-west Spain harbours great multitudes of migratory birds, as well as a wealth of indigenous flora and fauna. The only time of year that this wilderness is disturbed is during the annual pilgrimage to Rocío, when people in their thousands travel by grand carriage, horseback, ox cart or mule to honour the Virgin whose miracle stirred the imagination of the whole Peninsula.

The story is worth recounting, for its survival through seven centuries has made the pilgrimage to Rocío one of the most romantic and traditional features of Spanish life, and in the midst of it, inextricably woven with the essence of the whole occasion, looms the powerful figure of the horse – Spain's horse.

The Virgin of the Marshes, or La Paloma Blanca (the white dove) as the people know her, probably started her adventures in the times of the Moorish invasion, when Christians all over Spain stripped their churches in terror of losing their precious statues to the conquering infidel. These madonnas were buried or hidden in some safe, outlandish place until the time came when it was considered safe to retrieve them. Over the centuries of the occupation, many of these Christian relics were returned to their churches, but an equal number were probably lost for all time. When a missing madonna was finally dug out of the ground or discovered in a ruined cottage, this was usually accompanied by spiritual happenings, encouraged by the local priest.

On this particular occasion, which took place in the early thirteenth century, a hunter from the town of Almonte was out on the marshes with his dog looking for game. Examining a thicket at which his dog was pointing, he was amazed to find the wooden statue of a Virgin caught in a hollow of a tree. Delighted with his find, he forgot his hunting and started on the long trudge home. Wearied by his burden, he stopped to take a nap on the way. When he awoke he found the Virgin gone, and thinking her to be stolen retraced his steps in the hope of finding the culprit. To his astonishment he was led back to the tree and there she was again. The Virgin had returned. This time he left her where she was and hurried home to Almonte to tell the village. Disbelieving his story, a group of local men set out and also tried to bring the Virgin home. During a stop on the way back, the Virgin again disappeared, and this time, thoroughly frightened, no one tried to remove her from her resting place. The outcome of this miracle (after much debate within the Church) was that the Virgin of the Marshes, by decree of the

Bishop of Seville, was to stay in her chosen place so that she could be worshipped there as she wished.

Since then, a settlement has grown up at Rocío, and every year pilgrims have travelled the long, desolate route through Las Marismas to pay their respects to La Paloma Blanca at Whitsuntide. We read in history that Columbus was forced to delay the departure of his 1498 voyage of exploration, the third to the New World, while his sailors joined the arduous, dusty march to Rocío. Today the pilgrimage lasts seven days and is highly organised with brotherhoods or *hermandades* from all over southern Spain taking part with their own standards and colours, leaving the special clubhouse of their village to attend this event for which they have prepared for many months. The men wear the traditional costume of *traje corto*: flat black hats, short sober jackets and black or grey trousers protected by intricately worked leather chaps. The

The salt flats of Las Marismas stretch towards the Atlantic Ocean as the bustling cavalcade of the Rocío throngs its way to the shrine of the Virgin of the Marshes, La Paloma Blanca.

women wear the traditional long, highly ruffled and brightly coloured Sevillana dresses, and each year it is a matter of pride to turn out in a new dress, with new colours and a new line. Flamenco dresses change with fashion as much as any other mode of costume.

At one time it was impossible to cross the marshes to Rocío by anything other than horse-drawn vehicle. Now, sadly, cars and coaches are to be seen although the true *Rocíero* insists on making the journey in the traditional way. Horses become inordinately difficult and expensive to hire for *Rocío* week and owners of carriages and carts make more money during *Rocío* than at any other time of year. Passing through countryside which is normally the private domain of the bee-eaters and spoonbills, the ducks and the flamingos, as well as roaming herds of deer and wild boar, the air is suddenly alive with the jangling of bit and spur, the creaking of carriages and the rumble of wooden wheels which heave over the uneven tracks. Galloping horsemen sweep past in a cloud of dust, sometimes stopping to swoop a child from an open cart high into the air for an impromptu ride on his *jaca*, disappearing far into the hazy cavalcade of horses ahead, before returning to hand it speechless and thrilled to its smiling family. There is song and laughter in the air, and at night flamenco, dancing and fireworks round the camp fires which burn far into the drum-filled night.

At the end of up to four or five days spent in the saddle and exhaustive late nights of eating and drinking and making merry, the pilgrims arrive in front of La Paloma Blanca on Saturday evening. As the different brotherhoods pass in front of the shrine, they salute the Virgin and make an imposing lap of honour of the village before going on to their individual community houses. Celebrations continue all evening; the noise and crowds swell until the central *plaza* is full to bursting. After the general parade, the evening gives way to a frenzied crescendo of music and dancing interspersed by wild race-riding as young bucks on fiery Andalusian *jacas* rip through the town in a kind of madness which may last well into the dawn.

Sunday morning is a sobering experience when Mass is taken in the *real* and a portable altar set up. Riders, quiet and dignified on motionless horses, as though lined up before going into battle, bow their heads in prayer and take the sacrament.

The climax of the pilgrimage takes place on the Monday when the Virgin is brought out of the church on a float in order to make a *paseo* so that she may bless the pilgrims who have trudged so far to do her honour. Everyone tries, through the tight, teetering throng, to touch her, and happy the man who can retire from the *real* knowing that even though he did not touch the precious Virgin, at least his fingers rested on her float for a blessed moment. Gradually, the pilgrims and their tired horses begin the long trek homeward. The kites circle high above as though in silent farewell and soon the marshes are tranquil again. The *Rocío* lives on in the hearts and minds of the people all through the summer, and by Christmas they are planning the next pilgrimage with even finer horses for next year.

The Great Horse Fairs of Spain

Not only has the Church provided an outlet for the special capacity of the Spanish to throw themselves into an ostentatious world of ceremony, participating to the full, the traditional countryside pursuits have also bestowed an excuse for extravagance, gaiety and flamboyance.

Up until the Peninsular Wars, Spanish culture had been deeply influenced by Paris, as we may still observe in the eighteenth-century architecture of the great cities, Madrid and Seville, where wide boulevards and elegant fountain-filled *plazas* appear more French than Spanish. After Napoleon had been driven out, leaving a bruised and indignant country behind him, Spaniards everywhere shrank from French cultural influence particularly in everyday matters of costume and entertainment. Instead, the rural traditions of the Spanish countryside became the rage. High-born ladies pursued rustic, native styles of fashion; bullfighting and flamenco took on a new importance with all classes of people; and music with old Moorish influences was welcomed back and viewed as a romantic symbol of the distant past.

At about this time the tradition of the Spanish fair assumed a new significance. The names of Spanish and Anglo-Spanish families involved in the sherry industry were not only synonymous with the production of fine grapes but also for the breeding of bulls and horses for the entertainment of their friends and workers with *ferias* (fairs) and *corridas*. Carriage driving, where the horses were magnificently festooned with colourful harness and baubles, became a feature of Andalusian life. Thus, the land of grapes, cotton, corn and cork, led the way from now on for a truly national way of life.

The coming of spring and the gathering-in of the harvest had always been followed by festivals of thanksgiving and celebration, and when for a time it became
politically unwise to do this in churches, the fruits of men's labours could still
be applauded in the agricultural festivals of the marketplace. Horses which traditionally carried men into battle, now carried the feudal sherry barons and their
ladies through the *plazas* and *avenidas* of prosperous towns, and the magnificence
of the parade of the great fiestas of Andalusia attracted young and old from the
humblest to the grandest home in the province. A nineteenth-century Spanish
natural historian, Antonio Machado Nunez, writing on the subject in 1869, says:
'the increase in luxury carriages in the most important cities in Andalusia is a
powerful incentive for the breeders who are repaid for their efforts and find greater
advantages in the competition to breed them.'

He goes on to illustrate how breeding was recovering from the disastrous days
of the Peninsular Wars, and it is clear that the Seville Fair (originally started by
the Romans) was enthusiastically attended in company with many others: 'From
all the provinces there are brought to the famous fairs of Sevilla and Mairena ten
or twelve thousand, among which are some 3,500 horses, 5,000 mares and 4,000
colts.'

Today, although the numbers of horses cannot compare with those thousands
and are assessed instead in hundreds, the enthusiasm is as strong as ever and visitors
flock from all over Spain and abroad to share in these truly ethnic occasions. Here
one sees the Spanish character at its most dynamic and vibrant. It is sometimes
hard to understand how a nation with such enormous capacity for enjoyment could
have become so divided only half a century ago.

Antonio Gala, a modern Spanish writer, sums up the spirit of the occasion as
only a native of the country can. He describes the tradition of the fair:

> 'in which the master recalls his rustic origins and stuffs himself into the
> traditional costume and tips his wide-brimmed hat over one eye and goes
> off to display himself in the promenade on horseback pretending disdain,
> looking into the distance, his chin high and half-covered by the chin-
> strap, one hand on the reins and the other doing anything so that the
> world will see that one hand is enough.'

Over the last 150 years, Spain has developed a type of horse especially for these
glittering occasions. Capitalising on the natural beauty of the Andalusian, *aficionados* of the fair have selectively bred a horse for the parade, whether carriage
or ridden, which steps even higher than the prancing war-horse, which rotates
its neat fetlocks in an elegant dish and which, roused by the cries of applause from
the crowds, snorts and stamps with impressive dash. This is a horse of pure luxury,
the darling of the people. As he trots, heavily caparisoned, past the *casetas*
(pavilions) which line the fairground, in a slow, almost suspended collected gait,
there is no prouder man than the *caballero* who rides him with studied arrogance.

The word *caballero* is as pregnant with meaning today as it was during the battles
for the Spanish crown. As well as indicating a man of substance, a *caballero* has
to be versed in the art and courtesies of good horsemanship. The prestige of these
occasions, which are almost mediaeval so steeped are they in tradition, generate
a glamour few can understand unless they see it for themselves. All over the city,

This modern Iberian drawing portrays the roundness which every Spanish and Portuguese horseman looks for in his riding horse. The convexity of the head and neck and roundness of back, chest and quarters are not exaggerated, but are repeated throughout centuries of ancient and modern art.

be it Seville or Jerez, handsome young men in formal riding habit, with white ruffled shirts, hand-tooled chaps and flat, wide-brimmed hats, set forth to join the parade area. The accompanying *senorita* is dazzling as she rides pillion, perched delicately sideways on the horse's croup, one arm passing round her *caballero's* waist, the other clutching the crupper. Dressed in gorgeous gypsy costumes of gold, vermilion, blue and yellow, these doe-eyed girls look sullenly sulky – all part of this week of unreality when anyone may be a prince or princess for a day, dreaming from atop the horse which gave Spain its great and glorious past.

These young men come from many walks of life: one may be the son of a wealthy merchant, another a croupier from a casino, or perhaps a waiter from one of the big tourist hotels who has invested all his savings in the dancing horse beneath him. Then there is another group: Spain's landed gentry. These are the powerful families who control the huge sprawling vineyards, the *haciendas* for the breeding of bulls and the lucrative cotton industry. Blue-blooded and elegant as any leading society in Paris, London, Venice or New York, the *clase alta* with their good looks and austere riding dress stand out as only the highly groomed and confident do.

The women ride astride in sober whipcord suits, their chaps close-fitting and narrow, their hats slimmer than the men's. Gleaming, plump, beautifully schooled horses curvette beneath them and the crowd exclaim in admiration. Their menfolk are well-known local figures. As well as employing on the land up to several hundred of the people who have come to watch, they may be famous as *rejoneadors*, familiar figures on the television screen, risking life and limb against Andalusia's deadly fighting bulls.

Carriage driving at fairs in Spain is something of a phenomenon. Two, three, four, five – even nine – in hand is not unusual to see at Jerez or Seville. Dozens of ornate carriages drawn by beautifully matched pairs of gorgeously bedecked horses pass under the trees, their occupants laughingly calling in on their friends to enjoy a glass of *fino* at each *caseta* as they make several circuits of the fairground and revel in the admiration of the world.

In the words of Gala, 'There is everything in the Andalusian fairs . . . carriages of every kind . . . horses of sorrel like newly varnished mahogany, dapples like grey pearls from the Orient, haughty blacks like feathered plumes . . .'

The Gypsies, the Music and the Dancing

People still talk about the days when the horses were outnumbered by the gypsies who camped for miles around. Today the gypsies are still drawn to the fairs, but in ever-decreasing numbers.

Jerez is the cradle of flamenco singing and dancing and there is still a thriving gypsy community in the two *barrios* of San Miguel and Santiago on the outskirts of the town. There is even a famous gypsy bullfighter. Rafael de Paula is an absolute idol to the Andalusian people. His artistry with the bull is superb but like all his race he is extremely superstitious and this has caused problems before a fight. In Spain if you decide not to fight a bull once in the ring, you may find yourself in prison. It is a legal offence to refuse a bull, for by law it must killed. Only once, perhaps in ten years, does one hear of the life of a bull being spared for quite exceptional bravery. On the last occasion when this happened spectators were rioting, screaming and throwing cushions or whatever else they could get their hands on, into the ring to force the President to stop the death by sword. When a bull is saved, he is never allowed to fight again. Instead he is kept for stud and legends grow up around his progeny. Old men on street corners and young men in tavernas talk for hours on end about the bulls they have known or worked with.

The climax of the great *ferias* are the championships for the pure-bred Spanish horse. The *Feria de Jerez* is dedicated to the horse alone and equestrian competitions of every type conceivable abound. We have already read of the games *à la gineta*, and in Chapters X and XII will learn more of the significance of the *Doma Vaquera* at these fairs, which are very popular with the crowds. But the Spanish fair is more than an opportunity to compete on horseback. Whilst no Spanish festival could be conceived without the horse, the carriages and the bullfight – the gypsies, the singing and the dancing, the circus and the wild flamenco are all essential parts too.

The dust rises, the music plays and the *fino*, which is drunk from noon onwards, puts fire in the belly. Days of honour and conquest, passion and triumph are remembered. Love of his country flows in a fierce burning current through the Spaniard's hot-blooded veins. The spirit of *feria* with its brilliant trappings, song, drinking and merriment blots out the bitterness of blood once spilt between friends, brothers, families. Fiesta carries one out of oneself; it heightens the senses and flaunts itself amidst the shouting and clapping. The only blood shed now is at the death of the bull in the hot sand of the *plaza de toros* (bullring) as Spain reverberates with a gaiety and a fervour which is peculiar to herself and her people.

At ten o'clock the restaurants fill up and the fun of the fair is underway. It is still building up at midnight, for the night is yet young and tender. Outside, in the soft Andalusian air, beyond the bright lights, the cubist shape of white buildings stand proud against a Van Gogh starry sky and the spire of a church and tiled rooftops glint in the moonlight. There, below the whine of the guitar, the laughter, the fierce clapping and the voices, can be heard a special sound: a steady munching, a contented snort, a rustle of straw, an occasional stamp. The night is scented with the good clean smell of a thousand horses, stallion next to stallion, each at peace with his neighbour. Such sights, such sounds, such realisations will dictate that there is nowhere else in the world to be at that moment but in Spain.

Magic is the sun glinting on two smooth milk-white backs, glancing off oiled leather and silver buckles, whilst the jangle of bells resound in the ear. (Photo by Arnaiz)

Overleaf-Top: *The Procession to Rocío is more than a religious pilgrimage: it is an excuse to take to the ancient route of the cavalcade as it stretches mile after dusty mile through the desolate flats of Las Marismas, southern Spain. (Photo by Arnaiz)* Bottom: *Spanish jacas at work on the harvest field. A typical Andalusian scene. (Photo by Soskia Mesdag)*

Right: *Sharply pricked ears listen for the roll of the drums at fiesta.* (Photo by Soskia Mesdag)

Below: *Carthusian horses make a pleasing picture of three-in-hand as they pass down the hibiscus-lined road.* (Photo by Arnaiz)

The best Lusitanos are to be found at the great country houses lying deep in the Portuguese interior. Campinos dressed in traditional livery have known and worked with these horses all their lives and are proud to present them. (Photo by Sally Anne Thompson)

CHAPTER VIII

Portugal – An Insight into Her History and Culture

In dreary, doubtful waiting hours
Before the brazen frenzy starts,
The horses show him nobler powers;
O patient eyes, courageous hearts!

JULIAN GRENFELL
(*Into Battle*)

Portugal has a haunting story all of her own to tell. The Garden of Iberia, as some people call this fertile and pleasant land with its rolling mountains, green valleys, swift-flowing rivers and long white beaches swept clean by the booming Atlantic, remembers not so much a past filled with bloodshed and conquest, but a history of discovery and former glories that have drifted away like the blossom on the almond trees.

The Atmosphere of Portugal

The moment the frontier is crossed, whether via the water from Ayamonte into the neat, tiled town of Vila Real de St Antonio in the Algarve, or across the magnificent northern frontier of Guarda, where the shadows of coliseum-like Scots pine blot out the sunshine from the winding route south to Coimbra, there is a distinct feeling of wistfulness. Mingled with a curious sense of enchantment, it creeps down off the steep hillsides and rises up from the lovingly tended land. Small plots and carefully nurtured terraces cut into the red earth yield up a profusion of tempting vegetation and strong leafy vines, but even this wealth of nature's green bounty cannot mask the sense of longing in the air. The Portuguese call this sensation *saudades*, which is described as a nostalgic yearning for the grandeur of the past, the mighty discoveries and the greatness of an empire which spanned every corner of the world. Now, the last remnants of those rich colonies as they once were, are crumbling away, and where in another country, disillusionment might have led to bitterness, in Portugal the people shrug their shoulders and give a gentle smile of resignation. Acceptance tinged with regret – but life goes on.

Here, the azure skies of the Atlantic are as different from the dazzling cornflower Mediterranean skies as the stark Spanish plains which sweep across Andalusia seem from the homely looking farms tucked into the undulating Portuguese hinterland of pungent cork forest and bamboo-filled riverbed. All around is the scent of oregano, tarragon and eucalyptus and there is something earthy, comforting and motherly about Portugal which contrasts sharply with the disturbing, fierce, fatherliness of Spain.

The Portuguese Temperament

To understand a little of Portugal's history is to understand the people and their special relationship with the horse. Portugal's past has shown a notable lack of cruelty to the underdog, whether man or beast, and in this Latin country you rarely see a starving cat, a cringing cur or an emaciated donkey.

The Portuguese love animals. They may lack the sentimentality the English display towards their pets, but the poorest household surrounds itself with creatures great and small, and if sometimes treated with ignorance, they are never knowingly made to suffer. Plump dogs roam the streets and sleep undisturbed in the midday sun. Round every small café in the remotest village square will gather a collection of hounds of every shape and size, all waiting for, and more often than not, all receiving, a tasty morsel dropped by a kindly hand.

In the Portuguese bullfight there is no death in the sun. The bull will, it is true, be put down in the normal humane way after the fight, for meat, or he may be saved for breeding, but the Portuguese do not revel in the act of death. We shall be examining the Portuguese mounted bullfight in detail in the next chapter, but it should be pointed out that to the Portuguese, the *corrida* on horseback is no more cruel or unsporting than the shoot or hunt is to the Englishman. The emphasis – as in hunting – is on the whole way of life which accompanies the sport, the breeding and training of horses and the traditions of the countryside upon which so many families depend for their livelihood.

As for the spectators, it is the expertise of the horseman and his horse which attracts the nation to the arena, rather than the climax as the final dart is placed. The courtly discipline of the *alta escola* (High School) and the sympathy which exists between the *cavaleiro* and his Lusitano fill an emotional void in the hearts of the onlookers, recalling an age when Portuguese noblemen mounted on just such a horse swept this small country to unprecedented heights of empire, and fiercely defended the *patria* against the ever-encroaching Spanish invaders.

Ecologically, socially and culturally, Portugal would be a very much poorer country without her elegant mounted *corridas*.

Portuguese Cavalry

Whilst never reaching the power and proportions of the Spanish cavalry, Portugal, through the Carthaginian, Roman, Swabian and Visigoth attacks and occupations of early history, had by the Middle Ages slowly developed a cavalry of which to be proud. So effective was it that by the mid-thirteenth century, coupled with an excellent infantry who understood and used the rugged terrain to advantage in making swooping attacks against the Moors, Portugal was able to drive the infidel from her shores two hundred years in advance of the Spanish Reconquest.

The Iberian horse with his collected balanced movements could pick his way carefully between the rocks and ledges of the granite hillsides, and his courage and obedience gave the cavalryman the element of surprise, for a Portuguese horse will stand all day without fidgeting or fussing in the lee of a cave, quietly waiting for the command for action. Thus, the Portuguese knights fought a war of daring and cunning, combining the resourcefulness of their horses with the special attributes of their soldiers. All over the kingdom, castles and watchtowers were built by the Christians on outlying heights to defend themselves against the Muslim forces. Beacons were lit in times of danger and hornblowers rode out with the cry *'Mouros na terra! As Armas!'* ('Moors on the land! To arms!') Any knight who disregarded this challenge was punished by fines and his horse would be docked for all to see. The rank and file had their beards cropped. Afonso Henriques, later D. Afonso I, took the first important initiative against the Moors at Ourique (a small town which lies today on the new road from Lisbon to the Algarve) in 1139. The *Book of Testaments* of Santa Cruz de Coimbra speaks of his skill in all the arts of kingship including fine horsemanship, and he is traditionally depicted in much the same *genre* as El Cid, dashing, virile and with a flowing black beard.

Friendship with England

Both seafaring peoples, with strong Celtic connections and a further interrelationship through the Swabians (whose Angle branch established the English system of monarchy and whose Quadi branch created the first Catholic kingdom of Europe in what is today Portugal), it is natural perhaps that the English should have proved useful allies to the Portuguese of the twelfth century. Crusaders from Kent, East Anglia and London, as well as Germans and Flemings, poured into Oporto and, flattered and bribed with 'good cheap wine and other delights' by the shrewd bishop Pedro Pitões, were persuaded to divert their attentions temporarily from the Holy Land and assist in the siege of Lisbon, which Afonso was to wrest from the Moors in 1147.

Having driven the Moors southwards (with this verbal broadside from the Archbishop of Braga: 'Go back unbidden to the land of the Moors whence you came with your baggage, money and goods, and your women and your children, leaving to us our own . . . you Moors and Moabites fraudulently seized the realm of Lusitania from your king and ours . . .') many of the Crusaders continued on their way to Palestine, taking along with them as much booty as they had been able to pillage after the siege. Horses were amongst the most prized acquisitions. Many of the English adventurers liked the country so much that they remained, or paid deposits on land to be claimed on their return from the Mediterranean. The trend for British people to settle in Portugal has continued since then until the present day, and still for many British people Portugal is a home from home, with its many Celtic customs and strong similarities of national temperament.

Although trade had existed for many centuries between the Celtic tribes of Lusitania and those who dwelt round the coastal areas of Cornwall, Wales, Lancashire and Ireland, the first official maritime treaty was made between Portugal and England in 1294 and this activated sea commerce and expansion for both nations.

Portugal's royal navy was formed in 1317. Educational and agricultural reform led to the setting up of the University of Coimbra in 1290, and the founding of agricultural colleges to introduce new methods of cultivating the land under King D. Diniz, known as the 'Farmer King'.

England's great Duke of Lancaster, John of Gaunt (1340–1399), ambitious to regain territories in Castile, arranged for his daughter Philippa to marry King

John of Gaunt, from a fifteenth-century engraving from Froissart. His daughter became Queen Philippa of Portugal, and the Anglo-Portuguese alliance (begun in the twelfth century) was greatly strengthened during his lifetime.

João I of Portugal, and the fourteenth-century French chronicler, Sir John Frois-sart, gives a vivid account of the first meeting between John of Gaunt with his great retinue, and the magnificent reception laid on by the Portuguese king at Moncão: 'The king and the duke had each their apartments hung with cloth and covered with carpets, as convenient as if the king had been at Lisbon or the duke in London.' After feasting, sealing their friendship and agreeing to the marriage, the duke and his knights were escorted back to Galicia by one hundred Portuguese lancers under the Count of Novaire. Presents of horses, greyhounds and falcons were exchanged and from then on the two countries would fight together against the might of Castile.

In 1385, Castile attacked Portugal. England immediately intervened by sending five hundred English archers and the Castilians were utterly defeated at the Battle of Aljubarrota. Froissart records that the cavalry of Castile consisted of

> 'twenty thousand men on horseback. You might have seen these young knights full of vigour and gallantry, carrying themselves so handsomely that it was a pleasant spectacle to see; and they were, as I have said a large battalion of themselves.'

The following year, John of Gaunt reinforced the Portuguese army against Castile with five thousand English soldiers, and the Treaty of Windsor 1386 reconfirmed the alliance between Portugal and England. This was to be ratified by Henry IV, Henry V and Henry VI of England.

During this productive period, Portuguese expansion began overseas with the capture of Ceuta in Morocco in 1415.

The Period of Discoveries

It is possible that as Portugal was now turning her attention to building herself up as a great seafaring nation, there followed a decline in the breeding of war-horses. This is feasible; but we do know that wherever Portugal sent her great sailing ships, horses were taken aboard from the *patria*, reaching as far east as Goa in India and Macão just off the Chinese mainland.

Queen D. Philippa of Lancaster had a son. This Anglo-Portuguese was no ordinary boy and he grew up to become Prince Henry of Portugal, the Navigator Prince – a name that is synonymous with the spirit of the age. Those enquiring, exploring, searching qualities of his people were fired by Prince Henry's resourceful, brilliant mind and he was able to place at his captains' disposal the very latest, most up-to-date maps and charts, concise information on astrological and weather research, and the most modern technical instruments devised to assist them in their voyages of discovery.

Where the Spaniards had penetrated deep into the countryside of the lands they discovered, the Portuguese began a systematic exploration of new coastlines, and the African coast was the first to be scrutinised in this way.

By 1445 Senegal and Cape Verde were reached and in 1446 Alvaro Fernandes pushed on almost to Sierra Leone. There was colonisation in the Azores and Madeira, where sugar and wine were produced, but more important by far was the gold being brought home from the Gulf of Guinea under King D. Afonso V. In 1488 Bartholomeu Dias had passed and repassed the Cape of Good Hope, proving to Portugal and the world that the route to the Indian Ocean was accessible by sea, and by 1500 on the other side of the globe, Cabral (see Chapter XV) had claimed Brazil for the Portuguese crown.

The Portuguese Empire, 1499–1580

Portugal brought back many slaves to European soil and did not hesitate to use slave labour for her ambitious construction projects, but there was little wholesale slaughter of native populations as carried out by the Spanish during their expeditions. Portuguese settlers were actively encouraged to intermarry, and the crown's main concern was to build up a powerful empire and establish efficient trading posts and towns in the new territories, which would later magnify into great colonial cities. Still today in Lourenço Marques, Rio de Janeiro and Goa, we find breathtakingly beautiful examples of Portuguese colonial architecture which, with its rose-coloured buildings, ornate churches, exotic archways and entrances and intricately tiled rooftops, is peculiarly distinctive.

King D. Manuel assumed the title in 1500 of 'Lord of the Conquest, Navigation, and Commerce of India, Ethiopia and Persia.' Far from objecting to this grandiose form of address, Pope Alexander VI confirmed it in 1502. This gives us some indication of Portugal's image abroad as a leading world power.

A huge programme of colonisation ensued, particularly in the African Congo, and by 1540 Portugal had acquired a line of scattered maritime possessions from Brazil to east and west Africa, Malabar, Ceylon, Persia, Indo-China and the Malay archipelago. The most important settlements in the east were Goa and Malacca.

In the meantime, another Portuguese sailor, Fernão de Magalhaes – better known as Ferdinand Magellan – had made history by completing the first voyage around the world.

Troubles with Spain

Despite these conquests, Portugal continued her religious crusade against the Moors in North Africa. On one of these commercially unimportant missions King Sebastian was killed leaving the Portuguese throne inconveniently vacant.

After some fighting, when again England came to Portugal's side, it was decided constitutionally in 1581 that Portugal should be joined to Spain solely, not as a conquered country but by a personal union similar to the one which had existed between Castile and Aragon, under Ferdinand and Isabella. At Tomar, Philip II of Spain became Philip I of Portugal, and he promised to maintain the rights and liberties conceded by his predecessors on the Portuguese throne, and to create a Portuguese Privy Council.

Philip I was succeeded by Philip II, and slowly promises were broken and Spain began to exercise an authority over the Portuguese which was not in accordance with the original agreement. The only time in Portuguese history that this proud little country ever came directly under Spanish rule was when Philip III (IV of Spain) came to the throne and attempted to rule over Portugal as a possession of Spain. This was too much for the Portuguese nobles. Gradually they had seen their liberties and their resources whittled away, and this humiliating state of affairs could no longer continue. Spain was never to be forgiven for her treachery, and in 1640 the Portuguese seized various strategic points and crowned their own Duke of Braganza, King João IV of Portugal.

During the reign of Philip III, which had lasted nineteen years in Portugal, horse breeding had reached a particularly low ebb. In an attempt to weaken the Portuguese nobility and forestall any uprising, laws had been passed by the Spanish which effectively arrested the national output of cavalry horses. Recognising that from now on her cavalry would have to be swiftly built up again if she was to maintain independence, Portugal, under her new monarch entered a fresh era of resistance and self-protection. Stud farms which had been allowed to run down under Spanish rule, were refurbished and revitalised with new blood often smuggled in from over the border. Andalusian war-horses were purloined from Spanish *hidalgos* sympathetic to the Portuguese cause, for many frontier families were closely related and the new King's own wife – herself a Spanish noblewoman of the Medina Sidonia family – had actually plotted against the country of her birth to raise her husband to the Portuguese throne. Some Spanish families who had acquired estates in Portugal actually decided to remain there, and sixty years on – with the abolition of mounted bullfighting in Spain – many more aristocratic families who were not prepared to give up their heritage of classical riding in the arena, introduced whole new bloodlines of magnificent Andalusian horses.

To this day, all along the Portuguese–Spanish frontier, stretching from the Algarve in the south to the extreme north of the country, stand grim reminders of those jealous days. Great towering fortresses, hewn of massive blocks of stone, shadow the landscape and proclaim their resistance to the Spanish invader. And nearby, in the stables of one of the small towns or villages which huddle at their foot, are horses; horses of such fantastic calibre and breeding that one can be sure that they too, like the people who own them, are direct descendants of those troubled and defensive days.

King Dom José I presides over the Terreiro do Paço (affectionately known by Portuguese and English alike as 'Black Horse Square') in Lisbon. D. José I was a patron of the art of High School and developed the Alter Real Stud founded by his father.

When Charles II of England married Catherine of Braganza and sealed once more the friendship between England and Portugal, the royal dowry of the Portuguese princess, as described in Chapter V, included the Portuguese territories of Bombay and Tangier with their complements of Portuguese cavalry horses.

Spain did not acknowledge Portugal's independence as a nation formally until 1668, and for the next few years of peace, Portugal enjoyed great prosperity not only from her colonies in the east, but with the discovery in 1693 of the Minas Geraes, fantastic goldfields in Brazil which were to bring a vast revenue in royalties to the crown.

Sadly for Portugal, this rich, golden period of the late seventeenth century was already fading by the turn of the new one, when they joined the British in the Wars of the Spanish Succession. These put a heavy burden on the Portuguese privy purse, and when in 1711 the French sacked Rio de Janeiro and cut off the Brazilian treasure ships, the Portuguese financial structure was in danger of collapsing in the same way that the Spanish had experienced in 1640 (see Chapter VII) when no silver fleet arrived from America due to Dutch interception.

Further fighting with Spain continued intermittently throughout the remainder of the century, and by the time of the Peninsular War, Portugal was experiencing severe economic and political difficulties.

Whilst Portugal fought[1] side by side with British troops from the beginning of the war against Napoleon, Spain was making secret treaties with the French in an attempt to bring about the partition of Portugal. This again caused much bitterness amongst the Portuguese towards their troublesome neighbour, and

---

1. The Portuguese are still proud of a phrase written by Wellington from the Pyrenees in 1813 in which he described them as 'the fighting cocks of the army'.

although Wellington was eventually to unite Spanish forces under his command to rid the Peninsula of the French, it would have been impossible for the Portuguese to fight alongside their old sparring partners. Fortunately, this was not required as Portugal was too busy defending her own territory to become involved in Spain.

It is not always appreciated that when Napoleon rose to power, England had but two friends in Europe: Portugal and Sweden. Portugal might never have been invaded so viciously by the French had it not been for her refusal to comply with Napoleon's Berlin Decree of 1806, when he called upon all Europe to close her ports to British ships.

The following year Portugal was invaded. Napoleon's troops ravaged the Portuguese countryside, looting and burning and causing enormous hardship. People were killed in their own homes for their silver and gold. Many of the fine studs which had been built up over the past century and a half were pillaged, and there is a story of a very good horse from a particularly famous bloodline being hidden in a cellar for three years to protect it from the French.

Eventually, under the brilliant command of the Duke of Wellington, the Portuguese and English army won a major victory against Napoleon at Bussaco in 1810, and while the allied forces entered the Torres Vedras lines, the French started their long retreat, crossing the Portuguese frontier for the last time on 8th April 1811.

Political Unrest and Revolution

The period after the Napoleonic Wars was as internally disruptive and riddled with financial and political problems for Portugal as it was for Spain and the other countries involved.

Brazil became independent at the end of the nineteenth century, and although the African colonies continued to support the economy to some extent, in 1892 the government declared themselves bankrupt and the budget showed a huge deficit. In 1908 King D. Carlos was assassinated, but the revolution of 1910 was a mild affair compared to Spanish revolutions, and as usual the people who suffered most of all were the poor.

Portugal continued to show her loyalty to Great Britain through both World Wars, and after further internal uprisings and then a system of dictatorship in the years after World War II, the country at last seemed to be running on an even keel, bulwarked by her vital resources in Angola and Mozambique where whites and black had become well integrated and prosperity was being achieved for all classes.

Alas for Portugal, the encroachment of Communism began to make its presence felt in the form of African guerilla attacks, and with underground Communist forces working at home, the revolution of 1974 saw not only the loss of Angola and Mozambique to Cuban and Russian forces, it also brought about the near collapse of the home economy.

For two unhappy years, political agitators, burning with resentment kindled by Marxist propaganda of the most erosive kind, moved from the cities into the countryside in concerted attempts to stir up as much trouble as was possible against Portugal's landed classes. In many areas, estates were vacated and commandeered

Above: *There are repeated moments in the mounted* corrida *when the bull looks perilously close, but the Iberian horse, well back on his hocks, deftly copes by moving sideways away from the horns. (Photo by Susan Cole)*

Left: *From ancient traditions of hunting bulls through the dense Iberian countryside comes today's popular Spanish sport,* Acoso y Derribo. *Here two young* vaquero *horsemen mounted on* jacas *demonstrate their skill. (Photo by Arnaiz)*

Overleaf: *Lone horseman. There is an emptiness about Iberia's great sweeping steppes and plains which somehow complements horse and rider. (Photo by Ward Wallace, courtesy of Promark Ltd)*

by the *povo* (populace). Whole stud farms were broken up and many of the best horses sold to Spain, as it became politically unwise to continue with a way of life on which the ringleaders of the Marxist movement had focused their hatred. A programme of senseless dismantlement and laying to waste was effected in the worst hit areas, particularly the larger *herdades* lying between Evora in the south and the Alentejo districts where a certain amount of absentee landlordism had caused resentment in the past.

For a time, things looked black for the Portuguese people. In 1975, Lisbon, one of the most elegant cities in the world, became a sombre place where anxious people gathered in groups and looked over their shoulders before they spoke, in the lee of buildings defaced by every manner of red-painted political slogan.

In the countryside the story was the same. No one smiled for many months, and the neat white cottages and spotless *horta* (orchard) walls were daubed with the hammer and sickle and the names of countless unknown political factions which had sprung up overnight. At this time, there were few horses to be seen at the fairs and suddenly the price of horses, along with everything from bread to olives, had rocketed by over a hundred per cent.

As land was commandeered and confiscated, hundreds of Lusitano horses were sold abroad and Brazil, Mexico, France and Spain were to benefit as Portuguese landowners were no longer able to support the large herds of former times. Some stud farms, however, were fortunate. Deep in the heart of the countryside, far away from the towns, life virtually went on unchanged, although until the good news filtered through that the Communists had been quietly overthrown, with not one drop of blood spilt, there must have been uneasy moments.

Democracy Restored

Now that democracy has been restored to Portugal and she has moved into a new era of partnership with the rest of Europe, the horse world, together with the agricultural world, industry and commerce are recovering well from the damage which

Portugal boasts probably the finest collection of coaches in the world, housed at the National Coach Museum, Bélem, Lisbon. Left: The Berlinda of Queen D. Maria I. Right: The Ambassadorial coach of the Marquis de Fontes, an extravaganza of Baroque workmanship.

occurred in the mid-seventies. Many breeders philosophically regard what happened as a natural culling – for the best lines were saved, and therefore breeding which has now taken off energetically again, is from the cream of bloodstock which was saved by the canny Portuguese breeders.

Prices of Lusitano horses today simply cannot be compared with pre-Revolution figures. A good brood mare from one of the large breeders in those days could be purchased for around 10 to 15 contos (equivalent then, when the escudo was high, to £150–£225). Today, a similar mare will cost around 600 contos (about £3,000 with the escudo at its present all-time low). For a good bullfighting horse, the sky is the limit and with purchasers in Mexico, Brazil, Chile, Bolivia, and Spain prepared to pay up to £100,000 for one very good stallion, it is hardly surprising that breeders cannot keep up with today's demands.

The Horse Fairs of Portugal

The Portuguese as a race do not yearn for dazzling ceremony and a loud display of pomp and circumstance. Unlike the colourful *ferias* of Andalusia, their horse shows are on the whole sober occasions, destined to prove the usefulness of the riding horse rather than flaunt his beauty.

There are two important dates in the Portuguese breeders' calendar which attract *aficionados* of the Lusitano horse from all over the world. The first of these is the Feira Agricola de Santarem which is held in June and lasts several days. Here, domestic animals of every type and breed are brought to be shown and judged, but it is the Lusitano horses which dominate the showground and provide a daily spectacle of skill and agility as their owners put them through their paces on the curving parade ground.

The whole show complex is built round the site of the Santarem bullring, high on the clifftops of this ancient fortified Roman town and encompassing several acres of land, set aside from the main part of the town for this one annual purpose. As sedate families arrive, dressed in their Sunday best, from miles around to admire the animals and the latest in agricultural equipment at this the highlight of the farmers' year, there is no penetrating flamenco emanating from the wine-hall, no screaming guitar or stamping of a hundred pairs of feet. Instead, somewhere in the background are the muted strains of Portuguese folklore music, or the sad haunting notes of *fado*, and it is only the fanfare of the trumpet from the van which sells tickets for the afternoon's bullfight that really cuts through the air and sets the blood tingling.

After lunch, when the smell of charcoal-grilled pork and fresh sole hangs in the air, the horses come out to parade, and each stallion gives a beautiful display of High School work which is automatically expected of any horse of the blood. People gather to watch and comment in the stands, and there is much speculation as to who will win the championships in any year.

By early evening, the restaurants are filling up again and more people come from the town to swell the crowds who promenade the fairground. Hundreds of little stalls line the way, providing a tempting array of nougat, sweetmeats made of fig, and baskets of pink and green marzipan fruit from this almond-growing land. Smoke from the hot-chestnut stand curls against the darkening sky as a thousand lights come on to brighten the track where a few horses have been brought out again for prospective purchasers, this time perhaps from Germany and Switzerland. The Portuguese never seem in a hurry to sell. Many of them will bring their horses to Santarem just for the championships and to be seen. If they do not like the approach of a potential buyer, they will not sell. The price may be right, but it is important that the face fits. Horses are treasured possessions and it may take days or months of careful negotiation before a freight plane is ordered to carry the cherished gilt-edged stock of someone's stable from Lisbon to, say, South America.

The second and perhaps even more important week in the horseman's year is set aside for the Feira da Golegã in November. Unlike the agricultural fair of Santarem, this old horse fair is dedicated to the stallion alone. On arrival at Golegã, which takes its name from the Galician woman who reputedly kept a fine coaching inn there before the Napoleonic Wars, one might as well have stepped back two hundred years or more, for there is not a car, horsebox or tractor in sight. Only horses, horses, horses . . . everywhere. Close to the bullring, where some of the great bullfighting names of the Peninsula have fought and still do fight, in this small, rather nondescript border town, is a large market square where hundreds of stallions are paraded in front of their stalls. Every house in Golegã boasts at least two or three stables, and when these begin to overflow, garages, stores and even the basements of houses may be used to cram in magnificent Lusitano stallions. In other words, there are literally hundreds of horses spilling out of every nook and cranny.

Again, the championships are the highlight of this great show. Because in Portuguese equestrian circles, everyone is related to everyone else, foreign judges are called in to officiate, perhaps from Vienna, France or Germany. To win is, of course, everything. Family honour depends on success at Golegã.

Visitors to Spain and Portugal are constantly amazed to see stallion after stallion stabled cheek by jowl in confined areas, often with the children of the house playing around their heels. The Iberians laugh at their amazement. As all gentlemen must ride stallions – geldings traditionally are ridden by women or grooms – it would be impractical not to house the stallions together. It is only a question of horse temperament and discipline. It would be unthinkable not to stable all the horses together. The horse must learn manners, to suit its master's requirements. Do the other nations of the world allow their horses to dictate to them?

I shall never forget the words of one Portuguese gentleman, delivered in impeccable English, to a passing visitor who had exclaimed, in shocked incredulity, at his six grey stallions standing quietly together in narrow stalls at the fair of Golegã: 'You must not forget, my dear,' he said, smiling politely after she had finished her small tirade about stallions being vicious and dangerous creatures, 'our Iberian horses are noble. They do not bite; they do not kick. Is it not true that aristocrats the world over instinctively know how to behave?'

CHAPTER IX
The Corrida

. . . this pageant of proud horses, grey and bay,
sorrel and black . . . with blazing eyes and glistening
flanks, recalled a procession of gladiators marching
to some circus . . .

PETER SHIRAEFF

There are two types of bullfight in Spain, but only one in Portugal. Unfortunately, the term bullfighting, loosely used in the English language, sums up a vision of a Costa del Sol poster where the artist has run riot with swirling impressions of *matador* and scarlet cape: as the handsome hero arches his arrogant back, a snorting bull – forefeet invariably off the ground in a hurtling charge – plunges past. One can almost hear the crowd roar '*Olé!*' through the rising dust.

This is the unmounted *corrida*, and with it go the often detested *picadors* – burly men on horseback whose job it is to weaken the muscles at the back of the bull's neck with persistent jabbing from their steel-tipped lances. The horses are elderly animals which play a sad, stooge-like role in the ring. Had they not been saved for this job, they might have gone for slaughter some time before. Their job is not to fight but to provide a position of height and vantage for the *picador* to do his job. They are not to be envied. This bullfight, or *corrida*, should in no way be confused with the equestrian or mounted *corrida*, although it developed as a result of a ban placed on the latter which took place (as we read in Chapter VI) in 1702.

The mounted *hidalgos* had always had their *chulos*, now known as *peõs de brega*, their servants on foot who assisted in the fight. They were allowed to serve their masters during the individual fight or *lide*, initially with their bare hands, and later with the use of a decoy, pieces of cloth, a hat or a jacket, which if waved violently would distract the bull. Unlike their aristocratic masters who courted the favour of the new French king, they felt little obligation to give up the fight which over the centuries they had come to enjoy so much. The result was that although they could not afford horses, they continued to fight bulls on foot and so the unmounted *corrida* developed.

At length, horses were introduced again but only as a further distraction and only the very poorest specimens were used, for the life of a *picador*'s horse is not a long one. Those who love horses should think twice about going to this form of fight, although it is still by far the greatest tourist draw in the whole of Spain, as well as being loved best by the Spanish themselves.

The fight with which this book is concerned is only now being fully accepted back into Spain after over two centuries of non-existence in this complex country of bulls and horses. To distinguish it from the *corrida* on foot it is termed *rejoneo* – pronounced re-hon-ay-o – and the horsemen, *rejoneadors*. These should in no way whatsoever be confused with the *picadors* of the unmounted fight whose horses are destined to be buffeted by the bull and who suffer greatly. The *rejoneador*'s horse by contrast is a fighting horse and is never touched by the bull. If it is, not only is it a disgrace but it could also prove an expensive mistake for a good *rejoneo* horse can be worth anything up to half a million pounds.

The Ancient Art

In Portugal the only kind of bullfighting which exists is mounted, and it is simply called the *corrida* as there is no need to distinguish it from another form. The names comes from the verb *correr* (to run) which is an appropriate name for a sport which once involved hunting running wild bulls on horseback in the untamed countryside of the Peninsula. This deeply rooted practice dating back to prehistoric times, as we have learned from cave paintings, combined with the inherent riding methods of the war-like Iberian people to leave a legacy of breathtaking skill on horseback. It is most unlikely, as some historians have suggested, that the *corrida* is a left-over from the days of the Moorish invasion, just as it is a known fallacy that the art of riding was brought to the Peninsula by the Moors (see Chapter II). In *El Caballo en Espana* we read that Julius Caesar 'fought a bull in Cadiz from the back of an Andalusian horse in the centre of a ring formed by Tartesian[1] horses in silver armour.'

The main difference between the Portuguese *corrida* and the Spanish *rejoneo corrida* is that in Portugal the bull is not killed. Secondly, the Portuguese fight takes place in the relatively small *praca de touros*, while the Spanish fight is conducted in a large arena where the *rejoneo* horse is encouraged to gallop at speed using the whole large *plaza* in a way which the Portuguese *cavaleiro* would never ascribe to, for his craft relies upon subtle ruses, surprise acceleration and what amounts to highly disciplined equestrian tactics, all of which may be conducted in the tightest of corners. In Spain, the death by sword is still carried out. From now on this chapter will explain the sequence of the Portuguese fight, which is considerably less harsh in outlook. Portuguese bulls, for example, have their horns padded with thick stuffed leather guards, whereas in Spain they are left unprotected and deadly sharp.

Other countries' bloodsports are as incomprehensible to the Portuguese or Spanish *aficionado* of bullfighting, as their bloodsport is to us. I do not propose to argue or to defend the moral aspects of the national sport of Iberia. In this chapter I wish merely to draw attention to the superb horsemanship which is generated from this sport and to explain as simply as possible to the reader who is genuinely interested in the art of advanced equitation, how such high standards of horsemanship are still to be found in this part of the world amongst ordinary riding folk.

---

1. Tartesian – of Tartessus. This important commercial city, famed for its sea trading and silver mines in ancient times and believed to have been built by the Phoenicians, is thought by some to be the site of present-day Cadiz, whereas other historians believe it to be several leagues under the sea.

Bullfighting may well be morally wrong, but it has kept alive the practice of *haute école* not as a forgotten art to be revived for the sake of showmanship in a dim reflection of historical nostalgia, but to be used daily for a practical purpose.

The Iberian Peninsula, and to a lesser extent the Latin countries of South and Central America, as well as some regions of France, represent a living stage where the finest principles of classical riding are daily enacted and perpetuated. There is no doubt at all in my own mind that to observe this colourful and lively partnership of horse and man at its best, revitalises the serious student of equitation and helps him to understand a little more how bustling, enthusiastic and joyful the whole process can be. Great bullfighters, who, at the height of the summer season, daily court death with their beautiful horses, are unreservedly emotional about the relationship they share with their fighting horse. Alvaro Domecq (Snr) talks movingly of the symbiosis he shared with his great mare Espléndida, a truly exceptional animal since it is almost unheard of to use a mare in the arena:

> 'But what a good heart toward her rider, proven on so many difficult occasions! Espléndida . . . would have preferred that they kill her rather than that anything should happen to me. She was a model of fidelity and loyalty, she understood me so completely. I felt her so much mine beneath the saddle . . .'

Wherever *gineta* horsemanship is to be found in those sunlit lands, the whole art of equitation – the expression of the centaur, man and his horse moulded into a single form – is as profound and ageless as the hills themselves.

The Sequence of the Fight

The first part of the Spanish and Portuguese *corrida* is essentially the same. Upon a signal from *o presidente*, normally a local dignitary flanked by two advisers who are often retired bullfighters, a fanfare of trumpets announces the opening ceremony which is known as the *cortesias* (courtesies). The *cavaleiros* (or *rejoneadors*) enter and salute the authorities and then proceed to make their parade to compliment the public. Their mounts, rippling beneath them, are majestic horses, highly adorned and extremely fit; their coats glisten with health. Manes are braided in bright, glowing colours; the silver trappings of the magnificent high-pommelled, high-cantled saddles and bucket stirrups glint in the sunlight; and the clinking of chain from the long-cheeked bits lightly carried, mingles with the general sound of excitement and impatience which fill the air with anticipation.

Whilst the Spanish *rejoneador* rides in the provincial attire of short velvet jacket, leather chaps, with a flat black hat on his head, the Portuguese *cavaleiro* is as dandified as a *chevalier* from the court of Louis XIV with his splendid attire of pristine white jabot and lace ruffles spilling over an intricately embroidered satin coat of peacock blue, deep vermilion, emerald green or yellow gold. The frothy cuffs almost conceal the hand held at the waist, which holds the horse on the lightest of contacts. Then, as he raises the other to doff his cockaded, tricorn hat, the crowd roars its appreciation. In response, with chest puffed out like that of a turkey cock, he manoeuvres his horse into a series of classical steps.

The full passes, performed so effortlessly to attract attention head-on, the canter

'Majestic horses, highly adorned and extremely fit; their coats glisten with health . . .' (Courtesy of Country Life*)*

on the spot, the rein-back across the whole radius of the arena, soon have the desired effect and flowers are being thrown into the ring in greeting. The *cavaleiro* smiles graciously as his horse piaffes provocatively before the *sombra*[2] side of the bullring, where the ladies of the most important families are grouped behind the *barreira*. Equally graciously, they smile back, proud and erect behind their best mantillas which have been carefully spread to drape over the protective wooden cladding. The armorial designs and floral badges of the great landowning families hang in a riot of intricately woven colour, which is reflected in the sequinned costumes of the bullfighter's *peõns* as they flank their master with their huge pink and yellow capes folded over one arm.

Now that he has the full attention of the crowd, the man on the horse moves into the centre and puts his stallion into a full display of *haute école* which may be as fine as anything produced under the strict discipline of the Spanish Riding School of Vienna, or it may verge on the circus. It all depends where the fight is, who is fighting, and whether the *cavaleiro* has been correctly schooled in his art in the old traditions, or if he is a *novo rico* upstart who fancies himself and is lacking in the finer techniques.

Well performed, the arrogant steps of the Spanish walk and trot, the slow stately bounce of the passage, a courbette where the horse sits right back on his hocks and the dock of his feathery tail sweeps the ground, and a perfect canter with counter changes of hand at every stride, show the Iberian horse at his gayest and best.

The purpose of the fight is to place *bandarillas* in the fleshy muscular part of the bull's neck – just in front of the 'withers' – which will numb the nerve endings and cause him to lower his head. In the Spanish fight this enables the *rejoneador* to aim the fatal blow with the sword, for if the head is too high, the thrust is almost certain to be inaccurate and the kill will not be clean. In the Portuguese fight, the *bandarillas* are also employed to lower the head, but the reason for this is to enable the second phase of the fight to take place. This is conducted with unarmed boys, which will be explained later.

There are stringent rules as to how these darts must be applied. When, in the

2. *Sombra* meaning shade does not only indicate a more comfortable seat, but also one of the more prestigious seats. All *cavaleiros* and *rejoneadors* make it their business to work the bull as close to the President as possible so that he may observe all the action of the fight, and this place is very naturally centred in the *sombra*. *Sombra* seats are considerably more expensive than those in the *sol*.

eighteenth century, the Marquis of Marialva (see Chapter V), who, in the tradition of Portuguese noblemen was himself a great bullfighter, rewrote the sporting laws governing the fight, specific requirements were made. Correct positions and angles were laid down for the entry of the dart so that had a sword been plunged into the bull's neck to full capacity, the bull would have been killed instantly. In this way, not only is the bull protected from unnecessary suffering, but it behoves the horseman to train his horse to the highest level of obedience.

When the bull is admitted to the arena and bursts in with his customary bullet-like charge, the horseman and his horse have only a few seconds in which to sum up the nature of their opponent. Each bull is different. It is vital before the first *sorte* is made to assess his speed, the way he charges and the mood. Some bulls may appear highly aggressive initially but then slow down and become almost indolent to attack. Others, apparently mild and uninterested can prove the most cunning and savage. What is true of all bulls is their capacity to remember, which

Left The Lusitano stallion Trigueiro (out of a Veiga dam by a Veiga sire) is ridden here by the cavaleiro tauromatique Emilio Pinto. As the horse makes his sorte, *the ears are pricked with excitement. Right A moment later the same horse demonstrates his agility as he bends sideways and around the bull's horns. Note the aggressive attitude of the horse as momentarily he lays his ears back for the plunge of the dart. (Photos by Luis Azevedo, courtesy of Alfredo Coelho)*

is why the horseman must be careful to use a different approach each time. A repeated move which the bull has learned to circumvent in the short time he has been in the ring, can prove fatal.

It is a code of conduct that at no time must the horseman attack the bull with the dart. Instead of the fluttering cape of the fight on foot causing the bull to charge, it is the provocative movement of the horse taking classical steps which incites the attack. Only when the bull is coming headlong at him, may the *cavaleiro* make his *sorte*, gallop towards the oncoming horns, swerve, and place the dart.

It is no easy task to insert a *banderilla* in a specified spot at a combined speed of around forty miles an hour. This is sometimes accomplished with no rein at all when the *cavaleiro* is armed with two *bandarillas* instead of one. These will be placed simultaneously and in some miraculous way, the horse swerves from the impending collision by less than a hair's breadth, guided only by the rider's legs, seat and back. If the *bandarilla* is placed too high up, or too far back on the neck, and not in the exact position prescribed by Marialva, the crowd boos and hisses. There is little tolerance amongst spectators at the *corrida* especially for inaccuracy or apparently unsporting behaviour.

Once the dart has pierced the muscle and the horse pirouettes to make his getaway, yet again the code of conduct dictates that the bull should have his chance. The essence of a good fight is when the horse's tail remains between the bull's horns for at least thirty seconds as he is pursued round the ring. It is a thrilling and extraordinarily beautiful sight to see the horse canter with apparent ease and grace and totally without fear round the sand filled arena, almost keeping pace with the bull and just sufficiently in front not to be touched by the wicked horns. The man on his back turns round – almost as though in salute – continually watching the bull, assessing his mood and measuring his momentum. Just for a second the three of them in frieze become a superb example of all that is noblest in man and beast – a trio of magnetic physical presence. The cunning competence of the man, the courage of the horse and the crystal-clear determination of the towering mass of black *toiro* in pursuit to vanquish. Those who sneer at the sport and say that the bull is never given a chance are wrong. The bull does have his chance; it is just thankfully rare that the horseman is not superior.

Up to six darts may be placed in the bull's neck before the purpose of this exercise is over. Finally, the head is sufficiently low and the second phase of the fight may begin.

In Spain this is the death by sword. In Portugal no more than a symbolic gesture of a sword thrust is made. Normally, this is performed with a rubber sword struck in the appropriate place; sometimes it is done with the hand. Having made the point that he could have achieved his kill if he so wished, the *cavaleiro* departs from the ring. To tumultuous applause, horse and rider canter out sedately. Upon a new note of the trumpet a group of eight young men enter the arena on foot.

Tackling the Bull by Hand

Although this part of the Portuguese fight is non-equestrian, the horse having played his part, it is worth recording the next and final stage for it is probably the oldest method in the world of man dominating bull with his bare hands.

The youths, clad in the bull-herders' ceremonial costume of soft buckskin shoes, white stockings and shirts, fawn breeches and floral jackets with a wide red cummerbund, stride boldly into the ring – daring to undertake this sport for the honour and glory of their home town. They may be university students, or local farmworkers; whoever they are it is very much a team effort. It is not difficult to pick out the white faces of those who are about to confront the bull in public for the first time, but en masse they look brave enough. After all, it is a test of manhood to take on a bull, a show of virility in this sunlit land of past glories.

Barehanded, the tacklers, or *forcados* as they are called, line up one behind another in a straight row opposite the bull. Their leader calls to the bull, swaggering as he does so, until the movement catches the animal's eye. '*Toiro! Toiro! Preto!* [black one] *Preto!*' Daringly brave, the lad advances, inciting the charge.

As the bull, now very angry indeed, plunges forward, the leader runs a few steps backward to reduce the thrust of the lowered head. He takes the full force of the bull's impact on his chest and as he is swept into the air, the seven supporting *forcados* run swiftly forward to fan out and arrest the bull by their sheer combined momentum. Now that the leader has been lifted off his feet, he straddles the bull's face like a frog, his arms round the neck in a firm hold so that the horns stick out beneath his armpits, his body covering the bull's eyes. If the back-up team misjudges the charge and is not swift enough to come to the aid of the leader, the bull will carry on in his forward charge and hurl the leader against the barricade. This happens more often than one might think and the ambulance does not stand outside the *praça* gates for nothing.

If all goes to plan, however, the combined strength of the eight youths stops the bull in his tracks and whilst one young man takes hold of the tail, the others hold the bull until he becomes quiet and still. The leader disentangles himself from the horns and provided that *o presidente* is satisfied that the bull has been truly outwitted and has succumbed and remained motionless for a minimum of thirty seconds, the trumpet is sounded once more and the fight is over.

It is a somewhat Quixotic ending to a fight which started off in such deadly earnest. Despite the very real danger in which the *forcados* often find themselves, the Portuguese spectators tend to treat this part of the proceedings with light-heartedness, almost as a joke. If everything passes off safely, everyone is happy. If not, well, that's the way of things – the bull had his chance and used it. Again, that curious sense of Portuguese resignation makes itself felt. There is certainly a very different attitude apparent in the audience between the finale of the death in the sun in one country, and the grapple in the sun of the other.

However foreign the idea of bullfighting may be to the more phlegmatic races of the northern climes, the British included, it would be wrong to condemn it out of hand without having attended at least two or three mounted *corridas* with someone who understands the technique of the art, in order to appreciate the superb competency and courage on the part of horse and horseman.

Unforgettable Moments

One of the most famous bullfighting horses I had the good fortune to see a number of times, including the last official fight[3] of Alvaro Domecq Jnr in his home town of Jerez de la Frontera in October 1985, was a Lusitanian horse called Opus. (See also Chapter XI.) Opus is loved by the Spanish people for he has been with Alvarito (to distinguish the son of this great bullfighting family from his father also named Alvaro) since he was first purchased from the Portuguese in 1969. As Opus is the favourite *corrida* horse from the Domecq stable, his name has become a household word all over Andalusia. On this particular occasion, which was to be a very moving day with the stadium packed to overflowing to honour the last fight of a dynasty of bullfighters, Opus was as usual amongst the several horses that Alvarito would ride that afternoon.

The first two *corridas* had been highly successful with the *presidente* bowing to the demands of the crowd and awarding Alvarito with an ear of the bull he had slain, a great honour for work expertly done. The last four bulls, there are always six altogether, had been tricky, particularly the final one, a huge tan-coloured beast which exploded into the ring like a torpedo. Even amongst ten thousand people sitting in an October sun, most of them seasoned spectators, you could feel the tension building up. There had been two horrific deaths in the arena earlier that year, both of them highly experienced and well-known bullfighters, which had deeply shocked the whole of Spain. Admittedly, these two were not – like Alvarito – *rejoneadors*, but nevertheless when faced with a ton of raging bull, whether on horseback or on foot, anything may happen. Superstition is never far away after such tragedies, and now, as Alvarito approached his last bull, the atmosphere could be cut with a stockman's knife.

Fortunately, all went well. The horses worked in their customary honest and brave fashion, and whilst the death was not as accomplished as it had been with the first two bulls, the crowd was well satisfied. Then, Alvarito made an unprecedented and amazing gesture which brought tears to almost every eye in the packed stadium, including to his own hardened helpers and rugged cape-men. Whilst the crowd watched with bated breath, he asked for all his bullfighting horses, still saddled and adorned with the customary braids and ribbons in their manes, to be led into the arena. He walked around each one of them, exchanging a word here and there with an obviously well-loved favourite. Then he came to Opus. There was a hush; everyone knew something was going to happen. Someone came to assist. First the saddle was removed; then the bridle. Opus was free! The great grey stallion stood there in bewilderment at first, reluctant to leave the group of men and all the other horses. Everyone watched. Then, for one unreal moment, at an indication from his master he trotted off into the space of the wide arena and gave his solo canter of freedom round that huge amphitheatre. The crowd rose as one to its feet and roared. It was a magnificent salute to a great horse.

What impressed me more than anything that day was the reticence of the horse to leave the little conclave of humans and horses standing there in the centre. He looked naked and vulnerable without his trappings, and somehow this brilliant horse which had been so much in control in his last fight, so poised, balanced and athletic, now in his moment of liberty was sprawling and awkward. One had the distinct impression that had, by some awful mistake, a bull been allowed to

---

3. This fight, which took place on Saturday, 12th October, 1985, was unique in that three generations of Domecq participated: Alvaro Domecq (Snr), Alvaro or Alvarito Domecq (Jnr) and Luis Domecq, a nephew of Alvarito's.

Another famous Lusitano Veiga stallion, Opus, canters a lap of honour in complete freedom on the occasion of his master's retirement from bullfighting. (Photo by Jane Hodge)

enter that arena, Opus would not have stood a chance. Separated from his master, he would have been defenceless as a lamb.

It is the combination of man and horse which constitutes such a formidable partnership. The Iberian horse with his master are a symbol of complete dependence, one upon the other. The centaur – man and horse-joined in a way that no other equestrian sport can adequately demonstrate.

Something deeply primaeval within us is touched when we see such perfect empathy between a man and his horse.

CHAPTER X

Present-day Horse Breeding in the Peninsula

With flowing tail and flying mane,
Wide nostrils, never stretched by pain,
Mouths bloodless to the bit or rein,
And feet that iron never shod,
And flanks unscarr'd by spur or rod
A thousand horses – the wild – the free –
Like waves that follow o'er the sea,
Came thickly thundering on.

LORD BYRON
(*Marzeppa*)

The Great Families

Old traditions die hard, and despite the revolutions, horses are still principally bred by the established, landed families.

Visitors to the resorts of Spain and Portugal are often puzzled because the only horses they ever see are the tired animals pulling buggies round the esplanades of the Costa del Sol, or giving rides to tourists on the long beaches of the Algarve. More often than not these stables are run by foreigners and whilst some maintain high standards, others are abysmally poor. The horses therein are usually of mixed blood and in no way represent the pure-bred Iberian horse.

To find the breeding grounds of the Iberian horse one needs a very good map and letters of introduction, hopefully followed up by an invitation from one of the families who are in the business of breeding. Of course, there are many small breeders who produce excellent horses, but to get a bird's-eye view of the whole spectrum of breeding one cannot do better than to visit one of the famous studs belonging to one of the great names in the Spanish or Portuguese Stud Book. Names such as Miura, Escalera, Cardenas, Domecq or Perez Tinao are only a handful of highly respected breeders that exist in Spain; and in Portugal the names Veiga, Andrade, Ervideira, Nunçio, Infante da Camara, Palha, Ribeiro Telles and Raposo Cordeiro dominate the stud books. Both Spanish and Portuguese are extremely hospitable once they know with whom they are dealing, and they will go to the most enormous trouble to show you their horses even if it means consider-able inconvenience to themselves and putting the services of several employees at your disposal in order that you might see everything at its best.

The Hidden Life of the Interior

More often than not, the big *haciendas* or *quintas* are situated deep in the countryside and unless you know exactly where you are going, it would not be difficult to lose oneself in the heart of cork forests or sprawling empty plains. Even armed with directions, one may bump down a sandy track between thick umbrella pine trees for hours before coming to a clearing and a marvellous oasis of habitation. There lies the great family house, the enormous impressive stable-yard and the indoor manège. Surrounding this establishment, which may be starkly square and practical or rustically Baroque – the highly ornate is normally reserved for the town or summer residence – but with an unusual beauty all its own, will stand the agricultural workers' cottages, each painted in the colours of the main house, often yellow ochre and white, and forming a quadrangle to enclose the whole agricultural emporium. The only relief to soften the glare of the fierce midday sun, is the cornucopia of blazing bougainvillaea, dripping wistaria and brilliantly blue morning glory weaving its way up from the cobbles and under the overhanging eaves.

Nearby, cut into a slice of hillside, will be the home bullring, and if the house is unusually set on flat land, the arena may be built from a strong fence of bamboo and eucalyptus. In the stables, close to the house, are the riding and driving horses, nearly always stallions, from youngsters being trained at three and four years to the fully fledged stallions of the *haute école*. If it is an important establishment there will be at least three superb breeding stallions, and until recently these might well have been horses of the *corrida* as well as being designated for stud use, but it is becoming increasingly rare to find many of these horses at any one particular establishment such is their demand from abroad. Occasionally there is an elderly 'gentleman' amongst the stalls, a much-loved older horse who, now that he is in his late twenties, will still be ridden in the school by the master of the house to stop him from getting stiff and put him through those beautiful exercises which recall memories of the past when crowds applauded and music played as he made his entrance. Worthy bullfighting horses are revered all their lives and are not pensioned off into an arid field. Instead they are groomed, fed and cared for as well as any younger horse, and they may still teach learner riders in the family a thing or two about the classical art. Today, however, even these elderly schoolmasters are in short supply such is the demand from abroad for a High School horse.

Husbandry and Care

Stallions are normally kept in stalls, despite the fashion overseas for looseboxes. They are correctly secured with plenty of freedom from two cross-ropes with a log to take up the slack, and there is usually a communal manger running the length of the stable. Gleaming brass furnishings and tiles decorated with equestrian scenes are commonplace inside the stables. By this method the horses are kept disciplined, cleaner and warmer. The stallions learn to get on with their neighbours – an important requirement of Iberian equestrian life – and the system also prevents the loosebox tendency to boredom. The horses become accustomed to the grooms coming in and out, and working round and about (and underneath) them, thus the superb temperament of the Iberian horse is further enhanced by this method of husbandry.

Diet is similar to that of an English horse, but the Iberian horses receive smaller quantities and the oats are not always crushed. The Iberians use more pulses than we do in Britain and dried broad beans – *favas* – are very popular and rich in vitamins. In the southern regions, home-grown dried carob (which is at least a year old and has had the oil extracted and the stones removed), with the pods chopped into black pieces about two inches long, is especially nutritious. Depending upon the farm, and whether there is sufficient water or irrigation to grow hay, hay or oatstraw will be fed for bulk, and alfalfa, which is very expensive, is something of a luxury.

It is not normal for stallions to graze out, unless they are running with the mares for breeding from February through to the end of May, but only ten per cent of breeders still run their stallions out in this way, and covering is generally carried out in a covering yard near the stables. State stallions are never run out.

Iberian horses are incredibly good doers and will get fat almost on thin air. Owners like their horses to look round all over, and as the Iberian horse tends to build up big muscles in the neck and shoulder area with concentrated school work, as well as in the quarters, it is important that he should be allowed excess fat to begin with. Iberian horses which are allowed to become lean or rangy through neglect or due to some imbalance in their metabolism, may look surprisingly ugly. Their proportions do not suit a loss of weight, and they may lose all their presence and could almost be mistaken for an indeterminate breed.

As with all quality blood horses, a little extra fat certainly does not slow them down, if anything it acts to the contrary. Sweating occurs as a result of demanding work where courage and concentration are required of the horse by the rider. Before entering the bullring a horse is very often covered in sweat, not due to fear but simply because he is aroused and excited, looking forward to performing his duty and serving his rider. The difference between the sweating Iberian and many other breeds, is that the Iberians *never* lose their heads, never panic, and never run away.

After work, it is customary to hose the stallions down, curry off all excess water, and allow them to dry in the sun until they shine again. Normal grooming is similar to our own methods at home.

The Iberian Foot

Shoeing is normally carried out cold by a visiting local blacksmith who may himself arrive by horse and cart, and in the case of a very large establishment may even be resident on the farm. Visitors to Spain and Portugal are often surprised by the length of the Iberian horse's heel and how the smith does not cut it back to the same extent as that of an English, French or German horse. They are also surprised at the depth of sole and the fact that very rarely does the frog of an Iberian horse's foot come anywhere near the ground.[1] The answer is simple. The

---

1. Xenophon described a good foot in a horse as being 'thick not thin, high and with hollow hooves and hard to be fit for service.' This would suggest that the foot of Greek and probably Roman horses of that period were similar to the Iberian foot which prevails to this day.

terrain of the Peninsula is singularly hard and often very rocky. Over the centuries, horses have adapted by walking on the wall of the hoof and due to their sloping, springy pasterns seem well able to cope with the shock and percussion presented by the hard ground. A Thoroughbred horse shod in the normal way, having to deal with such conditions, would (and does, as I have seen from experience) very quickly develop bruised soles and be unable to contend with the going. Iberian horses have hard, slightly 'boxy' feet and rarely have leg problems. The size of bone is not generous, but like the Arab it is very *dense* and in pure-bred horses it is extremely unusual to find splints and curbs.

Another amazing thing about the Iberian horse is that he may be left in a stable on hard concrete or cobbles for literally several days without being exercised and yet his legs remain firm and unfilled. Bringing Lusitano horses from southern Portugal to south-east England some years ago, by train, we were advised not to bandage their legs. Due to a number of hold-ups at both the Spanish and French borders, the whole journey lasted ten days. When we eventually reached our destination, not one of the horses came out of the box with any ill effects whatsoever. It was a remarkable testimony to the hardiness of the Iberian race.

Such observations over the years have led me to believe that there are many misconceptions about the necessity for the frog to be close to the ground. For racing on soft Irish or Yorkshire turf it would appear to be important; for work on roads or in a rocky environment, a lesson could be learned from the blacksmiths of the Peninsula.

A Surprise Display

After each stallion has been led out and trotted up and down the yard in the sunshine by an energetic groom for the visitor to admire, the owner, dressed in the traditional straight dark trousers, half boots and spurs will show him off in the customary fashion from the ground. Every *cavaleiro*, even if his day is spent at the farm office or family factory, maintains this simple riding dress in the country and part of the outfit is a long flexible stick, measuring about three or four feet and usually made from a type of thornless dog-rose which grows on every Iberian hillside. Moving round the stallion, he passes the stick lightly over the horse's back and loins and the horse begins to piaffe on the spot. As the yard is often flagged or cobbled, the beat of the hooves on the stone rings out like a double pair of castanets, and the stallion may continue to display perfect cadence in this movement for several seconds, lightly guided by the caress of the stick. Every so often this is brought just below the croup to encourage the in-hand stallion to bring his hocks more deeply underneath him. The whole rider-less display is quietly and accurately executed and with no fear of the stick. Another touch just behind the horse's elbow, and out stretches a forelimb in a perfectly held breast-high step of Spanish walk. The horse is patted, his ears prick and he nobly accepts the piece of proffered sugar. It is time for him to return to the stable and for the visitor to climb again into car or Land Rover and take once more to the sand tracks. It may be a further hour before one is sufficiently deeply into the interior of this rural paradise to find the mares.

Above: *Lusitano mares and foals stand at peace amongst the cork trees. Horses have been bred in these hills and valleys since time itself began. The chestnut foals will later turn to grey (see Chapter II). (Photo by Ward Wallace, courtesy of Promark Ltd)*

Left: *Carthusian mares enjoy the stubble of the sunflowers. Docks are often shaved to protect against burrs. (Photo by Arnaiz)*

Above: *Throughout the land, Portuguese horsemen from every walk of life have their own* picadeiro, *where horses are trained to the highest levels of advanced dressage by their owners who are natural maestros. Here Manuel Sabino Duarte,* cavaleiro tauromatique, *schools his horse after a busy day at the office. (Photo by Susan Cole)*

Right: *The similarity of the Lipizzaner stallion to the Lusitano is plain to see.*

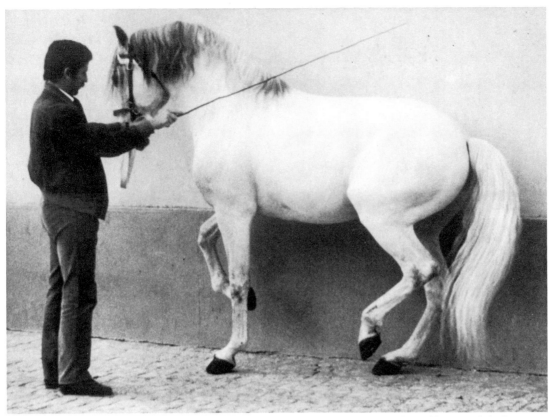

'Moving round the stallion, he passes the stick lightly over the horse's back and loins and the horse begins to piaffe on the spot.' Note the roundness of the horse, showing a complete lack of resistance.
(Photo by Jane Hodge)

Where the Herd Roams

Invariably the grazing lands or famous steppes of the Peninsula lie round a small tributary of one of the great rivers, the Guadalquivir in Spain or the Tagus in Portugal, and the wild life of these great, untouched reserves is breathtakingly beautiful and full of surprises. In central and north Portugal near the mountains, and on the northern slopes of Extremadura in Spain, there are still many wolves and some lynx, although the last wolf of the south in Andalusia was reputably shot just before the Civil War which was at about the same time that the brown bear disappeared from the hills of the south. Wild boar exist in their thousands wherever habitat is natural and undisturbed, and every year the Portuguese government organises *montarias* for thirty or forty guns in each region to carry out a systematic culling. In both Spain and Portugal, there are genets – a kind of wild cat with black spots on a greyish coat, reminiscent of a small leopard – and another rare creature is the mongoose, the species having been first introduced, it is thought, by the Moors from Africa. More familiar animals, such as the fallow deer, the badger and the silver and red fox, abound in the interior and the bird life is an ornithologist's dream, combining everything from bee-eaters to bustards, hoopoes to herons and hawks. Kestrels shadow the sun in search of prey on the remote hillsides, egrets perch on the backs of grazing bulls and the eagle owl with its five-foot wingspan (although extremely rare now) still haunts the forest.

Amidst this rich setting and embroidered with the most wonderfully delicate wild flowers in spring – bee orchids, hyacinths, irises, exotic bluebells and wild gladioli – dwell the mares. Hundreds and hundreds of free horses move in and out of the shade of the trees, the sun dappling their backs as they meander. Unhurriedly they pass the day as they and their ancestors have always done, quietly grazing.

Here the twentieth century might not exist. There are no unsightly pylons, no telegraph poles or wire fences. Miles and miles of gently undulating pasture, stretching down from the craggy hilltops to the wide brown river where bulrushes and emerald green bamboos harbour another whole form of life'in the banks and water, and the only sound to be heard rising above the haze of the afternoon is the steady munching of mares with their foals, and the clunk-clunk-clunk of the bells worn around the mares' necks.

Care of the Herd

Somewhere, far in the distance, just off the sandy track which led here, there may be a small whitewashed cottage, nestling below a cluster of stringy-barked eucalyptus trees. The eucalyptus not only provides protective shade but also emanates a delicious smell from its gum which wards off flies. In a simple lean-to stable where the roof is made of *canas* (bamboos), stands a saddled gelding waiting for his master to finish lunch and return to work.

Stock is constantly guarded and moved on when necessary by a stockman (*campino* in Portuguese; *vaquero* in Spanish), who may well have lived on the property all his life and whose cottage will be as close to the herd as is possible. Nearly every large estate which breeds horses, also breeds bulls, and whilst some farms may graze horses and fighting stock within sight of each other, other properties keep them miles apart. It is the sole job of the *campino* or *vaquero* to keep that stock together, to move them as required, and to ensure their well-being. Each farm has different methods of weaning and sorting out the youngsters that are born every year in the open air of the mild Iberian spring.

At one time, around two or three hundred years ago, we know that mares were used for breeding once every two years so that the young could stay with the mother for at least a year or even eighteen months, and this gave the mare adequate time to recover. About one hundred years ago the pattern changed with new, improved husbandry and better pastures, and the trend – which is still carried on today in many studs – was to wean the foals in August or September when they were around six months old. Recently, however, a few modern breeders have improved their pastures even further by adding nitrates, removing weeds and scrub and adequately controlling parasites, and are able to let the foals remain with their mothers for up to nine months with better results and with no detriment to the mares.

At the time of weaning, mares and foals are herded by the stockmen back to the farm and separated into corrals. Here they are branded with the badge of the family, which is officially recognised by the stud book of the breeders' association of Spain or Portugal. Whilst Andalusian horses are normally branded on the near-side thigh, and tattooed on the lip before they are weaned, Lusitano horses will be branded on the offside thigh and their stud number is branded under the near-

ALTER

FERNANDO SOMMER D'ANDRADE

DUARTE D'OLIVEIRA

MANUEL VEIGA

INFANTE DA CAMARA

COUDELARIA NACIONAL

*Famous twentieth-century Portuguese brands.
Although these symbols are normally associated
with horses, those families which breed bulls
use the same brands for their fighting stock.*

ESCALERA, D. JOSÉ LUIS

DOMECQ, ALVARO

MIURA, EDUARDO

FERNANDO A. DE TERRY S.A.

YEGUADA CARDENAS

GANADERIA LAS LUMBRERAS

Famous twentieth-century Spanish brands.

side mane for males, or the offside for females. A good future brood mare may also have the letter 'P' for *produtor* (producer) in the centre of the neck.

Once weaned, young females will not be returned to the main herd for a number of reasons. Firstly, if a stallion is to be run with the mares this is obviously not desirable; secondly, when the four-year-old mares are foaling for the first time, there is always the danger that the young fillies of one, two and even three years old will be attracted to the foal and try to play with it. It is not an old wives' tale but proven fact that if a young foal has been licked and caressed by another filly, the young mother will lose interest in her new progeny and as a result will reject it. Thus the foal is lost. Fillies are therefore kept separately in a smaller herd before the time comes for them too to join the sisterhood of *produtors*, and during their growing up years will learn all about the pecking order of herd life with those fillies from superior mares taking precedence over the youngsters of less-important mothers.

Young males will also be kept out at grass, but normally a little closer to home so they may be more frequently handled, until the time comes to decide what should become of them. By the time they are three, the stockman responsible for the colts, if he is conscientious, will have encouraged them to come to a call and a whistle and to enjoy being caressed and touched all over. It is unheard of for a pure Iberian horse to kick, even before he has been broken, and in Portugal the progeny of registered parents may be refused entry to the stud book if it is known to kick, for it suggests a throw-back to other blood.

Selection of the Colts

On big studs, the general rule is that mares are to be used for breeding and therefore the majority need never be broken; only the male horses are for riding. It is rare to geld a pure-bred Iberian horse, and gelding will only take place at a later age, say, around three or four years, if it is obvious that the temperament of the horse in question is not good, or that he lacks quality. It is, however, fairly normal to geld cross-bred Arab or Thoroughbred Iberian horses, but again this is not automatically done and will not occur until the horse is fully developed.

Geldings are not normally considered suitable riding horses for gentlemen. They may be ridden by women or by employees, but very occasionally an outstanding mare will be ridden by a man. The great Alvaro Domecq tells a wonderful story in *El Caballo en Espana*, of his mare Espléndida with whom he fought many bulls in the *rejoneo* fight. Espléndida, like all of her race, was full of courage and always eager for the fight. The only time her master ever felt hesitation on her part was during one notable occasion when:

> 'I realised Espléndida was pregnant because, for the first time, she trembled before going into the ring, but she controlled herself and fought better than ever. She was a mare of pure gold. Valiant, which is more than not being afraid; it is overcoming fear . . . resolute . . . the heart to face and cheat death.'

Only the very finest quality horses will be chosen for work in the bullring and, as we shall see, the long process of schooling for the *corrida* will halt if the horse shows any sign of not having sufficient courage or ability. However, even average horses will be schooled to the equivalent of advanced dressage standard in England, France or the United States, as this is the normal standard required of a gentleman's riding horse. This may seem strange to us at home, but it is far stranger to the Iberian horseman that we can put up with riding what they call totally unmade hacks, i.e. those which cannot collect, pirouette or produce at canter at least three-time counter changes of hand.

The large establishments may retain several geldings for their own workers. In this day and age, it may sound impractical to give employees horses to ride instead of supplying them with a vehicle, but the contrary is true. In both Andalusia and the Ribatejo, the terrain is not suitable for modern transport. Habitations and villages are few and far between, forests are thick, and often the landscape is interrupted with a Quixotic hillside generously scattered with rocks and ravines, which tumble down onto the plains. Since a horse is more versatile than the most modern Japanese truck and can not only traverse hill and dale with ease, swim across wide rivers, but also has a sixth sense for seeking out missing stock, it would be ludicrous to contemplate employing any other means of transport for everyday work on these huge and remote farms.

Brave Bulls

The breeding of bulls for the *corrida* is very different from the breeding of cattle for meat. First of all, *toros* or *toiros bravos* are a special race of bull whose genetic line of fighting characteristics actually dates back to pre-Roman times. These bulls, depicted in early cave paintings, were introduced to many Mediterranean countries, including Rome and Carthage, where they were used in the amphitheatres against the early Christians. Having constantly been selected for their fierceness and courage, they are not the sort of animals that one would choose to picnic beside; yet in the heat of the midday sun they may look extremely and misleadingly placid. There are many more *ganaderias* (cattle studs) in Spain than in Portugal to cope with the demand from the unmounted bullfights, and the small private *tientas* which are still a feature of Andalusian life and involve the running of bulls for would-be or novice *matadors*. At certain times throughout the agrarian year, young, immature bulls and heifers are exposed to men on horses and examined for their bravery and aggression. This is also a useful preparation for the training of potential bullfighting stallions, but it is the mounted stockman who first works with the bull to ensure that he grazes in the correct location. Therefore, in his early life, whilst having respect for a man on a horse, the bull is not afraid of him. It is very rare that grazing bulls will attack horses, but they would attack a man on foot.

The Life of the Stockman

Vaqueros and *campinos* are often excellent riders with hands of silk and a natural seat. They ride in a high-pommelled, high-cantled saddle and the hard seat is covered with a thick fluffy sheepskin held in place by a surcingle. The stirrups used in Portugal are similar to those seen in bullfighting, i.e. closed and bucket-shaped, but without the gilt trappings. In Spain they are of a similar style but open. The horse's bit is normally a long-cheeked curb. It is still customary in the Spanish countryside to see stockmen using the *cerreta* (spiked noseband), but with sheepskin wound over the spikes to protect the nose (see Chapter VI). The use of this gadget is important in the schooling of a young horse when being taught to heighten his poll and drop his nose. This is initiated by attaching the reins to a ring on either side of the noseband, so that the horse gets used to being long-reined and ridden in this method long before the reins are attached to the bit in his mouth. In this way, evasions are overcome and the horse has learned the basic rights and wrongs without ever suffering in the mouth. Properly and knowledgeably done, the Spanish argue, it is a practical and not unkind method, but it is no longer practised in Portugal, and as with all such practices there is always the risk of abuse.

In Portugal the horse's loins are usually

Fig. 11
Portuguese bullfighting stirrup.

protected by a *chairel* or piece of hide (usually cow for a working horse, or something more exotic such as lynx for a bullfighting horse) which is attached by two short lengths of leather buckled onto the cantle of the saddle. The numnah is normally a thickly folded blanket which will protect the *campino* should he spend the night with his herd. The saddle is always held in place with a crupper.

Whilst the specialised art of High School is not practised in the manège as such by the *campino*, it is interesting to find that most of the horses worked on the land in both countries are in fact schooled to a high standard. When one considers that these men have nothing to do except ride all day, it is not surprising that they emulate their employers. The Iberians take pride in their rank, and the head man at the home farm often knows more than anybody about the classical art of the manège.

The Portuguese traditional dress for the *campino* on high days and holidays is particularly attractive, and *campinos* from every horse- and bull-breeding *quinta* in the land wear the same navy breeches, white shirt and hose, brown shoes, red waistcoat and knitted Snoopy hat in the national colours of red and green with a pom-pom on the end. The stud's family brand appears on a smart brass badge pinned to the *campino*'s waistcoat, so one can see at a glance which stud he represents. As we have seen, the *campinos* have their own competitions on horseback, especially at the big annual fair of Vila Franca de Xira in Portugal, where hundreds of men ride together, and much honour is attached to the various championships. For this, the *campino* will ride his favourite gelding, which will be turned out to an extremely high standard with the mane loose but the tail braided and knotted.

In Spain it is the *jaca*, a gelding or mare of mixed blood, which performs the work around the herd, but in Portugal it is normally a pure-bred Lusitano gelding or occasionally a mare.

It is indicative of the way breeding is developing in Spain, that most *haciendas* no longer use pure-bred Spanish horses for herd work, or if they do, it is not advertised. There appears to be a stigma attached to the idea of a pure-bred Spanish horse carrying out agricultural work, and the *jaca* is reputedly of two or three bloods, either Hispano-Arab, or Hispano-Anglo-Arab. To differentiate them from pure-bred Spanish stock, the custom is to dock the tail (to facilitate work in the long-grassed *campo*) and to cut short the mane. The forelock is removed altogether and replaced with a leather flyshield, a *mosquero*, which being deeply fringed is very effective and also looks rather smart. One talks about two types of *jaca* in Spain: the *jaca vaquera*, which works specifically with the cattle, and the *jaca campera*, which is any working horse of the countryside, perhaps the horse of the foremen who tend the vast estates, or of the guards who patrol the perimeters, or they may be horses used by the small farmer to go between shafts.

At the great fairs of Spain, the *Doma Vaquera* contest literally means dressage for the *vaquero* horse, and this is a popular feature for it is highly specialised and the work involved is suited to that performed by the horse in his natural environment amongst the *toros bravos*. Only two gaits are required in this skilled competition: a good walk and a lightning fast gallop. The essence of a correct *vaquero* walk is when the *mosquero* swings rhythmically like a metronome from side to side of the horse's face indicating that he is stepping out and maintaining a good four-time rhythm, which will earn him the best marks. The gallop has to end in a dead halt in front of the judge, with the reins thrown down. The horse must stand like a rock, collected and totally obedient and square. For those visitors from abroad who have always ridden their horses on the forehand where the horse relies upon a balancing contact on the bit, the successful and brilliant execution of this gallop to halt must forever remain a huge mystery.

The Rationale of Traditional Breeding

As with all large organisations, the marrying of the work with the horses, the fighting bulls, the domestic cattle, the sheep and the goats to the production of wheat, maize, beans, oats, cork, olives and, of course, the grapes for wine, sherry, brandy and pure alcohol, must be accomplished harmoniously and smoothly so that no one facet of the whole complex, unbalances or mars the other. The maintenance of horses could be described as the luxury end of the agricultural scale, but since Franco's death in Spain, and the 1974 Revolution in Portugal, owners have become well aware that the horses cannot be subsidised by the commercial success of other aspects of the farm and therefore all breeders nowadays have to ensure that their stock is not a burden to the *hacienda* or *quinta* but is instead self-supportive. The export of good horses for large sums of money is one way of ensuring the continued success of the stud farm, and the Portuguese in particular are well aware that the value of their horses lies in their inherent ability to work. The next chapter describes how horses are schooled towards the High School, whether for use in the bullring or for pleasure riding in the manège, and examines the selection process amongst the breeders' associations of both countries involved.

Before we leave the secret, unspoiled interiors of the Iberian Peninsula with its green mysteries and soft, still air which only the bright birds and the deeply coloured flying insects know as they swoop between the *toros bravos* and the soft bell-tonging mares, I would like to quote this passage from Nicholas Luard's book, *Andalucia*, which reminds one of the ecological aspect of raising horses and bulls for the *corrida*.

> 'Paradoxically, the campaign to save the fighting bull by ending the *corrida* would, if successful, have only one certain result – the bull's extinction. It is not an efficient converter of grass into protein. Other modern strains of cattle can do the job better and more economically. Theoretically, with the bullring lost as a market, the ranch-owners would replace their *corrida* herds with one of these new strains. In practice they would almost certainly make a different choice. The way bulls feed allows their pastures to be shared by a host of other plants and creatures – the orchids, wild flowers, birds, butterflies and animals. However, modern technology has shown that almost any space of Andalucian land can be exploited much more profitably than through beef production by methods like hydroponics. The intensity of the new methods excludes any competitors. There is literally no living-room under a plastic canopy for an otter, a nightingale, a swallow-tail butterfly or a wild hyacinth. So if the *corrida* disappeared not only would the fighting bulls vanish, but great tracts of ancient countryside and the communities of wildlife they have supported for hundreds of thousands of years would be lost too.'

CHAPTER XI

Breeding for a Purpose

His ears up-prick'd; his braided hanging mane
Upon his compass'd crest now stands on end . . .
His eye, which scornfully glisters like fire,
Shows his hot courage and his high desire.

WILLIAM SHAKESPEARE

The Old Iberian Factor

As we have seen in Chapter II, which describes the origins of the modern Spanish and Portuguese horse, there is no doubt that the active progenitor of today's Andalusian and Lusitano as well as probably the Barb in North Africa, was the ancient Iberian horse of sub-convex profile.

The characteristics of this original breed are still remarkably dominant today and certain features appear genetically linked together so that they cannot be separated. In the Iberian horse, the obvious example of this is that the slightly convex profile of the head would appear to be genetically coupled with a gently sloping croup and low-set tail. Consciously or subconsciously assimilating these facts, we begin to develop an eye for a certain type of horse, and to those who have an eye for the Iberian breed, it is often possible to distinguish Iberian looks in other breeds, later to confirm that indeed in their recent evolution, Iberian blood has been present at some stage along the line.

These ancient distinguishing features, which may now be called the Iberian Factor[1], are as follows:

A slightly convex profile of the head which includes:
  a somewhat rounded forehead
  a long narrow, finely curved nose.
Large, generous eyes, usually almond shaped.
Well-defined, generous ears.
A long, powerful neck, deep at the base and set at a rather wider angle
  to the shoulder than is normal in the Thoroughbred for instance, giving
  the appearance of being more upright.
High withers.
A short-coupled body with wide powerful loins, the back almost appearing rounded.

1. The essential ingredients for the Iberian Factor are taken from a vast source of information which exists in ancient books, paintings, engravings, sculptures, etc., spanning thousands of years. The study of modern genetics with information supplied by leading specialists in this field have helped the author to define and collate the main genetic features, and for the sake of simplicity, give it a name.

The hindlegs positioned well underneath the body axis producing excellent hock action and thrusting forward impulsion. (This leads to the
development of a strong second thigh which helps the horse to flex
and collect.)
Small, round, high hooves.
A temperament of exceptional courage, willingness and kindness.

All these characteristics have withstood the passage of centuries and despite the
mistakes of breeding and the results of occasional infusions of other bloods introduced during periods of war and conquest, they continue to manifest themselves
to this day. There is no doubt that the best fighting or working horses of the Iberian
Peninsula still display most or all of the old Iberian Factor in both conformation
and temperament.

The Theory of Use Determining Physical Appearance

Those Spanish and Portuguese breeders who specialise in producing horses for
the bullring have, over the generations, discovered that by working their stud stallions to the highest level of *haute école* prior to being used for stud, certain ancient
characteristics are returning more strongly in resulting progeny. One could argue
that this is not a genetic phenomenon but merely the result of selecting functionally
only from stallions that perform best in the ring. On the other hand it is hard
to explain away the case of the two stud stallions which were saved from gelding
in 1936 by the late Dr d'Andrade when he realised that the Alter Real Stud was
about to be dismantled. Instead of the breed being weakened, line breeding from
these two stallions, which were both fine examples of High School horses, and
eleven remaining mares, has resulted in today's Alter Real horses displaying more
than ever the ancient Iberian characteristics. As the twentieth century draws to
a close, Alter Real stock more closely resembles the original horses of the time
of King D. José I than ever they did in the last century.

Another factor of great interest is that although the fashion in the past fifty years
– especially in Spain – has been for grey horses, amongst fighting stock, many
of the old colours are returning. It would therefore seem logical that the use to
which these horses are being put is helping to determine the genetic pattern of
future generations.[2]

In the case of horses being bred for bullfighting, we are seeing a return to the
old battle colours of dun, mouse-dun, dark brown, bay and dark chestnut. Of the
greys, instead of the popular pale, dappled colour, we are seeing a return to a darker
dapple, a dark flea-bitten grey (like the horses of the Celtiberians), and even near
black flecked with white. There has also been evidence of the Sorraia trait of zebra
stripes appearing on legs, despite the fact that the stock concerned has had no
infiltrations of Sorraia blood for hundreds of years.

By way of contrast, the theory of use determining physical appearance is supported by observations made from studies of horses bred for the parade, showing
in hand or light carriage driving. These horses are appearing to diverge in a com-

---

2. Collaborating information supplied by Arsenio Cordeiro, Director of the Lusitano Stud Book, Lisbon.

pletely different genetic direction. They are, in some cases, actually losing the Iberian Factor as well as retaining more strongly the characteristics of possible early infusions of other blood, such as Arab, introduced more than one hundred years before.

Whether these interesting differences are being brought about merely by man's selection for type is unclear. A process of natural selection does, however, seem possible and the next decade or so will prove enlightening. The fact remains that in 1986 it is possible to divide the Iberian horse into two definite types. This situation simply would not have existed 150 years ago. Despite the fact that some studs have always bred a lighter horse, and others a heavier strain, all Iberian horses from *bona fide* studs shared the Iberian Factor and were of the same stamp.

The Emergence of Two Types within One Breed

Today, there are many breeders who continue to produce the traditional horse of function, the fighting and working horse. These horses retain the Iberian Factor and could accurately be described as Great Horses or war-horses. They are superb at their work. Like all Iberian horses their action is high and rounded, they are forward-going and extremely nimble. As well as being excellent riding horses, unrivalled in the bullring, they are also extremely efficient for sporting driving. To look at, they are noble rather than pretty with aristocracy written all over their fine, slightly hawked, long faces. They develop a powerful neck and shoulder which causes them to look extremely majestic in front. The quarters are not large but the loins are wide and strong and the hocks long and wiry giving them the power to bound forcefully forwards with masterful impulsion. Deep flexion is obtained from the developed second thigh and the longer than usual cannons and pasterns.

On the other hand, there are the breeders, particularly in Spain, who aim to produce an all-round pleasure horse of symmetry and elan. He must cut a dash in harness at the *ferias*, carry a beautiful girl in her flamenco dress behind her lord and master on his croup, and shown in hand present a vision of beauty and uniformity. In this horse, the high-stepping action is encouraged but in order to eliminate features which have become unfashionable, such as the sub-convex profile or Roman nose, and the short-coupled back with its sloping croup, breeders favouring this more modern look have often sacrificed much of the agility which gives this horse his forward thrust, his handiness and his practicality. For *fiesta*, quite naturally this does not matter. The horse which does not track up behind, is easier to sit to – and the delicate beauty of a more oriental head is undeniable. So popular has this horse of the parade become, that at one time many people in Spain were in danger of convincing themselves that this type was the true type, and horses bearing the Iberian Factor were shunned in certain circles. Fortunately, however, sense is once more prevailing.

The Influence of Arab Blood in Spain

The divide between the two types has further been accentuated by historical events. After the Peninsular Wars, the effects of the revolutionary upheaval wreaked so much havoc in the old Spanish studs that by the middle of the nineteenth century horse breeding was in a poor way. There was simply a shortage of good breeding stock. It was, therefore, very properly decided by the Spanish crown that something must be done to improve the situation.

In her book *The Arab Horse in Europe*, Erika Schiele reports that a responsible decision was taken and attention was focused on the Arab horse. In 1850 a Spanish delegation brought twenty-six Arab stallions, twelve mares and three foals to the royal stud near Aranjuez. King Alfonso XII imported three Arab stallions from France between 1884 and 1885 and in 1893 a royal order laid the foundation for the breeding of Arab horses by the state. In the grounds of Moratalla in Cordoba, the Yeguada Militar (Army Stud) was established and Arab blood nourished the existing military herds of Spain. According to Miss Schiele, 'The original purpose of the Yeguada was to provide a sound foundation for the Andalusian horse-breeding operation, and the choice for its upgrading now lay upon the imported Arab horses.' The first priority therefore was to breed first-class stallions for the state stallion depots, where people might take their mares and have them covered for a nominal fee. This operation took off well and the first crosses were exceptionally good horses.

Military Control of State Breeding

At the same time as the Andalusian was being improved, pure Arab breeding became popular not only amongst the military, but amongst a number of private breeders such as Ybarra, D. Antonio Egea, Vazquez and the Duke of Veragua who pursued further importation and breeding with great enthusiasm. A number of these herds were later sold off to or acquired by the state, and since the 1930s the business of breeding the Arab and the Andalusian has remained the province of the military. Under the General Directorate for Horse Breeding and Remounts all flourishing new stock was and is strictly controlled, and the policy for state breeding, as well as the standards for the Stud Book were laid down by the Directorate.

By 1920 the all-over breeding situation in Spain looked much more promising. By now the Andalusian breed had been healthily re-established, and in addition to the pure-bred Spanish studs, there were many excellent studs up and down the country of pure-bred Arab, English Thoroughbred and in the north, of Breton horses. The well-organised studs in the various military establishments at Cordoba, Jerez, Baeza and Valladolid made it possible for private breeders to take their mares to state stallions of the finest calibre.

The Spanish Stud Book was formed in 1912, with a royal order of January 13th, which created the *Registro Matricula de Caballos y Yeguas de Pura Raza Espanola* and brought together Andalusian horses from all over Spain. From this point onwards the resolve of the Directorate was to establish uniformity within the Spanish breed. Colonel Carlos Kirkpatrick O'Donnel writing on behalf of Spanish military breeding policy in *El Caballo en Espana* states that the Spanish horse

> 'may be brought into conditions to compete with the other improving breeds . . . to achieve a complete transformation of our stock to arrive at the horse we know today as oriental, with a square profile, an animal

A typical Certificate of Registration for the pure-bred Spanish horse.

which finds nothing to envy in constitution and temperament in the stock of other countries as a saddle horse, there having been produced a type of harmonious proportions.'

This idea of 'transformation' appeared to be in complete contrast to the old war-horse type bearing the Iberian Factor. Whilst the presence of early Arab blood is today fashionably denied in Spain, there is no doubt that the early crosses made in the late nineteenth century did influence popular opinion away from the traditional Iberian horse, particularly as regards facial shape.

The Warning of Dr d'Andrade

What happened over the next couple of decades began to cause concern amongst traditional Iberian breeders. Not only was the Iberian Factor being bred out in the appearance of the horses which were being selected for future breeding, the accompanying hereditary make-up of strong hock action and impulsion, coupled with the superb temperament of the old war-horse was also being diminished, albeit unintentionally.

Many people felt uneasy as these subtle but increasingly obvious changes were noted within the breed. They recognised that a return to the old progenitor stock was needed. This, after all, had enabled the first successful twentieth-century herds to re-establish themselves in the first place.

Unfortunately, the Directorate for Breeding appears to have ignored this simple requirement (which forms the basis of all breeding principles whether in dogs, pigs or horses) and pressed ahead regardless to bring about the desired 'transformation' referred to by Colonel O'Donnel and similar-minded people within the army. As the progenitor Iberian horse was eschewed in favour of the new type that was emerging, and this pattern repeated itself in state-controlled studs up and down the country, people felt bewildered at what was happening within their precious breed, yet powerless to intervene.

At length, matters came to a head. Such was the concern of Spanish breeders of the old school, who required a practical horse for working the bulls, and of the Portuguese, who were helping the Spanish to re-establish mounted bullfighting, that in 1946, Dr Ruy d'Andrade wrote a book which he presented to the breeders' association, the Cria Caballar, entitled *The Crisis of the Andalusian Horse*. In this he warned that unless breeders returned to their original Spanish foundation horse – the Iberian prototype – and studiously avoided the new oriental look, they were in danger of losing their breed altogether.

This situation had been exacerbated by the fact that since September 1926 the administration at the Cortijo de Vicos[3] in Jerez, the new centre of horse breeding in Spain, had decreed that to obtain a uniform Spanish horse, any horse bearing the sub-convex profile might from now on be rejected for breeding.

The consequences of this decision were radically to change the Spanish horse. From 1926 onwards, the selection process excluded horses, no matter how pure their lineage and how excellent their performance, if they did not conform to the new approved pattern. It is hard to imagine how many excellent stallions and mares of the 'old type' were thus rejected for procreation. No matter how superb their body conformation, how good their past record for work and temperament, whole lines could be discontinued simply through the shape of the nose.

This process of repudiation of the old type and selection for the new continued unchecked until 1975 when it would appear that past concern had crystallised. Whereas the 1971 edition of the Spanish Stud Book upholds a 'straight profile head of oriental origin', the 1975 edition allows the head profile to be 'straight or slightly convex'.

---

3. Cortijo de Vicos in Jerez became the new headquarters of the Military Stud which had been set up by royal decree on 26th June, 1893 when the lease on the old premises at Moratalla, near Cordoba, ran out in 1956.

During these confusing times, there had always been a number of Spanish breeders who had clung to the prototype Iberian horse. Not surprisingly these were also the breeders of fighting bulls who were not oblivious to the significance of the Iberian Factor in their working and fighting horses. Conversely, these breeders often won championships at shows when their horses sported a superior action as they were trotted out, particularly in front of foreign judges, and the names of Domecq, Miura[4] and Perez Tinao are synonymous with a handsome horse of outstanding action.

At the same time, however, the military continued to exert strong influence which pulled in other directions. With their Thoroughbreds and Anglo-Arabs proving themselves for polo, showjumping and other competitive modern equestrian sports, it is possible they viewed the bullfighting horses of the *rejoneadors* as something of an anachronism.

Two schools of thought were clearly emerging, and that of the military was to bring the Spanish horse into line with the other breeds.

Conflicting Arguments

Certain writers[5] whose background is perhaps more academic than traditional, in an attempt to justify changes within the breed, suggested that the modern look was closer to the very early Andalusian horse. They argued that the horse portrayed by Velasquez and Van Dyck in the seventeenth century was a hybrid. This idea is taken from a reference in a book entitled *Paintings of a Colt*, written by an unknown author who was thought to be a stud groom, dating from the second half of the seventeenth century. The manuscript was found in the Duke of Osuna's library and describes the nose of the Spanish horse as being 'long, straight, narrow, smooth, and gradually diminishing until it reaches the nostrils'. Another writer, Dom Barnado Vargas de Machuca, describing the Spanish horse in his book, *Teoria y Ejercicios de la Gineta*, states that 'the horse's head should be small with a wide forehead', which is somewhat in contrast to the first description, but fortunately this has not prevented horses with a long face being admitted to the Stud Book.

The point that seems to have been missed by the new school of thought is that if we turn back to random dates from the Roman Empire upwards, when pottery, coins and statues, as well as pictures, stained-glass and portraits, give us ample evidence of the main features of conformation in the Spanish horse, there is a distinct regularity in overall shape, and whether the face is Roman-nosed or straight is not of prime importance when in entirety the look is basically the same. There is indeed a preponderance for the sub-convex profile, but this certainly does not rule out the straight-profiled horse when all the other characteristics of the Iberian Factor are so clearly present.

---

4. Don Eduardo Miura, probably Spain's greatest breeder of fighting bulls and a magnificent horseman (now in his late seventies), was featured in *The Sunday Times Magazine*, April 20th, 1986.

5. E.g. Colonel Llamas, whose book *Caballo Espanol, Caballo de Reyes*, clearly does not admire all the facets of the Iberian Factor within his concept of modern breeding, and Colonel Kirkpatrick O'Donnel, who, in *El Caballo en Espana*, advocates the 'oriental look' on a number of occasions.

To explain away the beautiful horses of noble sub-convex profile painted so prolifically by great artists such as Velasquez, Van Dyck and Goya, advocates of the modern oriental type of Spanish horse draw attention to the fact that Juan Jeronimo Tinti, the Italian mentioned in Chapter IV who was in charge of the royal stud at Cordoba, crossed many Spanish mares with imported German, Norman, Flemish, Danish and Italian stallions in order to breed an altogether heavier horse for cavalry purposes and thus changed the facial structure. It is certainly possible that some pictures painted during this period do portray a cross-bred Spanish horse; it is more than unlikely, however, that every Spanish equestrian portrait scattered across Europe depicting the Spanish horses of the Duke of Newcastle, King Louis XIII of France, Prince Mauritz of Orange-Nassau of the Netherlands, and many others, as well as all the horses of the Spanish royal family over a period of four to five hundred years, should be influenced by the breeding experiments of one relatively unimportant Master of the Horse.

The truly practical horseman and breeder has never denied the original Iberian type. In Alvaro Domecq's Prologue to *El Caballo en Espana*, he refers to the Spanish horse, the Hispano, as having 'more class than the Berber, greater height and classic heads – valiant, enduring, fast, serious, docile, sub-convex profile and with erect necks – and a dropped crupper . . .'

This is a very different horse from the type which has been promoted by certain Spaniards in the past sixty or more years. Breeders of fighting bulls, however, know the significance of breeding for action and function rather than for looks. Alvaro Domecq, Don Eduardo Miura and Perez Tinao are renowned for their horses which may not look pretty in the fashionable showing sense, but which are strikingly noble, muscular and energetic. Here the Iberian Factor has been encouraged through careful selection amongst riding horses, and the result is good hock action and straight, forward movement. Domecq's horses are not only used in the bullring, but for the physically demanding work of the High School in his Escuela Andaluza del Arte Ecuestre (see Chapter XII) where he also uses a number of Lusitano stallions.

Alvaro Domecq is also a strong advocate of the excellence of the Hispano-Arab horse and has been lobbying for years to have this versatile cross-breed accepted into a special section of the Spanish Stud Book. At the time of going to print, it would appear that this has been achieved. The important rule in cross-breeding is that sound pure-breds with well-defined characteristics are used on both sides, and the splendid Domecq Hispano-Arabs which have become famous throughout Spain clearly show more than a fair share of the Iberian Factor.

Many of Spain's best *jacas* used in the highly competitive *Doma Vaquera*, are of this stamp, and in some cases appear closer to the classic Iberian horse than some of the modern Andalusians where the oriental look has been encouraged for several generations.

A Change of Course

Breeding in Spain took a dramatic turn after the first Championship (*Campeanato*) for the Pure Bred Spanish Horse was held in Seville in 1979. Herr Dr Heinrich Lehrner from the Piber Stud of the Spanish Riding School in Austria judged all the in-hand and ridden classes and many horses which came from some of Spain's most celebrated modern studs were marked down for dishing and lack of impulsion. The outcome of this initial shock inevitably did good. Selectors are now rethinking their priorities and earnest efforts are at present being made to regain the straight forward action for which the Iberian horse was famed in history. The years ahead look brighter. The Andalusian of oriental look is beginning to lose its following, and those breeders who have clung doggedly to the Iberian Factor cannot keep up with the demand for their horses of superior action and temperament. Breeders continue to buy from Portugal which, because of the mounted *corrida*, has never diverged from its original prototype. In so doing they are proving successful in recapturing ancient bloodlines which may have come from Andalusia originally and certainly are proving beneficial to new generations.

Historically, the two nations are so steeped in rivalry that one may not wish to admit it needs the help of the other. Yet, looking dispassionately, everyone agrees that Spanish *rejoneadors* have always obtained their best bullfighting horses from the Portuguese; and at the same time everyone knows that many of the best bloodlines in today's Lusitano came from seventeenth-century Spain. Therefore one would hope that for the sake of the future of the Spanish horse, some help would be acceptable from over the border as has been shown in the past.

The Selection Process in Portugal

The Portuguese admit that in the past they too have made mistakes with the breeding of their Lusitano horse. A poorer country than Spain, lack of finance often led to indifference and not enough controls were imposed to stop occasional infusions of foreign blood being slipped into supposedly pure-bred lines. Records were not always kept up or simply disappeared in times of political stress.

Up until the second half of the nineteenth century, the Arab was unknown in Portugal. Then a number turned up in private ownership and in the royal stud at Alter do Chão. They were not greatly used at this stage for pure-breeding, but were popular for cross-breeding with Lusitanos and English Thoroughbreds. Luso-Arabs and Anglo-Luso-Arab crosses have always been recognised as separate breeds by the Portuguese Stud Book and this has helped to protect the pure Lusitanian horse, as those who preferred the oriental look could, without any loss of face, buy a legitimate Luso-Arab cross.

The real saviour of the Iberian Factor in the indigenous horse in Portugal was, as already discussed, the mounted *corrida*. Horses have always been bred and schooled towards this culmination of equestrian art, and because of this the necessary characteristics covered by the Iberian Factor were of paramount importance.

Both Portuguese and Spanish breeders for the *corrida* cannot to this day resist experimenting with a little English blood here and there to obtain that extra turn of speed in the arena, but they always come back to the same conclusion. Only the pure-bred Iberian horse has the temperament to cope with the strains imposed by the nature of the bull and the complexities of the fight itself. His courage is quite phenomenal.

Even showing in Portugal is inextricably bound up with bullfighting, therefore there is little danger of the selectors moving away from the classic type of horse.

The opening ceremony of Alvaro Domecq's last fight. A proud moment for the riders of the Andalusian School of Equestrian Art. (Photo by the author)

Above: *Sensitivity, courage and obedience in the horse are even more important when there is no guiding hand on the rein.* (Photo by Jane Hodge)

Above right: *An historic occasion shared by great men. Alvaro Domecq Snr in the foreground has become a legend in his lifetime. Note the brilliance of Portuguese Samuel Lupi's cavaleiro dress compared to the more provincial traje corto of the Spanish rejoneadors.* (Photo by the author)

Right: *Lusitano fighting horse caparisoned for the corrida.* (Photo by Sally Anne Thompson)

ASSOCIAÇÃO PORTUGUESA DE CRIADORES
DE
RAÇAS SELECTAS

REGISTO GENEALÓGICO PORTUGUÊS DE EQUINOS

STUD-BOOK DA RAÇA LUSITANA

CERTIFICADO DE INSCRIÇÃO

Nº 501

NOME DO ANIMAL *Cavante*   DATA DO NASCIMENTO 29/4/1980

SEXO *Masculino*   Inscrito no Livro Genealógico da Raça Lusitana N.º *IV* , a fls. *125*

Criador *Arqº Arsénio Raposo Cordeiro,*
Residência *Campo de Santa Clara nº 114 - Lisboa*
Vendedor *Arqº Arsénio Raposo Cordeiro*
Residência *Campo de Santa Clara, Nº 114 - Lisboa*
Comprador *Dr. Guilherme Borba*
Residência *Casal de Sto André - Póvoa de Sto Adrião*

IDENTIFICAÇÃO

Cor e sinais *ruço sabino claro, teta, cascalvo do bípede posterior*

Altura no garrote *1,59*   Marcas a fogo ☩ *na coxa direita*

PRÉMIOS OBTIDOS EM CONCURSOS
1983 - Feira da Golegã - Campeão de Campeões;
1983 - Concurso Nacional de Equinos de Lisboa - Campeão de potros de 3 anos
(Juiz General Albrecht - Director da Escola Espanhola de Viena da Áustria)

GENEALOGIA

Palpite	Bailador	Iguê-Bá
		Chamata
	Kinita	Berber
		Beleza
Quadrilha	Jipão	Pródigo
		Prenda
	Heroína	Selecto
		Urânia

O Secretário do REGISTO GENEALÓGICO PORTUGUÊS DE EQUINOS, certifica que *o cavalo* de nome *"Cavante"* , identificado no verso, está inscrito no LIVRO GENEALÓGICO DA RAÇA LUSITANA N.º *quatro* , folhas *cento e vinte cinco* e que os elementos constantes deste Certificado estão de acordo com os registos originais.

Lisboa , *14* de *Junho* de *1983*

O SECRETÁRIO,

A typical Certificate of Registration for the pure-bred Lusitano Horse.

The parade has never played such an important part in Portuguese culture as it has in Spain, and there would be little point in producing a horse without forward-going action. Despite her magnificent collection of royal carriages in the National Coach Museum at the Royal Palace at Bélem in Lisbon, carriage driving, so popular in Spain on feast days and holidays, is only just beginning to return to twentieth-century Portugal. In this small country, the stud system is not highly organised by the state or the military, it remains principally in the hands of private individuals, the majority of whom devote all their attention to the art of High School. The breeders' association which administers the Portuguese Stud Book is largely civilian controlled, with just two representatives from the government. It is therefore influenced by the traditions of the countryside rather than competitive riding, and it encourages its members to breed a strictly practical horse for the purpose for which it is required.

The national stud at Fonte Boa, near the ancient Roman town of Santarem, provides the services of state stallions of Lusitano, English Thoroughbred and Arab blood for mares throughout the country and is government run with knowledgeable people on site.

The system is similar to that of Spain, but where Spain boasts a number of state studs, Portugal only has two, those of Fonte Boa and Alter. The sixty Lusitano stallions at Fonte Boa are amongst the finest Iberian horses of the classic stamp one can hope to find. Kept in immaculate condition, their service is free to pure-bred or selected cross-bred mares anywhere in the country. Horses go out to various farms or depots to stand at stud from early spring onwards, and are scattered throughout the mainland and the Azores; alternatively mares may be brought to the national stud itself.

Here also stand the Thoroughbred and Arab state stallions to serve the mares of breeders who wish to cross. Dr Figueiredo, the Director, is naturally proud of the Portuguese stallions which include horses of the Andrade, Veiga, Campilho, Infante da Camara, Palha and Conde Belo Studs as well as horses from the Alter Real and of their own particular line at Fonte Boa.

As the Portuguese are convinced that only by work and application can stallions be selected for suitability for stud work, all the Lusitanos at Fonte Boa are worked regularly in the manège and undertake work trials before being selected for breeding. These will take the form of long-distance marches, cross-country speed competitions, jumping and, of course, of prime importance, dressage. In this way, the health, robustness, ability, agility and temperament of the breed is always being monitored so that the desired characteristics of the old fighting horse may be retained to produce the finest Lusitano foals.

The Veiga Horse

One of the most famous Iberian studs in the world is that of Manuel Veiga at Golegã. His line of Lusitano horses is reputedly closer to the old combat horse of the sixteenth and seventeenth centuries than any other type which exists. These horses have been developed exclusively for the bullfight and whilst in the stable they appear quite ordinary by Iberian standards: under saddle they transform. Swelling with presence, they become quite magnificent as they move forward, each bearing his *cavaleiro* like a precious treasure. Their beautiful light gaits give the appearance of an almost floating forehand and their hocks move so deeply underneath their bellies that their tails sweep the ground.

In-breeding has caused these horses to remain rather small, around 15 h.h. to 15.2 h.h., and with their great neck and fine, long, slightly convex head, they tend to 'run away' behind with a sloping croup which scarcely looks man enough for the job. This conformation, however, is misleading for whilst the Veiga horse is not handsome enough for the parade, these horses with their enormous energy, litheness and courage, are sought the world over for the *corrida* and for breeding.

Put this horse before the bull or in company with other horses and he grows. His 15 h.h. rise before one's very eyes and he looks every inch a sixteen hander. When he studies the bull before a *sorte*, his ears are pricked almost at right-angles to his face. He watches, measures, judges his adversary and his eyes never flicker or leave the bull.

You could be forgiven for thinking him a unicorn – a mythical, wonderful beast who has so much wisdom he can perform super-human deeds. The Veiga horse is worth his weight in gold, literally. Famous horses from the Veiga line include

Novilheiro, the famous showjumper now in England, ridden by John Whitaker; Opus, the bullfighting mount of Alvaro Domecq (Jnr), and Neptuno, the mount of Vidrié, the two most famous horses in the arena today. All three horses are out of a Veiga mare by an Andrade stallion. The list of important bullfighting horses dating back to old times is interminable, and today we find Veiga horses all too often abroad, in France, Germany, South America and so on, where only foreign gold can pay the going rate.

Breeding for the Future

People who love the Iberian horse, whether he be Andalusian or Lusitano, all over the Peninsula and amongst the small coteries of Iberian enthusiasts in Australia, the United States, Germany, France and Great Britain, must encourage the great studs of the Peninsula to breed such noble horses as the Veiga and Miura lines and promote once more the classical Iberian horse. Fortunately many horses of the old stamp have found their way abroad in recent years, and breeding also from these may encourage a healthy international stock of horses.

It is vitally important that breed societies and agricultural commissions press for the retention of the Iberian Factor whether the horse be Spanish or Portuguese bred. It would not only be irresponsible but also tragic if breeders should deviate from those characteristics in their foundation stock which have made the horses of the Iberian Peninsula so famous and so revered for so many centuries.

With Spain and Portugal's entry into the European Common Market, the temptation to produce an all-round Eurohorse with little to distinguish him from the other breeds of Europe is understandable, but ultimately such a transformation of a breed would end in tragedy. The Peninsula should be proud of the fact that her horse is different, and second to none when it comes to tackling the impossible where courage and supernatural agility is required.

Twentieth-century committees of the great and the good have shown themselves to be so obsessed with raising standards that they become oblivious to the obvious. Improvements can so often be the death-knell of a certain facet within the finely balanced precision of nature. We raise the standard of housing, and we lose our communities. We raise the level of entertainment, and communication between people breaks down. We improve our agricultural programme, and we lose some of our countryside. We improve a breed of horse, and we lose our progenitor.

The wise Ruy d'Andrade showed his deep care and his genuine concern for the future of the Spanish horse when he wrote the following:

> 'I consider it a duty for the history of Spain that the Spanish horse should be conserved . . . With his help, Spain achieved her greatness particularly, for example, in the wars against the Romans, the Moors, Italy, France and Germany, and the conquest of the New World. Without her incomparable *caballo espanol* Spain could not have been victorious, so it is her duty to cherish him, in the same way that one protects cathedrals, libraries, armories, paintings and so on. All of these things together form the character and demonstrate the nobility of Spain; better still of the whole Peninsula . . .'

The 4th Marquis of Marialva, Master of the Horse to King Dom José I of Portugal (from Luz da Liberal e Nobre Arte da Cavallaria, *1790). Note the extent to which the hind legs are flexed beneath the horse's centre of gravity. This impressive athletic control is typical still of today's Iberian horses.*

CHAPTER XII

Classical Horsemanship and the Great Iberian Schools

Well could he ride, and often men would say,
That horse his mettle from his rider takes;
Proud of subjection, noble by the sway,
What rounds, what bounds, what course, what stop
    he makes.

WILLIAM SHAKESPEARE
(*A Lover's Complaint*)

Iberian Horsemen

An enigmatic question dogs the equestrian visitor from home as he travels the Iberian Peninsula for the first time and catches a glimpse of life behind the scenes at one of the private yards, studs or schools. It is hard to understand the extraordinarily high standard of horsemanship being displayed by the majority of the riders. What is even more perplexing is that all Iberian horses – whether used for work with cattle on the hills and plains, for carrying the master of the house in a remote village to the market place, or for simple pleasure riding by a busy city industrialist – appear to be 'dressed' or schooled to movements which in England or America would come under the heading Advanced Dressage.

Portugal has always been the home of the Baroque School. Post-Renaissance classical riding methods reached a natural zenith of artistic skill under King Dom José (1714–1777) when the 'Art of Marialva' (see Chapter V) on horseback developed new standards of chivalry and gallantry amongst the riding population of the land. Whilst principally a nobleman's pastime, the collapse of the monarchy after the assassination of King Carlos and the Crown Prince in 1908 did nothing to diminish the classical traditions of schooling horses, and the nagsmen, the grooms, the *campinos* and any countryman of humble birth who had the good fortune to own a horse, still took a pride in turning out their horses to the same level of obedience as that of their superiors.

In Spain also, land of the great empty plains and towering rugged mountains, horsemanship had always been of a practical and highly skilled nature from the days when Spanish cavalry had virtually controlled the Old and the New World. With the banishment of the mounted bullfight, however, equitation in the manège largely disappeared until the early twentieth century, but riding in the countryside continued to be highly dextrous and adroit, with perhaps more emphasis on speed, due to working and herding the extremely nimble Spanish bull. Now, with the

*The Marquis of Marialva (*left*) demonstrates head to the wall. Note the similarity in riding style between this Portuguese maestro and his peer La Guerinière (*right*) who is executing the pirouette.*

return of the mounted (*rejoneo*) fight, the popularity of work within the manège is on the increase again, particularly in Andalusia where the Domecq family has led the way with its magnificent training establishment for High School riders, which we shall be discussing further on in this chapter.

Thus, in every manège generously scattered throughout the main horse-breeding areas, and in the field, the market place and the fairground, we find horses and horsemen performing at the most brilliant levels of equitation. It would not be unusual to enter an indoor riding school at, say, the Jockey Club[1] in Lisbon and watch, at any random moment, at least five horses and five different owners practising and perfecting piaffe, passage or Spanish walk all within a few feet of each other. This is done quietly and uncompetitively, for the pure joy of seeking harmony between horse and rider.

In Chapter X we explored the interior of the Peninsula and learned that the breeding of Iberian horses, as well as their schooling, is inextricably interwoven with the sport of mounted bullfighting. Surprisingly, perhaps, in addition to this we learn that the successful city lawyer or doctor from Oporto, Lisbon or Madrid, who has no connection whatsoever with the countryside and the breeding of bulls, is also a competent High School rider. How has this extraordinary situation come about? The answer is three-fold.

> Firstly, and of paramount significance, the Iberian horse is so clearly suited to this type of work, that High School is simply the most natural outlet.

1. The Jockey Club, as it is normally termed by its illustrious members, is officially the Hipodromo do Campo Grande.

Secondly, Portugal and Spain, despite their rapidly growing industry, are still economically very dependent on a rural economy and this has led to country traditions being preserved in a way which was swept aside in England with the Industrial Revolution. Thus methods of horsemanship which were a whole way of life to a large sector of the population have become firmly embedded in the national consciousness and continue to this day.

Thirdly, the terrain of Spain and southern Portugal, baked hard by the hot Iberian sun and the long, dry days of spring, summer and autumn, when occasionally not a drop of rain will fall in seven months, are hardly suitable for prolonged hours of hacking on horseback. The sandy tracks of the home stud farm are one thing, but when one leaves the river basin and climbs high into the Andalusian hinterland and experiences the sharply rocky paths of the bare *sierras*, where snow falls in winter and Siberian-like nights of cutting winds drop below freezing, riding out is something normally undertaken only by the stockmen and a few brave tourists who enjoy the romance of adventure. Thus other forms of equestrian sport have never seriously flourished in the past.

Only now, with the comparatively recent growth of the middle classes, do we see signs of a change within the Peninsula. This, however, cannot be compared to the huge spectrum of equestrian sport open to those of us at home. In England and New England, France and Germany – in fact any country where there is a year-round rainfall – we tend to take our springy green turf and the equestrianism it promotes for granted.

Iberian hunting, which once involved the chase of wild bulls through thick forests, has, with improved agriculture, retreated to the confines of the bullring. There are still, however, occasional mounted culling expeditions for wild boar in the north of the Peninsula; and in the hills behind Malaga in Andalusia, and in many other remote provinces, *caçada à lebre com galgos* – coursing with greyhounds for hare – on foot and on horseback is a popular sport.

Foxhunting, as we know it in Britain, has never been a national pastime and was first introduced to the Peninsula by the English.[2] It is very properly conducted by the Iberian anglophiles who indulge in it, but it primarily attracts the foreign residents and as with hacking out, cross-country riding and Pony Clubbing, it remains a somewhat artificial pastime to the average Iberian horseman. There are only two established packs of hounds, one at Equipagem de Santo Huberto near Lisbon, and one, recently started, at the large tourist development of Sotto Grande in southern Spain.

Neither does the terrain lend itself to flat racing, steeplechasing, point-to-pointing or polo. Where there is wealth, and enough people to support and administrate the venture, a *clube hippico* will be formed. Then, on a section of real estate, a clubhouse, stands, an outdoor showjumping arena with possibly a

---

2. In his article 'Those Peerless Lusitanos' which appeared in *Country Life*, June 18th, 1981, Major J.N.P. Watson describes foxhunting in Portugal as follows: 'It is parochial, expensive and exotic – its customs, its foxhounds and its official language are English, for it derives from those hectic far-off days when Wellington's officers kept hounds during the Peninsular War.'

tan race-track round the outer edge, will be set up close to one of the big cities such as Seville or Lisbon. Here, provided that the bulldozers and excavators have really done their job well and the Club can afford to run a dozen large water sprinklers a day to keep the Bermuda grass from burning up, a certain amount of equestrian activity other than High School and *Vaquera* riding may thrive.

Racing will probably take the form of trotting in harness and where *Garranos* were once popular, they are now being crossed with other breeds such as Thoroughbred and Arab. Polo will be limited to the very few who are enthusiastic for this imported sport; but showjumping will be well attended, particularly by the military and mounted police force. Showjumping is now appealing to a growing number of civilians and while there are many excellent Iberian showjumpers particularly within the forces who use national stock, the Anglo-Hispano or Anglo-Luso is proving a brilliant horse over showjumps. There is, however, a certain snobbery amongst the newly established showjumping fraternity to own an imported horse, and fabulous prices will be paid for a really talented English, French or German showjumper.

Cross-country jumping, once the province of the military, is beginning to be very popular in the Peninsula, and here the Hispano-Arab has proved himself particularly useful. This sport is still in its early stages of development in the Peninsula and because of climate and terrain is not always easy to organise. Certainly it does not offer a natural outlet for the Iberian horseman.

The Doma Vaquera

Although High School riding in the manège is returning rapidly to Spain with the reintroduction of mounted bullfighting, the majority of Spaniards still pursue the *Doma Vaquera*. Hours will be spent on the *hacienda* training horses to this specialised end, and although English blood is frequently introduced to provide speed and dash, it is those special Iberian qualities of temperament and short-backed conformation which help to make the *vaquero* horse so adroit at his art.

The *Doma Vaquera* is based on the following functional exercises: *recular* (halt and rein-back); *arreon* (a sudden surge forward into full gallop); *la media vuelta y recular* (half-turn and rein-back), and the famous *vaquera* walk (as already discussed in Chapter X). All the former movements require tremendous impulsion and the horse's ability to round his back and bring his hocks well underneath him. Although this form of 'dressage' is far less polished and sophisticated than classical High School, for no lateral or elevated movements are required, the *vaquero* rider equally relies upon a short-coupled, malleable horse whose natural agility he can develop to the full. As with High School, a strong, firm seat is a necessary feature on the part of the rider.

The *vaquero* horseman in his leather chaps and short jacket, riding by with one hand poised at the hip and the other on the rein, is as elegant in his own way as the more extravagantly attired *cavaleiro* in the Portuguese *corrida*.

Although not required of him, many a *vaquero* horse may naturally offer the rudiments of passage and piaffe when excited, and counter changes of hand come naturally to all Iberian horses and are used in everyday work with the cattle and on the farms. The more spectacular the movements of the *vaquero* horse, the more his owner will enjoy showing him off at *fiesta* time. It is all a part of Spanish tradition and combines gaiety and levity with practicality.

The High School of the Picadeiro

In Portugal, such is the strength of tradition that every horse owner has his own small *picadeiro* or school. These are now being seen more frequently in Spain, but nothing can compare with the beautiful indoor manèges of the Portuguese landed families. Every *castello, palacio* and *quinta* boasts a cool, highly vaulted manège in which the family and their servants have worked their horses for generations, and some of these, particularly those built in the eighteenth century are ornately Baroque with stunning handpainted tiles portraying equestrian scenes from the past inset into thick whitewashed walls. But in contrast even the most humble yard will boast a *picadeiro*. All one requires is a level piece of land, a couple of trailerloads of sand, some easily constructed bamboo fencing and the school is ready. The problem of mud is not encountered; no complicated drainage is required. Horses work happily in areas varying from 10 × 20 metres to 20 × 40 metres, but the popular *picadeiro* normally averages 12.5 × 25 or 15 × 30 metres.

I shall never forget being shown one Lusitano stallion, a huge chestnut animal of not much under 17 h.h. which was led out by hand into a large room. Here, in an area of approximately twelve metres square, interrupted in the centre by two Corinthian pillars, this horse was loose schooled over a four-foot jump and then ridden in front of an astonished audience through all the movements of the High School. One of my companions had just arrived in Portugal for the first time from England and was a British Horse Society dressage judge. The house was a nobleman's derelict country residence and the wooden floor had been dug out and replaced by sand. Such was the balance and precision of horse and rider that everything appeared quite normal to the Portuguese family who had taken over this property and were endeavouring to sell us their horse. They certainly looked puzzled at the gasps of horror (turning later to admiration) of the visiting *inglesa* who has never stopped talking about that day ever since. No doubt, she, like me, still has a vision of that big horse turning on a sixpence and successfully avoiding us all as his muffled hoof-beats reverberated off that panelled room.

With the strong historic influence of battlefield and bullfighting manoeuvres, coupled with a chauvinistic pride in working horses to such highly demanding standards, it is hardly surprising to find that the approach to riding in the traditional equestrian home is still one of chivalry and gallantry.

From a very early age, the young horseman is mounted on schooled horses and there is no place therefore for rough hands or crude aids. No obliging pony awaits the seven- or eight-year-old boy, who will one day face a bull across a packed arena. If the Portuguese child digs his little heels in or 'jabs' his father's stallion in the mouth, there will be a severe lecture which will be remembered for several weeks – perhaps all his life – and he will soon learn the manners of the manège and to respect the magnificent animals of *categoria* he has had the honour of riding.

Sitting still, using the back strongly and the hand lightly, are the Iberian's horseman's secrets for obtaining perfect balance in hand. There is no requirement for the rider to drive the horse forward into a strong contact, for with his hocks well engaged and his back soft and receptive, the horse becomes a veritable gymnast and is able to execute the most athletic manoeuvres on a feather-light rein.

Later we shall discuss the disparity between High School in the small manège and competition dressage for the Olympics, where a longer, more horizontal outline is required with more prominence given to medium and extended gaits. It is hardly surprising, therefore, that traditional methods of schooling are changing course, and many Iberian horsemen are striving now to extend the action of their horses in their desire for freer, forward movement. In some cases this has worked well, but some breeders have, conversely, lost the age-old characteristics of good hock action and impulsion in the attempt.

Those who love the Iberian horse for what he is – the Labrador of the horse world – so willing, so kind and so attuned to a close partnership with man, are glad that there still exists another school in Spain and Portugal. This school does not frown on competition for competition's sake, but its foundations are deeply rooted in the attainment of total oneness between horse and rider, and a state of supreme balance within the concept of equitation as an art.

Within the traditional High School training of the small manège or the bullring, impulsion is all-important, but it must be *contained* impulsion which may then be urged upward into wonderful airs above the ground, or into life-saving lateral movements, pirouettes and so on. Energy held in *suspension*, ready to be distributed instantaneously and without question in literally any direction, holds far greater potential than a steady stream of energy forward and 'out the front door'.

The greatest maestros therefore, and there are many in Portugal – Mestre Nuno Oliveira, D. José Athayde, Dr Guilherme Borba and Francisco Cançela d'Abreu – will school their horses in the correct forward gaits from the very beginning, but once these are well established, emphasis will be switched to containing that impulsion in the collected gaits.

Anyone who has seen the Lipizzaner give his piaffe and then leap with a surge of tremendous impulsion into the surprise moment of suspension in the capriole cannot deny that this ability to go forward is of the most enviable quality. Similarly, the spectator at the ringside of the *corrida* is amazed by the ease with which the fighting horse may execute a full pirouette and without any fuss or pause to gather himself, will make the transition into gallop, for example, to evade a sudden charge from the bull. A moment later he is cantering sedately on the spot again.

As the training for the mounted *corrida* must be closer to the classical training of the old combat horse than any other form in the world, let us now follow the education of the Portuguese bullfighting horse from the breaking and schooling process, to its logical conclusion from whence the horse emerges as a perfectly trained High School horse. His is the world of lightness in hand and total self-balance. A horse correctly brought to these levels dances into his transitions.

The Young Lusitano

Having been handled, but still living a relatively herd-like existence, the Lusitano colt is brought into the stable at the age of three and a half (depending on how early in the year he is born), when the summer sun has dried up the pasture and he has developed beyond the somewhat gangling stage of two and a half to three. Lusitanos are reasonably slow developers and young horses may gain a couple of inches in height in their fifth or sixth year. It is worthwhile to start as late as possible as this horse is long-lived and may successfully work well into his twenties, in even the most athletically demanding school exercises.

Stallions are always selected for training as we have seen in Chapter X. Quite apart from the loss of a potentially valuable sire, gelding an Iberian horse will cause him to lose presence and physically he will never make up to full-bodied capacity in the same way as the stallion. But the strongest case against gelding is that he will lack lustre and have no desire to fight. Stallions have traditionally been used in battle in the Peninsula since recorded time and they enjoy bullfighting. Certain bullfighting horses from distinguished lines, bred only for that purpose for scores of years, will actually face a bull without a rider, make *sortes* and literally challenge him with pure enjoyment. This is an assertion that one might not believe unless one had seen it with one's own eyes, but it does happen and is typical of the stallion's brave temperament.

In the castrated horse some primitive element is lost, and whilst he may be perfectly adequate for hacking, hunting or jumping, there is a loss of courage, interest and the close awareness and care of his rider which is so vital in the good fighting horse.

It is the custom in Portugal for the sons of every great house to acquire the art of schooling the stallions. Thus, even though he may be the director of a large company to which he must commute daily, the dedicated father will endeavour to work regularly with his son in the manège, teaching him in the family tradition so that together they may bring on the cream of their youngstock.

One famous Portuguese family, the head of which, David Ribeiro Telles, became one of the world's greatest *cavaleiros*, now has four members fighting in the ring. David himself, a true artist on horseback and the gentlest man one could hope to meet, still fights occasionally, and now his eldest son is making a name for himself with the next two eagerly following suit.

Of course it is always easier for the farming *cavaleiro* who has no beckoning city desk to spend time on his horses, but even the businessman who breeds horses on a small scale at his weekend retreat of no more than a hundred acres, will somehow find the time to school his horses himself. If not, he will employ a good nagsman, a highly experienced stud groom, or former *campino* who will do the job for him. Imagine in Britain finding a local farm worker who could school one's youngster through the basic movements and onto passage and piaffe. Such an idea is unthinkable today, yet it is very likely that such a situation did exist in the time of Charles I when as a nation we understood what was meant by '*on dresse le cheval*' . . . and 'dressed' meant *fully* schooled.

The basic training to go forward in walk, trot or canter is normally accomplished on the lunge, under saddle. Backing the young Lusitano stallion is remarkably free of problems, and he quickly regains his balance once he is used to the weight on his back, a factor greatly facilitated by his conformation.

By the time he is four he will be ready to start leg-yielding which he does so naturally that this does not interfere with his basic forward movement. Once the horse is showing good, free paces with plenty of energetic activity behind, collected and lateral work in all gaits will commence. This normally starts at about four and a half. As already discussed, the Iberian horse finds it relatively easy to round his back and shorten his gait, and it is often tempting to encourage this at too early an age when it is offered so readily. The good trainer will, however, be patient and only when the horse is versed in all his basic movements, and is confident in his lateral work and turns, will the specialised work of the High School begin. By now the horse is about five.

Training for the Bullring

Most *cavaleiros* prefer to teach passage and piaffe from the ground with the assistance of someone at the horse's head and the use of one or two long switches. The horse is made to lower his croup, which has the effect of lightening his fore-hand, and allowing his hocks to come deeply underneath. Light taps on the horse's rump and in sequence on the back of the legs to make him lift his feet soon have the desired effect. With patience, the horse develops a lively lifting of the diagonal pairs of legs and with the encouragement of the chuck-chuck-chucking noise of the *cavaleiro's* tongue, a rhythm is gradually established.

Work in hand gives way to ridden training, and these movements will gradually be perfected over the last phase of training when the horse is introduced to preparatory work with the bull. More exotic movements such as Spanish walk and Spanish trot will be added, and in all probability the levade. The capriole, however, has no place traditionally in the bullring.

At approximately five and a half years of age, if not before, the horse learns to become familiar with the sight of two formidable bull's horns approaching him. From now on, something more than the Iberian's inherent tractability is required, he must have courage. If the horse is not mentally suited to the demands of the *corrida*, it may become painfully obvious even at this early stage, and such a horse will never ever appear in an arena.

The introduction to the horns is made by a groom wheeling a *tourinha* into the manège, an artefact which is basically a pair of horns mounted onto a square of cork and supported by what looks like a large bicycle wheel. A good stallion will not shy away from the rattling *tourinha*, but will study it closely, judging its distance and the speed at which it is pushed. The horseman will practise with his horse the placing of a dart into the cork, and gradually the horse learns the routine of the approach, the slight lateral swerve as the horns come perilously close, and the moment of suspension to allow the horseman to plunge in the dart. In a surprisingly short time, the horse is able to respond to the aids and requests being made of him, without a moment's hesitation.

As the groom and *tourinha* grow meaner with the passing of the weeks and new threats and new attacks made, lateral work becomes not only second nature to the horse, it assumes a new meaning. A great deal of side-stepping, sudden turning, and repeated changing of leg at the canter is required for this cat-and-mouse game. Above all in this phase of training, the horse learns to anticipate and to obey without question.

People talk about the submission of the horse, but, again, like the good Labrador and his master, it is rather a process of partnership. The rider and his horse form a bond of complete understanding and unification as together they pit their wits against the wily *tourinha*. During this period, the new High School steps will also be rehearsed and improved, and the excitement caused by the work with the *tourinha* will encourage the horse to raise his poll and lighten his steps as he prepares himself for the advance from a perfect piaffe.

The next phase in the stallion's education will be to work with a tame bull, or *toiro manso*, and for the first time the horse will feel the weight and thrust of an animal stronger than himself, as the *cavaleiro* allows him to be buffetted once or twice only. The *toiro manso* will be an excellent schoolmaster, chosen for this work because of his age or his unaggressive approach. Instead of hurtling himself at the horse in a full-blooded attack, he will make lazy, half-hearted charges which should not deter an intelligent horse. Working with a bull of this type gives the horse confidence before he is introduced to an animal of more fiery temperament, a young heifer.

Although not so large as a bull, and unable to do the horse any serious harm, a heifer of good fighting stock is a formidable opponent. Heifers, due to their lightness, are extremely quick and nimble and a clever one can run circles round a young horse before he learns to anticipate exactly what is going on. They can also be extremely pugnacious. It is at this stage that the talented fighting horse will often be singled out from the unsuitable ones.

As the horses which finally go to the arena constitute only about a tenth of those selected for training, such a horse is a very valuable asset. A good horse will not show fear, only mild surprise at this invasion of black quicksilver energy. Swiftly, he will gather his senses together and respond, in the way that he has been prepared, to every aid that his master gives him. There is now a relationship of deep trust, and on occasions it will be the horse which may take the initiative. Nothing concentrates a horse's inbuilt senses for a task better than this stage of training, and the young stallion has now developed an alert and watchful eye, and his ears are sharply pricked as he listens to every change in the huffing and puffing of the angry heifer. It is evident that the best bullfighting horses clearly enjoy their work, and although they never relax into it, as to do so would be certain death, they throw themselves wholeheartedly into working with their master to outwit the opposition. It may sound sentimental but there is nothing more moving than following the look on the horse's face during a mounted *corrida*.

Not until the horse is perfectly schooled in all these phases will he be let loose in the arena. From practice at home with the *novilhas*, which are being tested too for their future breeding (as only those with sufficient ferocity will be used), the first fight in public for the now fully-fledged horse will probably be at a small local *corrida* with another *cavaleiro* and his more mature horse present. The two *cavaleiros* will take it in turns to make *sortes* and thus the young stallion will gain confidence. By the time he is fighting on his own, he will be used to the fanfare of the trumpets, the cheering of the crowd, the capes, the colours and the tremendous sense of occasion. From now on the *corrida* will be a way of life and from April through to October, he will be travelling the length and breadth of the country in company with five or six other horses from the same stable. Every small town in Portugal has its own bullring, and one of the most famous, Campo Pequeno in Lisbon draws huge crowds and the best-known names in bullfighting. Simao

Classical horsemanship correctly done is the same all over the world. The principles laid down by the Spanish Riding School of Vienna are no different from those practised in the Iberian Peninsula.

da Veiga, and the great João Nuncio, the most revered name in Portugal, fought here, as did Manuel Condé and Mestre Baptista. That great *cavaleiro* with the silken hands, David Ribeiro Telles, is a frequent visitor although his place is being taken more and more by his elder son João. Of the younger generation, Gustavo Zenkl, Françisco Zoio and the highly popular João Moura are but a few of the most respected names. Many Portuguese will cross the frontier into Spain to fight at Seville and Jerez and as far afield as Santander or Valencia. Ronda bullring, high up in the *sierra* on the road from Arcos de la Frontera to Malaga, is the oldest existing arena in Spain and was reputedly built in the fifteenth century.

One of Spain's most popular stars of the *rejoneo* is a Portuguese *cavaleiro* Samuel Lupi, but the *rejoneadors* of Spain are equally great horsemen and the famous Peralta brothers, Angel and Rafael, are admired the world over as are the Domecqs (both now retired from public fights), D. Fermin Bohorquez, and Manuel Vidrié, all of whom enjoy the highest reputation and ride to the topmost standards of equestrian skill.

In the winter, there is a chance to fly abroad with one's horses, and now that the Peninsula is enjoying a particularly brilliant epoch of mounted bullfighting, which has been greatly helped by Spain's participation again after so many decades, countries which traditionally have only been interested in bullfighting on foot, such as Mexico and Ecuador, are now participating in this sport. This can only raise the standard of horsemanship in these countries and should inspire a return to classical equitation.

The Classical Schools of the Peninsula
NUNO OLIVEIRA'S SCHOOL

You do not even have to be a horseman to see the closest semblance to perfection between man and horse when you set eyes on Mestre Nuno Oliveira. This great Portuguese classical riding master is acknowledged the world over as probably the most brilliant dressage rider alive. He might well be described as the Guerinière of the twentieth century, and in true Portuguese tradition, he passes on to his worldwide pupils the disciplines laid down by his seventeenth-century predecessor, Marialva. As with all Portuguese teaching, the emphasis is on softness and lightness and this is achieved by a strong active back and seat which give an outward impression of tremendous stillness in the saddle, for there is no apparent sign of leg and hand aids.

Horse and Hound's well-known dressage correspondent, Colonel Anthony Crossley, writing for *Riding Magazine* in an article entitled *At The Feet of the Master*, expounds the Oliveira concept of equitation in the following clear and concise way:

> 'The Oliveira theme, unmistakably apparent in the horses they [Oliveira and his son João] train for themselves and for clients, is embodied in the three principles of collection, impulsion and lightness, the first and the last being taken to a degree beyond the conception of most riders. But of the three it is lightness that makes the most vivid impression on the average visitor and which is Nuno Oliveira's greatest contribution to twentieth-century dressage. Such heights of artistry may be out of reach for the average rider, but the visual awareness that they are a practical reality, and not just something that occurs in books, must raise and enrich the conception of what dressage is all about for any devotee who makes the pilgrimage.'

Mestre Nuno Oliveira's school is situated north of Lisbon at Avessada, near Malveira, and here pupils flock from all over the world to be taught by this great man and his talented son, predominantly on Lusitano schoolmasters. Nuno also travels and teaches widely abroad, especially in the United States. Colonel Crossley's final paragraph, describing his lasting impression of the Mestre is typical of the standard of skill of which one catches so many glimpses in this classically orientated country.

> 'When all was over the writer bade his farewells and took with him for ever the memory of Mestre Nuno Oliveira on a splendid 16.3 h.h. Andrade Lusitanian stallion called Levant, riding small circles in an incredible collected canter, slower than a walk in speed; steady as a clock in tempo; so supple that the three-time beat was impeccable; the position

Nuno Oliveira performing the levade with Beau Geste, a Lusitano stallion from the Ervideira stud.
(Courtesy of Fernando d'Andrade)

of the head unvarying; and with rein contact unbroken but almost invisible. The pirouette that followed was of identical quality. That picture alone justified the whole excursion.'

Nuno Oliveira's books, *Reflections on Equestrian Art* and *Notes and Reminiscences of a Portuguese Rider*, are an invaluable contribution to modern understanding of the subject.

THE PORTUGUESE SCHOOL OF EQUESTRIAN ART

In contrast to the privately run school of Nuno Oliveira, A Escola Portuguesa de Arte Equestre, which has only recently been recreated, is a cultural product of the Ministry of Portuguese Agriculture and Trade. It is not only aimed at educating the public – including many tourists – about the Portuguese art of classical equitation, it is also a useful outlet to test the tractability, endurance and suitability for this work of the stallions from the old royal stud. Thus the school uses at the present time only stallions from the Alter Real line, and its lead rider, D. José Athayde is the director and chief instructor at Alter do Chão. Another important representative of the Portuguese government breeding programme is the second rider, Dr João Filipe Figueiredo, director of the national stud at Fonte Boa.

At present the school practises for its demonstrations and displays in the manège of the Jockey Club at Lisbon, and performances are then given in the open air in the magnificent Versailles-like gardens at the Palace of Queluz, one of Portugal's most beautiful royal residences just to the west of Lisbon. It is here that Queen Elizabeth II stays when she comes to Portugal, and recently both the Queen and the Duke of Edinburgh, and subsequently the presidential party of Mr and Mrs

Left: *Pas de Deux. Perfect rhythm, cadence and matched elevation is maintained by the talented horses of the great Iberian Schools. The horses clearly enjoy their work and there is a fluidity and flamboyancy about their performance. (Photo by Jane Hodge)*

It is hoped that visitors who previously have only visited the great Spanish Riding School of Vienna (below) will also take the opportunity to visit the cradle of classical horsemanship, the Iberian Peninsula.

Preceding page: D. José Athayde and Dr João Filipe Figueiredo (Graçiosa) demonstrate levade on their Alter Real stallions from the Portuguese School of Equestrian Art, in front of the Palace of Queluz, near Lisbon. (Photo by Eduardo Tomé)

Nuno Oliveira practising a salute with Ulysses, a pure-bred Lusitano. (Courtesy of Country Life*)*

Reagan, enjoyed a display of Portuguese classical horsemanship in this rich setting.

A varied and interesting programme is presented with eight team members working through a quadrille, pas-de-deux, work in hand and between the pillars. The elevated work of the Alter Real stallions is of a very high standard indeed, but for the capriole and ballotade a smaller *isabella*[3] stallion is also used which literally surges high above the head of the trainer, in a series of splendid leaps.

Most impressive about the Portuguese school, who ride in eighteenth-century traditional court dress recalling the days of chivalry on which their equitation is based, is their calm, soft, yet tremendously effective approach to the horse. Stately and still in the saddle, their aids are scarcely visible, yet their work is accurate and their horses move through their transitions with enviable fluidity.

The Portuguese School exists due to the dedication of a handful of men working under their director, Dr Guilherme Borba (one of Nuno Oliveira's most talented former pupils), who was instrumental in instituting a programme of work for the Domecq School in Spain when it was first set up. None of the riders is paid for what he does, which has to be fitted in after work hours and in his own time.

It is, however, hoped that the Portuguese government will set up a special centre for the development of this important cultural activity, as at present horses have to be moved between the outlying district of Alter in the Ribatejo, to the city centre, and there exists no facility to bring on young horses except at the stud.

The Portuguese School gave a stunning display of High School in England in the presence of Their Royal Highnesses Prince Charles and Princess Diana when the team came over to participate in the Treaty of Windsor Sixth Centenary

---

3. The term *isabella* is still used in the Peninsula to imply a coffee- or cream-coloured horse.

celebrations which took place in June 1986. This was preceded by a display at Goodwood House, Chichester.

THE ANDALUSIAN SCHOOL OF EQUESTRIAN ART

Although unconnected with the *corrida*, the classical school of Spain – La Escuela Andaluza del Arte Ecuestre – has strong associations with the art of *rejoneo* fighting, and the *Doma Vaquera*. This is not surprising in the light that it was started by the Domecq family.

Whilst many treasures and traditions of Portugal so often remain unseen and unsung by visitors to that small country, the Spanish have always been well aware of their own attractions to overseas travellers and in much the same way as their art has been well exhibited and presented (as in the recently modernised Prado) so department ministers have been quick to recognise the cultural importance of a national centre of Spanish equitation. Originally started in 1973, the Domecq School reopened in 1982 in the centre of Jerez, at Avenida Duque de Abrantes, within the grounds of a splendid Baroque palace which is a fitting background for this magnificent centre. At a cost of 200 million pesetas a marvel of modern architecture was constructed which accommodated not only the *picadero*, but seating for 1450 people and stabling for sixty horses. All this was incorporated into a building which, far from looking like a typical indoor riding school, could well be a modern version of the eighteenth-century palace next door.

Now run by the Ministry of Information and Tourism, the aim of La Escuela Andaluza is to provide the country with a permanent site for the pursuit of the high ideals of classical equitation. Here, specially selected pupils from Spain and outside the Iberian Peninsula go to study the art under experienced instructors on schoolmaster horses. These pupils learn how to school young stallions and bring them on to the standard of the older schoolmaster horses which are versed in all movements.

Not unlike the Spanish Riding School of Vienna in its aspirations, one notices, however, a striking difference in the national flavour. It is perceptibly non-military and more relaxed in its attitude towards its pupils and programme of training than the Prussian-style regime of the Austrian school in Vienna. Every Thursday, a display is given in the 20 × 60 metre indoor arena of the Jerez school for the benefit of the Spanish public and tourists from all over the world. The programme describes this as 'the great equestrian ballet of classical and Andalusian-style dressage, fruit of the purest and most prestigious art.'

The show is expertly and dramatically presented with eight riders dressed in Spanish Goya costume mounted on grey Iberian stallions. The lead horse, currently being ridden by the senior rider[4], Francisco Javier Garcia Romero, is a seventeen-year-old Lusitanian stallion, Jaguar, and the youngest horse in the opening quadrille, is Volapie, aged six.

The arena is theatrically lit with the Spanish flag mounted on the central pillars through which the horses pass, and looking down from the lofty vaulted upper

---

4. Since retiring from public mounted bullfighting, Alvarito Domecq is again beginning to take up the role of lead rider in the quadrille.

wall at the end of the school is a portrait of King Juan Carlos I with the Spanish government coat of arms fluttering underneath. The riders salute the standard as they enter the arena and with a roll of the drums the show begins.

The quadrille is spectacular and artistic. The white coats of the eight horses gleam in the spotlights, as they move effortlessly through half-pass in collected trot and canter, into their one-time changes in sequence across the diagonal, and canter pirouettes where luxuriously long, thick tails sweep the ground. There is an upward surge of energy into the piaffe, and the crowd gasps as two horses accomplish a complete circuit of the Olympic-sized arena in a perfectly sustained high-stepping passage. The sheer beauty and gentleness of these strong, muscled, deeply flexed stallions is moving, and here and there one observes a moist eye in the enraptured audience.

The Andalusian School of Equestrian Art may cost the Spanish government a fortune to maintain, but whatever the cost, it is a small price to pay for keeping alive the highest ideals of horsemanship and for providing a solid base for the correct teaching of equitation on schoolmaster horses. It is regrettable that the latter is not yet part of every country's training scheme.

Spain deserves to be proud of her classical school and it is a fitting tribute to a great family that the name Domecq will ever more be associated with restoring classical equitation to Spain.

Readers who visit Spain and Portugal can help to promote the government support these two schools need if they are to continue and expand, by insisting that they are provided with information about them and given the opportunity not only to see performances but also to see the horses in their boxes behind the scenes.

Worldwide recognition for the horses and horsemanship of the Iberian Peninsula was the raison d'être *of the late Dr Ruy d'Andrade, pictured above at the age of eighty, riding Vulcano, a Lusitano stallion.*

CHAPTER XIII

The Royal Mares of England

... And now as proud as a King of Spain,
He moved in his box with a restless tread,
His eyes like sparks in his lovely head,
Ready to run between the roar
Of the stands that face the Straight once more ...

JOHN MASEFIELD (*Right Royal*)

Unlike the Arab horse, which is now bred in almost every country of the world and therefore constantly reminds us of its links with so many of our quality modern breeds, the Iberian horse, which is bred on a comparatively small scale in only a few countries of the world, is easily forgotten as a progenitor.

Even in the most knowledgeable equine circles, it may come as a surprise to learn that this horse has played an important part in the family trees of the cream of our horses. Many a finely arched eyebrow has been raised in disbelief that the Spanish or Iberian horse exerted as much influence as the Arab in the original foundation Thoroughbred stock of England.

The appeal of the Iberian horse as a progenitor has not been accentuated furthermore by the writings of Arab breeders and enthusiasts. The foremost of these was Lady Wentworth who published her *Thoroughbred Racing Stock* in 1938. This admirable publication accomplishes what it sets out to do, i.e. draws attention to the magnificent contribution that the Arab has made to the racing world. Unfortunately, in so doing, a somewhat inaccurate and unconcerned interpretation has been given of the contribution of the Iberian horse to early Thoroughbred racing stock, which is perhaps all too understandable from someone whose interest in horses lay in other directions. Lady Wentworth's chapter entitled 'Spanish Horses' takes up only five pages of print, and these dwell mainly on the mistakes of Tinti at the Court of Cordoba and take little account of the importation of Spanish horses into England which was most concentrated in the Tudor and Stuart periods.

In our appraisal of the foundation period, it is important that we recognise the Barb as being closely related to the Iberian horse, and in all probability descended from him. It must also be remembered that in many cases where reference is made to a Barb or Barbary horse in old records and documents, the animal in question has in fact been obtained from the Iberian Peninsula. An example of the haphazard use of the word 'Barb' by English recorders of the time can be found in the case of the 'Mantuan Barbs' which were so highly prized at the time of Henry VIII of England. These, as we have seen in Chapter V, were more often than not the result of judicious crossing with Spanish and Barb foundation stock. However, even without relying on the evidence of so-called Barb blood, in our search for the progenitors of the Thoroughbred and other breeds, there is still ample proof of the presence of pure Spanish blood in those early quality lines.

The Development of the Racing Horse from Early Times

We tend to think of flat racing as something relatively new[1] and only undertaken by a certain type of horse, namely our modern Thoroughbred racehorse. What is often overlooked is that racing in England might never have developed in its present form had it not been for the importation of Spanish and Italian coursers long ago.

In King Stephen's reign (1135–54) we hear of the first mention of 'royal mares' being served by imported stallions. Unfortunately, history does not relate whether these mares were home-bred or imported, but from then on the stallions being used at the royal studs were normally referred to in books and manuscripts as 'hot-blooded' or 'imported'.

Two centuries later, quality breeding had become so important to the national effort to improve English stock that King Edward III (1327–77) sent overseas to Spain for fifty stallions. Their safe arrival in this country was of such concern that special permission had to be sought from the kings of France and Spain to secure their passage through those kingdoms. By the time these Jennets had reached the royal stables, it is calculated that each horse cost £160, a truly fabulous sum in those days when the average light horse could be purchased for around £4. Today this discrepancy is almost equivalent to the difference between the cost of a son or daughter of Troy, Shergar or Northern Dancer purchased at a Tattersalls sale and an agreeable hunter from a local dealer.

The first mention of a formal race being arranged for prize money in England occurs in the reign of Richard I (1189–99) when at Whitsuntide a number of knights competed against each other on their best destriers over a three-mile course for a purse of £40 in ready gold.

Breeding received a severe set-back during the Wars of the Roses. It has been recorded that many owners of good horses were anxious to avoid having them 'impressed' for the Civil War, and instead sold them to foreign buyers in France and Germany. Also, a number of noble families who had become impoverished during the wars, in which they lost men and horses to the cause, resorted to selling their most valuable horses abroad to help fill the family coffers again. It was not long, however, before Henry VII put an end to this practice by passing an Act in 1494 which forbade the export of all stallions and of any mare worth over six shillings and eight pence. The act bewails the dearth of quality horses at that time for the defence of the realm and points out that many such horses had already been sent abroad.

Worldwide, the earliest records of horse racing date back to somewhere around 1500 BC with details of the royal stables of the Assyrian kings of that time laid down in meticulous order and indicating that the sport had already been in existence for perhaps some thousand years before that, if not more. In those days,

---

1. We also know that the Romans raced ponies in the North of England throughout their occupation of Great Britain.

chariots were employed for both galloping and trotting races, but by Xenophon's time, flat racing had become popular and large sums of money were wagered.

In England, the earliest written record we have of the sport of kings is in the middle of the twelfth century. During Henry II's reign a lively account is given of racehorses assembling at Smooth Field (London's Smithfield) which in those days was 'without one of the London City Gates'. Here we find a gallant company of horses being paraded for sale, and amongst the worthy citizens who have come to participate and spectate, we fine such important personages as 'Earls, Barons and Knights' who we are led to believe are on the look-out for a 'War-horse of elegant shape, full of fire and showing every proof of a generous and noble temper.' The writer, a Canterbury monk, one William Stephanides, talks of a match between these clearly blood horses, and the atmosphere is immediately captured,

> 'When a race is run by this sort of horse, and perhaps by others which also in their kind are strong and fleet, a shout is immediately raised and the common horses are ordered to withdraw out of the way. Three jockeys, or sometimes only two – as the match is made – prepare themselves for the contest. The horses on their part are not without emulation. They tremble and are impatient, and are continually in motion.'

It is certain that these war-horses were Spanish or Barb. The Arab was unknown in England in those days, and hot blood, which we now tend to call oriental, came from the best Spanish studs or those along the Barbary Coast. As well as importing from the south, Henry II also brought into England Norman and Flemish breeds, but it is highly unlikely these heavier war-horses would have been used for racing, and the trembling with excitement and being constantly on the move is characteristic of the blood horse. We know that these highly prized horses which belonged to the king were kept in the royal stables at Winchester.

Henry VIII and His Love of Fine Horseflesh

People tend to remember only the unreasonable, selfish side of this king in his latter years, but Henry VIII is owed an eternal debt by English horse breeders. A great sportsman with a feeling for the arts and the pursuit of beauty, Henry VIII was committed to matching his magnificence at court with the very finest imported horses in his stables. Deeply interested in racing, he attended the first established site for an annual race meeting in Chester. Participated in by the king's horses (if not by the king himself) this race was contested over the Roodee, just outside the old city on the site of the present-day Chester racecourse. Henry VIII kept in force his predecessor's laws on the exportation of horses,[2] and even forbade the sending of horses over the border to Scotland. He also passed laws to encourage the breeding of bigger horses. He is the first English king to have made definite distinctions between the heavier war- or jousting horse and the lighter blood horse.

---

2. The Laws on Export (23 Henry VIII (1532)) are similar to those of Henry VII and state furthermore that it was a felony to 'sell, exchange, convey or deliver unto any Scottish man within this realm of England or Wales, the town of Berwick or the Marches of the same with intent to be conveyed into Scotland, any horse, gelding or mare.' This shows the English king's concern to protect the Border.

Henry's agents were sent forth far and wide to scour Europe for the very finest stallions to be brought home and crossed with the best of the existing English mares, which by this time were at least of part-imported if not wholly imported blood. With importations of quality horses from Spain and Italy arriving in a fairly constant stream and new legislation encouraging a national breeding programme, the situation in England began to improve out of all recognition.

The King's energetic efforts were well rewarded. J. P. Hore writes in the *History of Newmarket and Annals of the Turf* in 1885 that 'in the spring of the year 1514, Giovanni Ratto was sent by the Marquis of Mantua with a present of Thoroughbred horses to Henry VIII,' which implies either Spanish or Barb or a mixture of both. Ratto also informed Henry that the Marquis had a stud of 'Barbary mares' and of 'Ginetes' and also of 'great mares' which he offered to the King.

Mr Hubert Reade, who wrote *Sidelights of the Thirty Years' War*, discovered in his intensive researches among the royal archives of Turin and Mantua, that there was a very active trade in hot-blood horses between Mantua and the royal stud in England, and one of the stud farms which is mentioned as a main supplier to Henry VIII belonged to the Duchess Catherine, daughter of Philip II of Spain, and wife of the Duke of Savoy. As a kinsman of the King of Spain, the Duke was able to procure stallions direct from the royal Cordoba stud, home of the famous Andalusian *genets*. According to Mr Reade, 'of this privilege he made ample use'.

There is also on record a conversation which took place between Henry VIII and Ratto, during which the Spanish Queen Katherine was present. A bright bay Mantuan Thoroughbred was led forward for the King to admire and was put through his paces in 'the Spanish fashion', which would again indicate a horse from the Peninsula.

In 1515, Henry received a gift of two pure-bred Spanish Barbs from the stable of Ferdinand of Aragon, and in 1519 he sent forth one of his agents, Sir Gregory de Cassalis, to buy the best horses procurable in Spain and in Italy. In 1539, the King, ever open to gifts of flattery, received a present of twenty-five of the finest Spanish horses directly from Emperor Charles V of Spain, and throughout this period of royal acquisition, Henry continued unremittingly to promote and build up his prized stock.

Carefully organised and maintained studs were set up not only near London at Hampton Court, but when this began to overflow, the cream of the King's imported stock was sent to Cole Park at Malmesbury in Wiltshire, to Tutbury in Staffordshire and to Ripon in Yorkshire. Of these three principal studs, Tutbury developed into the most important, but there were several others scattered throughout the country, wherever Henry deemed the land was sufficiently suitable to graze his precious mares. It can therefore be said that Henry VIII paved the way for today's superbreed of Thoroughbred. The progeny of his imported coursers were to constitute the foundation lines for the Royal Mares[3], destined to be served by oriental stallions a century and a half later, making England the home of the finest racing horse in history.

---

3. From this point in our text the term 'royal mares' will be allotted capital letters to indicate the foundation lines for Thoroughbred racing stock as opposed to any royal mares of any royal stud, or the earlier royal mares which were not necessarily connected with racing.

Elizabeth I and Her Master of the Horse

The Queen's delight in worldly pleasures cannot be compared to her father Henry's. When it came to horses, however, she allowed herself a little indulgence. She must have seen the wisdom of breeding a lighter strain of horse, although her principal aim was to improve the horse of England's cavalry.[4] She obviously enjoyed becoming a patron of the turf and set up a notable racing establishment at Greenwich for the blood horses she had inherited from her father.

The Earl of Leicester was Master of the Horse to Elizabeth from 1558 to his death thirty years later (the longest tenure of any holder of this noble office until the late Duke of Beaufort in the present century) and again, England gained from having such an enthusiastic supporter of the turf and of the blood that went with it. Leicester tried very hard to import the famous Iberian Jennets, but he was often thwarted by the Queen, who did not encourage overtures with Spain. There is one amusing incident when Leicester tried to buy twelve Spanish Jennets but could offer only dogs in exchange and his exasperated envoy in Aragon had at length to report that the deal was a non-starter. But despite these material difficulties, Leicester did succeed in bringing much Spanish and Barb blood into the royal stables and continued breeding with the now well-established 'English' bloodstock mares resulting in a further increase of quality horses as first initiated by Henry VIII.

At the same time, Leicester was interested in the art of the manège and he arranged for some of the best known exponents from Italy to come to London and teach at court. One of these was Prospero d'Osma,[5] a Neapolitan, not only well versed in the noble art of equitation but also an authority on stud management and breeding. D'Osma was taken into the service of the Queen and was appointed by Leicester to make a detailed report on the royal studs.

The Royal Mares

D'Osma's report, which has only turned up in recent times, is an invaluable contribution to our understanding of the early bloodlines of the Thoroughbred racehorse. Until its discovery, the term 'Royal Mares' was a nebulous description and rated no more than a paragraph or two in the first edition of Mr Weatherby's *General Stud Book* in 1791. They are in fact erroneously referred to as having been imported by Charles II. Now, thanks to Mr Alfred B. Maclay of New York, who purchased the report in 1927 through Sotheby's in London and generously supplied an admirable translation[6] from the original Italian, a faithful description of the royal studs of Malmesbury and Tutbury is now accessible to the general reader.

Prospero's report takes up 117 leaves and was bound by the Earl of Leicester for his own library. The front cover bears the cognisance of the bear and ragged

4. In 1580 Queen Elizabeth I sent forth a *Proclamation for Horsemen and Breeding of Horses for Service*. This chided her lord lieutenants and sheriffs for not enforcing the 'most necessary and profitable laws provided for the breed and encrease of horses.'
5. Prospero d'Osma had been a pupil of the Neapolitan School, working closely with Giovanni Pignatelli.
6. Translation from the original Italian by Mr Charles B. Lombardo A.M. of Columbia University, U.S.A.

Tutbury Castle, Staffordshire housed one of the great early royal studs. It was divided into paddocks, named Castlehay, The Trenches, Stockley, Rolleston, Little Parke and Obholme.

staff of that great English family. The report is entitled *Explanation and Account of My Sojourn at the Stud of Malmesbury and then of Tutbury by Prospero d'Osma* and is dated 1576. It is dedicated to Leicester thus: 'Grand Master to Her Majesty, always my revered Master.' The report gives a detailed list of all the Royal Mares at these two great studs, as well as discussing and advising on general conditions and husbandry at the studs. Much of the guidance offered would be as applicable to breeders today as it was in 1576 and the whole study makes fascinating reading. For example, 'Soundness should originate in the body of the dam. When a foal, within its dam's body, is reared on damp grass which grows in such soil that wherever the mare puts her foot mire will rise and mix with the food, both the mare and the foal will become sluggish and heavy.' Prospero appears to have a thorough knowledge of the best feeding methods, and the veterinary notes are also very interesting.

What makes the appearance of this document in the twentieth century so exciting is the positive proof that there were Royal Mares of England, contrary to popular public opinion, long before Charles II's reign and we now have written evidence of their exact type, colour and markings, as well as the recommended stallion for each mare.

For the purpose of demonstrating to the reader the strong influence exerted by Spanish blood, a number of these lists of mares are reproduced as an Appendix to this book and it will be seen that a large proportion of the animals listed are none other than the Spanish Jennet. At the same time, it is likely that the courser blood mentioned may also include Spanish and Barb blood, as without doubt these will have come from Italy where, as already discussed, there was a preponderance of the best Andalusian blood from the court of Cordoba.

The Tudor period may therefore be looked upon as the early foundation period of breeding in this country. The work of Henry VIII and his daughter Queen Elizabeth I should never be underestimated and it was a natural consequence of their desire for better quality home-bred horses that led to the Stuart era being remembered for the rise of the turf as well as the consolidation period of breeding.

The Establishment of Newmarket

James I is not looked upon with great affection by the British people, but it is to him we must attribute the permanent establishment of Newmarket as the chief racing centre of England. Ironically enough, James really preferred hawking and hunting to racing, and his comfortable house at Newmarket was originally built to accommodate his horses and hounds. The land around he turned into a magnificent game reserve and hares were reared in their thousands (which still abound in this part of Cambridgeshire today) to provide sport for his hunting, shooting and hawking.

James had first patronised racing in Scotland and after he acceded to the English throne, he sponsored racing at Croydon and Enfield in the suburbs of London, which brought the city folk into the countryside and gave them a taste for field sports. This was later to explode into a passion in the hearts of the people in the care-free days following the Restoration. During James' reign, race meetings were established at Salisbury, Huntingdon, Doncaster and Carlisle.

The Great Duke of Buckingham

History again paid bloodstock a handsome favour in the form of another fanatic for quality animals. George Villiers, Duke of Buckingham, may not have been king of England, but he shared Henry VIII's sense of occasion and surrounded himself with magnificent horseflesh. Buckingham made himself indispensible to the King and very soon rose to the position of court favourite, becoming affectionately known by his patron as 'Steenie' from whence he was able to indulge in his favourite pastime of breeding and racing with as much licence as though he were the monarch himself.

During England's flirtation with Spain over the proposed marriage of Prince Charles, James I's second son, later to become Prince of Wales, with the Spanish Infanta, Buckingham played a game of great diplomatic skill and succeeded in bringing out of Spain some of the finest horses of the royal stud of Cordoba. C.M. Prior in his book, *The Royal Studs of the 16th and 17th Centuries*, puts so much importance on these transactions that he remarks:

> 'The event, however, which was destined to affect the future history of our Thoroughbred race, more than any other, was the projected marriage between Charles, Prince of Wales, and the Infanta of Spain, with the

result that a large number of the highest bred horses in Spain, then *the best in the world*, were sent to this country as presents from the court of Madrid.'

History records how the proposed marriage was not popular with either the British public or indeed the Spanish people, and eventually the negotiations fell through. However, even when it was decided that the Prince Charles and Buckingham should leave Spain, once all idea of a royal match had been aborted, Buckingham was able, as only a true entrepreneur may, to inveigle out of the King of Spain a parting present for the English crown of twenty-four pure-bred horses, together with brood mares and a number of foals. At the same time, he was also able to achieve for himself a 'dainty present of Horses already made, and Coults of the Breed of Cordova'.

There is a story that James I first spotted Buckingham on the course at Newmarket, and such was the charm and ability of this son of an impoverished Leicestershire knight, that he was quickly elevated in 1616 to the prestigious position of Master of the Horse. In 1619, already one of the most powerful men in the land, he became Lord High Admiral. These two offices gave him *carte blanche* in his horse dealings, which seem to have greatly preoccupied him. There are many amusing letters in existence, such as one from the naval commander Sir Richard Bingley, who was ordered against his will to remain in port at Santander until he had received a consignment of an important horse from Lord Bristol, the British Ambassador in Madrid. He comments in an injured tone, 'My respect to the honour of the King's ships makes me sorry to have them used for the transporters of beasts.'

In another consignment, Buckingham himself writes to the Commissioner of the Navy making arrangements for the transit of thirty to thirty-five horses which were being shipped from Madrid, 'His Highness having had divers horses presented unto him in this Court, the which are ready to be sent into England, Theis are therefore to desire you that there be a shipp provided, and made ready presently [i.e. instantly] for this service, and be sent unto San Sebastians.'

In a detailed inventory of the Hampton Court Stud made in 1623 (see Appendix) we again find many mentions of the Spanish Jennet and there is reference to those coming 'newly out of Spain'. Even the King himself is moved sufficiently by the excellence of the animals coming from Madrid to urge the Admiralty and their Commissioners to lose no time in getting these large and valuable consignments home to England. 'His Majesty's thanks if it be done, his reproof if it be not done, and his commandment that it be done with all expedition,' were the orders received at the Admiralty.

As well as filling the royal studs of England, many of these imported Spanish Jennets and Barbs were finding their way into private hands. Foreign-bred horses had for more than a century become the fashion of the day and through the auspices of a succession of sympathetic British diplomats in Madrid, such as Sir Francis Cottington and Sir Henry Rich, there appeared an apparently never-ending stream of supply as long as Buckingham remained Master of the Horse up until his murder in 1628. As Prior points out, 'every breeder wanted a Spanish jennet', and Buckingham certainly sent horses from the royal stud to a number of private estates throughout England with the idea that they could be reared to more advantage on certain pastures. Whether Buckingham was playing a double game and lining his own purse with these transactions will never be clear. It is possible he may genuinely have arranged for the horses to be returned to the king at a later date, but it would seem that many Spanish Jennets went out into private hands, which naturally did nothing but good for the future of British breeding.

Following in the footsteps of Buckingham, the Duke of Newcastle, as we already know, puts the Spanish horse before all other breeds but what is interesting is that as well as recommending them for breeding, war, the manège and ambling, he names the following 'running' horses as being Spanish. These were Conqueror, Shotten, Herring, Butler and Peacock. He adds that they 'Beatt all the horses in their Time, so much, as No Horse ever ran near them.' The Duchess of Newcastle in her *Life of the Duke* testifies to her late husband's appreciation of them: 'But of all sorts of horses, my Lord loved Spanish horses and Barbs best; saying that the Spanish horses were like princes, and Barbs like gentlemen in their kind.'

Newcastle himself mated Spanish stallions to English mares and in all probability raised a quality stamp of medium-weight horse, but the general opinion at the time was that crossing imported stock with native-bred horses only succeeded in producing 'bastard horses'. According to Lamb, however, 'he thus helped to lay the foundations of our Thoroughbred stock which was due to the careful selection and rearing of English mares as much as it was to the mating of them with Eastern stallions.' Lamb's statement would more accurately describe the true situation at that time if he had said 'imported English mares'. Undoubtedly, early racing stock in England was imported,[7] and the so-called English mares being crossed with the excellent Spanish, Barb and Italian horses that were so prolifically imported during this period were warm-blood horses, and not as is sometimes suggested cold-blood native strains from the forests and fens.

The Abolition of Race Meetings and the Dispersal of the Royal Studs

Charles I had little real interest in racing, but efforts continued to produce a super-breed of racehorse, particularly at Tutbury. These activities suffered a huge blow after his execution in 1649 when the victorious Cromwellian forces ordered the dispersal of the royal studs. Only six horses, undoubtedly the best – for Cromwell had a good eye for a horse – were retained by Cromwell himself. For the sake of politics this former cavalry officer was obliged to suppress his own deep love of blood horses and his secret zest for the turf. It must have been hard for him to banish his sporting instincts and abolish race meetings, but he and his followers could not afford the risk of mutinous assembly and especially at the courses of Newmarket and Croydon with their royalist connections. So racing meetings were forbidden at every racecourse in the land. Such a ban must have made the sport of racing all the more attractive to the people of England after the Restoration, and Charles II's love of the turf created a huge revival.

---

7. This view is supported by the majority of equine researchers including Colonel Sir Richard Glyn Bt, C.M. Prior and Lady Wentworth of the 20th century, and a host of writers from earlier times, e.g. General Lord Fairfax writing in 1664, Bradly in 1727, Osmer in 1761 and Berenger in 1771.

In many ways, the dispersal of the royal studs under the Cromwellians probably proved of lasting benefit to the country. Regarding the bloodlines of Tutbury, Cromwell expressed the wish 'that the breed be not lost', and perhaps in his strait-laced but philanthropic way he saw more chance of a good future for these lines in smaller, private studs than as the exclusive property of the royal stables and even the state. Whatever his motive, the cream of England's bloodstock was sold off and the progeny thereof dispersed widely throughout the land so that wealthy private breeders now had the chance to carry on the good work of producing horses of immense quality in conditions which may even have proved more suitable than those that had been left behind.

In an inventory of the goods of Charles I, which was discovered in an archive of the House of Lords and which totals twenty-eight pages, not only is there a mention of six horses from the Tutbury Race[8] being allotted to Cromwell to be sent to Hampton Court, but it is recorded that another six horses were presented to Colonel Michael Jones, Commander in Chief in Leinster, as a reward for his services in Ireland on behalf of the government. Hore states that five of these were 'royal stud barbs' and that they were subsequently acquired by the Earl of Thomond, accounting for the latter-day success of the O'Briens on the Irish turf from the strain of blood thus introduced.

One of the most famous Royal Mares to be found in the General Stud Book was Grey Royal, who came from a line of mares by the same name dating back to long before the days of Charles II. The original mare is thought to have been presented to Lord D'Arcy by George Villiers, later Duke of Buckingham, who at that time was importing from Spain.

Contrary to many widely held beliefs, Arabian horses only became sought-after in England around the time of Oliver Cromwell.[9] Apart from the Markham Arabian[10] which was purchased by James I in 1616 and which gives us no clue of its history or how it came into the country, there is only one mention of an Arabian stallion in the inventories of the royal studs between the time of Queen Elizabeth I and Charles II. It was clearly a formidable task procuring horses from Arabia, and even the Lord Protector of England was to discover the near impossibility of importing these rare horses. In 1657 he had set his heart on obtaining a number of Arab horses, as we learn from two letters dated 10th September of that year and sent by the Levant Company to the British Ambassador, Sir Thomas Benyshe, at Constantinople and the Consul at Aleppo. The first commences:

'Upon intimation from his Highnes the Lord Protector of his desire to be accommodated with some good Arabian Horses, as a means to furnish England with a breed of that kind; we have now written to Aleppo . . .

8. In Tudor times the term 'race' in this context meant 'stud'.
9. In Lady Wentworth's book, *The Authentic Arabian Horse*, it is loosely stated that 'Cromwell imported Arabs' – the type of statement which has over the years given an erroneous impression of England's early racing stock. We now know from the historical research of a number of modern writers that Arab horses were extremely rare in this country until the end of the seventeenth century.
10. We first read about this horse in Gervase Markham's book *Markham's Maister-Peece* (published in 1599). The horse had 'travaild from a parte of Arabia called Angelica to Constantinople, and from thence to the highermost partes of Germanie by lande, and so by sea to England.' The Duke of Newcastle describes it as 'a bay but a little Horse and no Rarity for shape, for I have seen Many English Horses far Finer.' The *General Stud Book* describes the Markham Arabian as 'the first of that breed seen in England'.

to supply us with two of that sort if it may be; and we likewise propose the same to your Lordship namely to procure two others at Constantinople and cause them to be sent to England . . .'

The second runs in similar vein:

'His Hignes upon our late address to him hath expressed a desire to be, by our meanes, furnished with certain Arabian horses which we have promised our endeavours to procure; and because we conceive there may be of that sort there at Aleppo, We pray you to make enquiry; and if possibly you can procure two that are good . . . let them in the best way you can contrive be sent into England unto us.'

At an earlier date, Cromwell's agents had been successful in buying Italian horses at Naples, and a letter from Longland, dated 18th June 1655, who was in diplomatic service at Leghorn, warned him of the difficulty of buying an Arab mare, which he had obviously asked for at the same time:

'I gave order to the man I sent over to Tripoli . . . to bring a mare thence, which he did; but t'was so small a thing, genteel and thin . . . that I thought it not worth your acceptance; for a good mare to breed should be as well tall and large, as cleanlimbed and handsome. I know not yet whether I shall speed in the commission I gave to Aleppo for a horse; but if I do, I am confident, the world has not better horses than that place affords."

Eventually, it appears that having ordered four Arab horses in 1657, only one was obtained and shipped home to England on board the *Dartmouth* in the same year. Almost a decade later, the problem seems as acute as ever. In letters from Lord Winchilsea, who became Ambassador in Turkey on the accession of Charles II, sent to the Earl of Northumberland we read:

'Since your Excellency departed, I have not been able to buy one good horse, they are all either at the Court or going for Candia. I intend to try for some of the Turcoman breed, for I despair of getting any Arabs from Aleppo, where my correspondent cannot even procure any for the King.'

As Prior points out in his extensive historical researches into the ancestors of the Thoroughbred, 'Hitherto, [i.e. up until the time of Cromwell] the importation of horses had been mainly confined to Barbs and Jennets, and an Arabian was almost unknown in this country.'

Cromwell was to die in 1658, just a year after his only Arab horse arrived in this country, and although one school of thought might blame him for breaking up and destroying the most famous of England's studs in his contempt for the system of monarchy, another school would thank him for what he did.

Thus, through the ambitions of powerful men – a monarch's desire for magnificence, two noblemen's passion for excellence in blood, and a determined parliamentarian's radical ideals – we find that the scene is set in England for the next step in the advent of the Thoroughbred racehorse: the introduction of oriental blood to cement all the unstinting preparatory work for the new horse which was to emerge and be enjoyed today.

Resolving a Myth

Charles II won for himself the title of Father of the British Turf, a name which is well deserved for he adored his racing and was the only monarch of England ever to ride in flat races. He patronised all the great racecourses of the south and encouraged his followers to do the same. One of the famous races with which he is linked is the Newmarket Town Plate, which he founded in 1665.

What is completely erroneous is the idea that the Royal Mares, progenitors on the female side of the Thoroughbred, only appeared in Britain during his reign.

Regrettably, this misinformation came about from an inaccurate entry in the introductory volume of the *General Stud Book* published in 1791, which, apparently unsubstantiated, was copied again and again into successive volumes and remained unchanged until 1891.

It is plain from the original entry that Mr Weatherby had not researched beyond the reign of Charles II and the subject of the Royal Mares is written off in one cursory paragraph which reads:

> 'ROYAL MARES – King Charles the Second sent abroad the Master
> of the Horse to procure a number of foreign horses and mares for breed-
> ing, and the mares brought over by him [as also many of their produce]
> have since been called the Royal Mares.'

It is possible that at that time Mr Weatherby had no records at his disposal which would afford him the opportunity to trace back further; certainly it is unlikely that he would have had the benefit of Prospero d'Osma's recently discovered report. It was not until 1886 that long overdue research into the foundation stock of the Royal Mares was undertaken, and in his *Annals of the Turf*, J.P. Hore tracked down and made an inventory of the Tutbury bloodstock existing up until the time of Charles I, which threw a very different light on the subject and left Mr Weatherby's original statement looking more than inadequate.

Regrettably, even this wealth of information, which listed 140 animals, is obscured in the revised version of the *General Stud Book* of 1891 which proffers again no more than one misleading paragraph on the whole subject. How, then, was the general racing public ever to know that the Royal Mares had been established in Great Britain long before Charles II ever came to the throne?

Fortunately, today we have sufficient documents and specialised books on the subject at our disposal to enlighten us. As C.M. Prior points out in his book which covers the subject in minute detail,

> 'From the several lists of the royal studs covering the period from 1576
> to 1649 . . . it will be seen that there was already a considerable stock
> of 'foreign-bred' horses and mares in this country at the time of the Res-
> toration (1660), thus Charles II had no necessity to send abroad for them
> as stated [in the early edition of the Stud Book] and in fact did not do
> so.'

From the D'Arcy family papers we note that Charles II, on his return in May 1660 from exile on the Continent for nine years, made an immediate attempt to resuscitate the dispersed Tutbury Stud and for this task he appointed James D'Arcy as Master of the Royal Stud. Sadly, the estate of Tutbury was so despoiled that it was never restored as the home of royal bloodstock. Charles II was, however, more fortunate in retracing the cream of his father's breeding stock. The 'seven horses of Oliver Cromwell, said to be the best in England' were immediately seized for the crown, and many of the horses which had gone to private studs in the north of the country were happily put at the disposal of the King. Many of these were at Buckingham's estate at Helmsley, which had been given to General Fairfax. He presented one of the horses to Charles II at his coronation, and later Helmsley with all its horses was given as a wedding present to the second Duke of Buckingham, who became Charles II's second Master of the Horse. In the words of M.M. Reese in his book *The Royal Office of Master of the Horse*,

> 'It is not true that Charles restored the English breed by costly purchase from abroad. He did indeed import when it was practicable . . . but the horses he was looking for were not far to seek. In this way the crown regained access to the magnificent stud that Buckingham had created.'

On the subject of breeding, whilst it is generally accepted that Charles II's real passion was the sport of racing itself, we do hear of divers importations of unknown, untried foreign horses. One of these was a gift from the Moroccan Ambassador in 1681 of six 'most beautiful Barbary horses' which the King raced at Newmarket. Another was a group of Turkish and probably Arab mares which were incorporated into the royal stables under the very natural heading of the 'King's mares'. Unfortunately, no inventory or pedigree exists for these animals and whilst some enthusiasts have suggested that these alone constituted the famous Royal Mares this is clearly inaccurate. Probably of more consequence, although again we cannot be certain, were the Portuguese and Barb mares which arrived in England as part of the royal dowry of Catherine of Braganza. The Portuguese still refer to these as the Royal Mares and it is very likely that all these importations played their part in what was to follow.

What has become crystal clear from all the evidence which has recently come to light in the past 150 years, is that the real foundation line lay in those existing Royal Mares whose antecedents' arrival in this country was so zealously planned long before Charles II was even born.

Thus, only in recent times have we been able to grasp the full situation and appreciate that credit is owed to an earlier generation of Englishmen than has ever fully been acknowledged before, and that the first strains of 'blood' in England were largely dominated by Iberian genes. In the words of His Excellency, Senor Dom Ramon Perez de Ayala, Spanish Ambassador to Britain in the 1930s, in an account entitled 'Horses imported into England from Spain in 1623 and the Following Years', we may conclude this clarification of the true meaning of the words Royal Mares: '. . . and doubtless it was the descendants of the "Royal Mares" as they called those imported from Spain, i.e. the Valenzuela [Andalusian] breed, who were one of the principal elements, if not the predominating one, in the actual pure blood.'

Philip III of Spain by Velasquez, Prado Museum, Madrid. The horse portrayed is typical of those which were shipped into England during the seventeenth century.

Philip IV of Spain by Velasquez, Prado Museum, Madrid. During the reign of this king, extensive exportations of Spanish horses were made to England.

Enter the Orientals

Our libraries abound in many excellent books about the foundation stallions from whence descend, without exception, all our modern-day Thoroughbred horses, spread as they are throughout the entire world. These are the Byerley Turk, the Darley Arabian and the Godolphin Barb, and from these sprang the lines of Herod (1758), Eclipse (1764) and Matchem (1748).

One point which must be stressed here, for it is not generally understood, is that in addition to the large preponderance of Iberian blood within the female line of those early progenitors, through the Barb connection (see Chapter III) there was undoubtedly a modicum of Iberian blood in the male line.

The majority of the foundation sires were oriental or quasi-oriental, but the information on the antecedents of these is obscure. The terms 'Arabian', 'Turk' and 'Barb' were used in the very loosest of ways, and in the early eighteenth century the feasibility of bringing horses back from as far afield as Aleppo was fraught with difficulties. Turks, however, were somewhat easier to procure and had been imported into England since 1580, after Turkey decided to make peaceful contact with certain Christian countries (after centuries of warring) and trade was permitted with Britain.

On the other hand, many of the Turks we read about in the seventeenth century were in fact Arabs which had been brought back to Turkey as spoils of war. These were shipped to England from Constantinople, whereas Arabians straight out of the desert came via Aleppo. As well as the famous Darley Arabian, another important pure-bred Arabian to leave Aleppo in the early part of the century was Lord Oxford's Dun Arabian, in 1715, and the Bloody Shouldered Arabian in 1719/20. The Pagett Arabian, which was extensively used at the Welbeck Stud, was sent by Lord Pagett to the Duke of Newcastle as early as 1703.

I am paying the pure-bred Arabian horse no disservice when I draw attention to the fact that until two hundred years ago the term 'Arabian' was used by many writers to provide an umbrella for any horse of oriental origin, but certainly those pure-bred Arabs which survived the obstacles put forward to prevent them leaving their own country, were to contribute greatly to the transformation of the blood horse. As Lady Wentworth points out in *The Authentic Arabian Horse*, 'the Arabian was imported to get speed and the subsequent abnormal Thoroughbred speed has been developed by centuries of specialisation and forcing from selected stock as emphasised by Darwin.' To this should be added that speed was also obtained from the Turk and Persian horse and there are still those who claim the ancient sprinting Galloway blood may have played a part in the female line, though this is unlikely. The initial thrust and impulsion which gives meaning to the ability to sprint or to sustain speed should be ascribed wholeheartedly to Iberian blood.

The Male Foundation Line of the Modern Thoroughbred

Even today there is still some confusion on the subject of the three most famous foundation sires.

The Byerley Turk would seem to be correctly named. Although an early English source calls this horse the 'Arab' charger of Captain Robert Byerley, who rode him at the Battle of the Boyne in 1690, a Continental source goes back further and states that the horse was captured from the Turks at the Siege of Vienna in 1689 by a Dutch officer who sold him to Byerley for 100 gulden.

Most authorities now agree that the originally named Godolphin Arabian, now known as the Godolphin Barb, was indeed a Berber from Morocco. He was brought into Lord Godolphin's stud around 1730, originally as a teaser, and the resulting foal from his first mare, Roxana, was Cade who formed the famous Matchem line.

The Darley Arabian was more accurately named, having been sent direct from Aleppo in 1704 and certified an Arabian of the best Maneghi blood. He was a present given by Thomas Darley to his father Richard, of Aldby Park in Yorkshire where he remained throughout his career.

'They are Bred out of All the Horses of All Nations'

Whilst buttressed with the blood of many other strains, it was the blending of the blood of these three great stallions with a wonderful legacy of quality on the female side, that brought the modern Thoroughbred to his present state of excellence.

The Duke of Hamilton's 'Disguise' with Jockey Up, signed G. Garrard (A.R.A.), 1786. This canvas portrays the Thoroughbred with head, crest and shoulder still reminiscent of old Iberian blood, but the body is more elongated and the set of the tail shows the distinct oriental influence. (Courtesy of Arthur Ackermann & Son Ltd)

The second edition of *The Horsebreeder's Handbook* lists the following horses as Eastern sires: 90 Arabian, 46 Berber, 32 Turk, and 4 Persian sires. In the same book, Osborne goes on to remark:

> 'There can be little doubt, despite all that has been and still is written upon the subject of 'Arab' blood in our English Thoroughbred, that at the best very vague notions exist as to the distinctions of breed in the oriental sources . . . the distinguishing names, Arab, Barb and Turk are found in sufficient proportions as to nullify any special or singular claims.'

Colonel Ironside in 1800 describes the English Thoroughbred as being of Barb or Arab blood 'mixed with the breeds of every other country,' but perhaps our old friend, The Duke of Newcastle, sums up the English horse in the wisest manner of all:

> '. . . and some as Beautiful Horses as can be had anywhere, for they are bred out of all the Horses of All Nations.'

Truer words were probably never uttered, and taking a bird's eye view of the whole history of the English racehorse from its less-famed beginnings to the much celebrated present day, lovers of the Iberian horse may be proud that this breed also contributed significantly to that whole miracle of breeding.

CHAPTER XIV

British Breeds with Iberian Influence

...a horse is a thing of such beauty...
none will tire of looking at him
as long as he displays himself in his splendour.

XENOPHON

Britain's Rich Heritage

Britain has always been far richer in horses of blood than many people realise. This happy state dates back, as we have seen, to the Norman and Plantagenet kings and earlier. If we dismiss the importations of Iberian and Barb blood during Roman times as too remote, we should not forget the trading activities (started by the Phoenicians and advanced by the Brigantes) perpetuated by the seafaring people of south-east Ireland and the south-east and north-west of England throughout Saxon times, which went on well into the Middle Ages. (See Chapter IV.) Neither should we forget the adventurous spirit of the British throughout history. Those of us who travel today tend to think ourselves unique in our ability to jet from country to country. It is easy to forget the indomitability of those warring princes and crusading knights as they set off to Europe or the east not once or twice in a lifetime but on many separate occasions and expeditions.

John of Gaunt, for example, went to and from the Savoy, his palace in London, to Castile in Spain with all the apparent ease of a twentieth century executive on international company business. Horses then had to serve as plane, car, taxi, train and tank rolled into one, and it is scarcely surprising that on these trips, the best from abroad were procured and brought home.

We shall never come near to knowing how many Iberian horses were brought into Britain throughout these numerous expeditions. What we do know is that the Spanish horse was at the top end of the world market, and every British traveller of means would have tried to acquire one in his sojourn on the Continent. In this book, we have pinpointed as many of the known, recorded cases as possible but these would only have been the tip of the iceberg, and it is almost certain that every one of our saddle breeds would at one stage or another have received an influential infusion of Spanish blood.

At the same time, it is highly improbable that breeds developed for heavy draught work on the land, would have been crossed with Iberian blood as this would have adversely lightened their legs, which were required to be thick and stocky. It has been suggested that because many large draught horses are Roman-nosed, there may have been an Iberian ancestor at one time or another. This is unlikely. Although the convex-shaped head is shared by a number of breeds, there the resemblance ends. The muzzle of the draught horse is coarse and fleshy, whilst that of the Iberian is long and finely tapering and the throatlatch is clean. The forehead of the draught horse is flat and he is fleshy round the eyes which tend to look angular; the forehead of the Iberian horse is wide and rounded and his eyes are oval in shape.

Our story of the British breeds known to have descended from the Iberian horse begins in Yorkshire, which was renowned even in Saxon times for producing excellent horses – no doubt an inheritance from the days of the Roman legions stationed there. A sixteenth-century document from the Chapter House books of Jervaulx Abbey lists over 250 horses requisitioned there from the tenants of the Jervaulx estates which include, as well as trotters, amblers and pacers which were almost certainly of part-Iberian blood. Daniel Defoe's *Tour through England and Wales* relating to the year 1722 also refers to the excellence of the Yorkshire horse on several occasions.

The Cleveland Bay

No one is more knowledgeable about the history of the Cleveland Bay horse than Anthony Dent, writer and historian extraordinaire, whose letters and advice have been most helpful in compiling this book, as has his excellent book, *Cleveland Bay Horses*, published in 1978.

In simple terms Cleveland as it affects the story of the Cleveland Bay horse constitutes the eastern half of what was the North Riding of Yorkshire, and has always been closely linked with Whitby Strand. Cleveland and Whitby Strand formed the centre of a particular region which had for many generations been renowned for an excellent, sturdy breed of pack-horse which, in those days, was basically the only means of transport overland.

To cut a long story short, it was the Chapman horse which provided the cold-blood element for the future Cleveland Bay Horse, and the Andalusian and Barb which made up the hot-blood element. We have already seen how the royal favourite of James I, that powerful Master of the Horse, the Duke of Buckingham, cultivated an alliance with Spain which enabled him to bring into England so many of the best Iberian horses, particularly from the royal stud at Cordoba. After his marriage, a number of these stallions found their way to the Helmsley estate of his wife, Lady Katherine Manners who was the only daughter of the rich Earl of Rutland. Here, Buckingham was able to set himself up as a notable breeder with the acquisition of this beautiful estate, and as well as all his other dealings in the south, a superb strain of racehorse was bred at Helmsley with a steady infusion of imported Spanish blood.

It is only natural that local breeders should take their mares to the fine stallions which were available for service. The strict royal monopoly was a thing of the past, and according to Mr Dent, 'Buckingham freely dispensed the favours of his master's stallions. For love when flush, for money when broke.'

Mr Dent goes on to extol the obvious virtues of the Andalusian horse of that time which, he says,

'We can see painted as the throne of royal models for equestrian portraits scores of times over – by Velasquez in Spain, Van Dyck in England, by the Clouets in France. It was the only European hot-blood, short-coupled, with a superb outlook, around 15 h.h., very massive powerful sloping croup and superbly arched neck . . . We should not equate it exactly with the Andalusian of today, which has been much Arabised since about 1900, but it had the teachability and handiness still typical of the breed – a handiness dearly bought in training for, and practice of, the mounted combat (rather than hunting) with wild boars and half-wild bulls that was the supreme test of virility for Spanish hidalgos . . . The Andalusian came in all colours, including palomino, but the most frequent were black and bay and of them all the bay was most esteemed.'

As well as passing on the predominant bay colour, the Iberian horses used to service the Chapman pack-horse mares, also passed on the dominant gene for a slightly sub-convex face, and to this day the Cleveland Bay has a tendency towards this profile.

When Buckingham's fine stallions fell into Republican hands during the Civil War of the 1640s, another importation of Spanish horses had arrived in Cleveland, this time brought in by Sir Hugh Cholmley of Whitby, famous for his stubborn defence of Scarborough Castle, who returned from exile rather too soon and spent several years of Cromwell's rule in prison. His horses, too, together with his sequestrated estates fell into Republican hands. Fortunately, however, the pattern was repeated throughout the region. Even larger numbers of Andalusian stallions – now required for little else – became available to any owner of a Chapman mare. On the Barb side, again the aristocratic families were active in bringing these horses into the country during Elizabeth I's reign. The Cholmley family certainly boasted a Barb at Whitby Manor which could be used with a native mare to produce a 'Barbary' mare. More Barbs and more Iberian horses arrived in Yorkshire through Whitby after the Restoration when Charles II married Catherine of Braganza, and her father, the King of Portugal, gave as part of her dowry the port of Tangier in Barbary. Whitby ships carried out great quantities of supplies for the garrison, and it is certain that horses came back to make up part of the ballast. This gave Cleveland breeders the opportunity to buy Portuguese and Barb horses directly from the North African coast, and in this way, long before the Thoroughbred was finally fixed as a race, it seems – according to Mr Dent – that 'this Andalusian/Barb/Chapman amalgam had solidified' and the Cleveland Bay was firmly fixed as a breed.

The Cleveland Bay really came into his own during the reign of George II when it had no peer as a coach horse. The Yorkshire Coach Horse, another great driving breed was descended from him, and many people were unable to tell the two breeds apart. Many of these are to be found in the pedigrees of Continental coaching breeds such as in the Oldenburg Stud Book. As Elector of Hanover, as well as being King of England, George II exported Cleveland Bay stallions to the Electoral Stud at Celle in Hanover for his big German carriage lines.

Although the breeding of Cleveland Bay horses went into a sharp decline at the end of both World Wars, many people still associate the name with the Royal Mews and King George V owned twenty-six horses and mares registered in the Cleveland Bay Stud Book. Today, they are still popular with our Royal Family

H.R.H. The Duke of Edinburgh's team of Cleveland Bays at Sandringham Driving Trials 1985. The long faces and superb hock action of these horses are inherited from their Iberian forebears. (Photo by Brian Fisher)

as driving horses. As this sport becomes more and more attractive to the general public, it is certain that the Cleveland will come into his own again as king of the harness breeds as well as being a superb riding horse.

Even 360 years on from Buckingham's first introduction of Spanish horses to Yorkshire, the Cleveland Bays of today still retain many of the ancient Iberian characteristics. There is a marked similarity in fact to the Alter Real horse of the old Portuguese royal stud. Short-coupled and strong, with powerful neck, high wither and a tendency to the sub-convex profile, the Cleveland Bay is altogether bigger, longer and of greater bone than his Latin cousin, but he has inherited the same handiness and courage, and those who own him swear that he is the finest all-round horse that is native to England today.

The Welsh Cob

In delving back into the history of the Welsh pony and that magnificent native animal, the Welsh Cob, we again cannot ignore the Roman influence. There is a Roman road from Chester which passes Lake Bala in which locality the Romans are said to have founded a stud to breed pack-ponies. We also know that when the Romans withdrew from Britain during the fourth and fifth centuries, King Cunedda of the Votadini[1] (whose country encompassed modern Northumberland)

---

1. The Votadini were an early British tribe. The name came from the days when their ancestors, also known as the Votadini, were requisitioned by the Romans to protect the Hadrian Line. Other British tribes living to the north and south of the line were known by similar Latin names: Vocontii, Sarmati, Petriana, Pannoni, etc.

led his people southwards and westwards, driving out the Irish invaders who had slain many of the tribes of north Wales. The ancient bard, Taliensin, sang of this king, 'He would freely distribute war-horses in winter', thus helping the local people who needed protection. This would indicate that a horse of warm, if not hot, blood was introduced to Wales and would most certainly have found its origins in the Spanish or the Barb horse brought in by the Romans.

The Welsh Stud Book makes reference to the Romans crossing the ponies of the Welsh Mountains with the Arab, but in fact during the period of the Roman occupation of Britain, the Arab – as we know it today – did not exist, and, as we have seen, the term normally indicated a hot-blood horse from Persia, Libya, Syria, the Barbary Coast or the Iberian Peninsula. Taking into account all that we have learned so far about the passage of horses from Spain and Portugal into Roman Britain, it would seem practically conclusive that these imported horses were Iberian or Asturian.

In the reign of Edward II (1307–1327), the Earl of Shrewsbury began to cross Welsh ponies with imported Iberian stallions sent to his estate of Powysland in the centre of Wales, just south of Lake Bala. We hear of:

> 'most excellent studs put apart for breeding, and deriving their origin from some fine Spanish horses, which Robert de Belesme, Count of Shrewsbury, brought into this country; on which account the horses from hence are remarkable for their majestic proportion and astonishing fleetness.'

The progeny of this combination was to produce the Powys Horse or Powys Cob, highly thought of at the time and probably not so very different from the Welsh Cob of today.

Therefore, although the resilience, hardiness and pluck of the indigenous Welsh pony has continued into today's Welsh native breeds, the cob-like characteristics of the Powys Horse have not died out, adding the powerful hock action, strong shoulder and neck, and hard bone of the Iberian horse. From this came the splendid combination of the 'old blood' which is talked about with so much reverence in the early stud books of the Welsh Cob.

The Irish Draught and the Connemara Pony

Ireland has always been singularly independent from the rest of Britain in the breeding of horses. Only in the middle of the eighteenth century when breeding of the Irish Thoroughbred began to run on parallel lines to English Thoroughbred breeding (whilst still tracing itself back to a very different lineage from our own), did the two countries appear to come close in their methods. In the very early years of Irish horse breeding, we have seen how the Celtic tribes round County Wexford and Waterford imported horses from Northern Spain. This trend was to increase from the sixth century onwards when Ireland was regularly in direct touch with the Continent, exporting her wool, hide and fat to Spain, and in return importing oil, wine and horses.

At the beginning of this century, three fossil skulls of horses were discovered in a primitive lakeside dwelling near Dublin, and these showed features of the

Libyan/Barb/Iberian type horse which has led historians to be convinced of this strong foreign influence which may even have dated back before the Celts.

By the early Middle Ages, the popular saddle horse in Ireland was the Irish Hobby, which we discussed in Chapter I. Easily trained to amble they were favoured by ladies at court, for up until the time of Elizabeth I there were no stirrups on sidesaddles. In Chaucer's day, we learn that the ambling palfrey cost more than double a trotting hakenay (sic): 61 shillings against 24; and the majority of these would have been sent to England from Ireland, who in turn exported them to France.

In 1565, Blundeville, who has given us such a faithful account of the different breeds of horse in the sixteenth century, has this to say of the Irish horse:

> 'The Iryshe Hobby is a pretty fine horse, havening a good heart, and a body indifferently well proporcioned, saving that many of them be slender, thin-buttocked, they be tendermouthed, nimble, light, pleasant and apt to be taught and for the most part they be amblers and therefore very meet for the saddle and to travel by the way, yea and the Iryshe men both with darts and light spears do use to skirmish with them in the field. And many of them prove to that use very well, by means they be so light and swift.'

Readers will recognise so many features of the Spanish horse in this description, particularly in temperament and suitability for the battlefield, that there is little doubt from whence came the ancestors of these horses.

History records that Anne of Denmark, the wife of James I, sent six of these 'hobbies' to the court of King Louis XIII of France. Again, the genes of the Spanish horse would appear remarkably dominant, for although these palfreys eventually went out of fashion around the time of Charles II, it is still possible to purchase just such a palfrey or hobby horse in the north of Spain and Portugal today, which may be part-bred Iberian crossed with a Garrano or Asturian.

After the Norman invasion of Ireland, heavier horses of Flemish and Dutch origin began to be imported into Ireland and concentrated crossing over the centuries that followed brought about changes that would eventually deprive Ireland of this type.

Even as late, however, as 1771, Richard Berenger, Gentleman of the Horse to King George II, writes: 'Ireland has for many centuries boasted a race of horses called Hobbies, valued for their easy paces and other pleasing and agreeable qualities of middling size, strong, nimble, well-moulded and hardy.' Meanwhile, an earlier writer, Edmund Campion in a *Historie of Ireland* talks of the same horses:

> '. . . of pace easie, of running wonderfull swift . . . This broode [breed] Rafael Volateranus sais to have come first from Asturia, the country of Spain between Galicia and Portugal, whereof they were called Asturcones, a name now properly applied to the Spanish Jennet.'

Our only consolation for the disappearance of these famous ambling palfreys of Ireland lies in the fact that the Irish Draught is probably the direct descendant of the crossing, which took place from the Norman Conquest of 1172 onwards, with the heavy Dutch and Flemish breeds. Again the characteristics of clean limbs,

Countess IX, champion Connemara mare, owned by Miss Anne Hammond. Although today's Connemara has generally lost the old-fashioned head of its Iberian ancestor it still retains the powerful chest and shoulder and highly crested neck as well as the superb temperament. (Photo by Nigel Bloxham)

hard bone, and powerful hock action are reminiscent of the Iberian type, as well as a tendency to a slight convexity of the face.

The earliest direct reference to the Connemara pony would appear to come from the French chronicler, Creton, who accompanied King Richard II on an expedition to the western shores of Ireland in 1399. He describes them thus: 'they scout the hills and valleys fleeter than deer.'

Throughout early Irish history we read that the Irish warriors despised armour and rode their handy horses into battle bareback and often with merely a halter and a crooked stick to guide their mounts. In the *Historie du Roy Richard d'Angleterre*, by the Bishop of St Asaph, we hear of Arthur McMorough, King of Leinster, dashing down the mountainside to do battle with the Earl of Gloucester on a

> 'horse without saddle or saddle tree, which was so fine and good, it had cost him, they said 400 cows . . . In coming down it galloped so hard that I never saw in all my life hare, deer, sheep or any such animal run with such speed as it did. In his hand he bore a great long dart, which he cast with much skill.'

Such a price was high indeed by Irish standards, and it is probable that this horse had been directly imported from Spain. As these expensive animals were crossed with the local mountain stock, it would seem that whilst the 'hobby' evolved through repeated importations from the Asturias and therefore received a comparatively high concentration of Iberian blood, the Connemara might be assumed to have a stronger preponderance of the original mountain-pony blood with only intermittent infusions of Iberian blood. Professor Low, writing in his book *Breeds of Domestic Animals of the British Isles* in 1842, is of the opinion, however, that the Spanish influence in the Connemara area was very strong, and it is worth quoting this excerpt which Pat Lyne in her excellent book on the Connemara pony *Shrouded in Mist*, published in 1984, has also deemed of sufficient importance to quote in even fuller detail:

'The horses of Spain have been referred to as having contributed to form the mixed races of the British Isles; but it is not generally known that a race of horses of Spanish descent, nearly if not altogether pure, exists in this country in considerable numbers. They inhabit the Connemara district of the County of Galway. Tradition is that from the wreck of some ships of the Spanish Armada on the western coast of Ireland in the year 1588 several horses and mares were saved which continued to breed in the rugged and desolate country to which they were thus brought. But the aid of tradition is in no degree necessary to prove the origin of these horses since all their characters are essentially Spanish. They are from 12 to 14 hands high, generally of the prevailing chestnut colour [probably bay[2]] of the Andalusian horses, delicate in their limbs, and possessed of the form of head characteristics of the Spanish race. They are suffered to run wild and neglected in the country of mixed rock and bog which they inhabit, and where they are to be seen galloping in troupes amongst the rugged rocks of limestone of which the country consists . . .

'It must be regarded as remarkable that these horses should retain the characteristics of their race for so long a period in a country so different from whence they are derived. They have merely become smaller than the original race, somewhat rounded in the croup, and are covered in their natural state with shaggy hair, the necessary effect of a climate the most humid in Europe. From mere neglect of the selection of the parents in breeding, many of these little horses are extremely ugly yet still conforming to the original type. It would be desirable that the gentlemen of Ireland should direct attention to this remarkable race which would supply a class of horse of the Galloway size now much wanted. *By importing some of the best Andalusian stallions a wonderful change could be effected in the breed which would thus be rendered of economical importance to the district which produces it.*'

It is possible that Mr Low may have over-emphasised the importance of the Spanish influence, and there has always been some doubt about the likelihood of Spanish horses surviving the long swim from sunken ships far off the mainland to the Irish coast. What is more likely is that an Iberian influence from far further back still prevailed, including from those days when chariot racing was popular amongst the Irish Celts, and no doubt a certain amount of hot-blood was introduced to bring about a turn of speed.

2. Confusion often arises when translating old Portuguese or Spanish documents referring to colour in horses. To this day the word bay in Spain and Portugal denotes dun; the word chestnut (literally translated) implies bay.

As Miss Lyne points out: 'While it is fascinating to speculate it would be unwise to suggest that any one breed has had more influence than another in the make-up of the Connemara pony.'

Certainly, many of today's Connemaras appear to have moved far away from the type described by Professor Low in 1842 due to a large infusion of Arab blood brought in to revive a dying breed in the nineteenth century. One cannot help but theorise on the last sentence quoted from Low concerning the importation of the best Andalusian stallions which I have italicised. Had this advice been adhered to, we might now see in the Connemara all that was best of the 'old type', qualities which so many of the breed's admirers still yearn for after all these years, and endeavour against so many odds to achieve.

The British Appaloosa

Most people generally assume that all Appaloosas come from America, being the natural home of the coloured and spotted horses which the Indians developed from the Spanish horses brought over by the Conquistadores (see next chapter). Enthusiasts of the breed in Great Britain, however, are convinced that the early ancestors of the type in this country were direct descendants of Spanish and Neapolitan horses brought over in the seventeenth and eighteenth centuries.

Examples of spotted Spanish Jennets are to be found in the art collection of the Earl of Pembroke at Wilton House, and John Wooton's English painting of Lady Conway's Spanish Jennet is typical of the horse we now call Appaloosa. If the breed is not from America, the name certainly is, as we shall see. It is perfectly logical to suppose that those horses which were developed for this special colour in Britain could trace a major part of their ancestry back to the Iberian horse. Although the indifferent breeder could be accused of breeding only for colour and not for sound conformation, there is certainly a number of extremely well-made Appaloosas to be seen, particularly in junior showjumping events, which display all the Iberian characteristics of good hock action and agility.

CHAPTER XV

The Conquistadores and the Horses of the Americas

Horses are the most necessary thing in the New
Country because they frighten the enemy most, and
after God, to them belongs the victory.

PEDRO DE CASTANEDA DE NAGERA

Nobody reading an account of the Spanish and Portuguese invasions of the West Indies and the Americas, could ever disagree with that famous sentiment, written by Pedro de Castaneda de Nagera in his sixteenth-century contemporary chronicle of the conquest of the New World under Cortés.

Neither does anybody dispute that all the native horse breeds of America, the Mustangs, the Criollas, the Pacers, the Pintos or Paints, the highly reputed Quarter Horse and the more refined Saddle Horses, owe their ancestry wholly or in part, however diluted, to those early horses brought into the continent by the Conquistadores.

The aim of this chapter is not to provide a reference for all the different magnificent breeds which exist in the United States, Canada, Central America, South America and the West Indies of today. Rather it is an account of those first famous horses which set foot on the soil of the New World and the part they played in establishing today's modern breeds. There is a strong temptation to begin this account with the Quarter Horse of the United States, the most popular breed in the world, which can boast over two million *registered* animals spread today throughout fifty-seven different countries. To acquire a true perspective, however, in this remarkable story of the horses of America, we must start at the psychological point of the whole narrative. Then we will retrace our steps to the bottom of the chronological ladder of equestrian expansion and follow the Iberian horse through the Indies, Mexico, South America and finally the United States of America.

It is now known that a very mixed complement of horses set sail under the various exploratory expeditions to the West and as they left behind the royal studs of the Spanish and Portuguese crown, or the humble hillside farm of a peasant breeder in Andalusia or the Alentejo, one thing is certain: no one embarking those horses into the hold or onto the deck[1] of those sturdy small sailing ships, could possibly have foreseen the impact the Iberian horse would have on the pre-Columbian civilisations of America.

---

1. Robert M. Denhardt recounts in *The Horse of the Americas* how 'on the smaller craft the horses stood on the main-deck, side-lined or hobbled in fair weather, and tied down during storms.'

This engraving from Manejo real en que se propone lo que deben saber los caballeros *by Manuel Alvarez Ossorio y Vega (Madrid, 1769), demonstrates the method of loading and transporting horses on boats in the sixteenth century prior to sailing to the New World.*

Yet, as we gaze with the benefit of hindsight at the beautiful horses of the Americas today, and marvel at the way in which Nature's first law, survival of the fittest, adapted those early arrivals to cope not only with the rugged heights of the Andes, the Sierra Nevada and the Rockies, but also with the plains, the prairies and the harshness of the great American desert, we accept it all: the resilient Iberian horse was created for such an undertaking.

As we shall come to understand something of the character of those early Conquistadores and appreciate fully their almost total dependence on their Iberian horses, one virtue shines through above all else in both man and beast – courage.

Against all Odds

'And after God, to them belongs the victory.'

How fortunate the Iberians were to have their horses. As they landed in the West Indies and prepared to make their assault on the lands jealously held by the great Aztec and Inca civilisations, they enjoyed this one great advantage. Praise of God and praise of the horse are repeated time and time again by all the Conquistadores in the several chronicles that have been handed down to us, and certainly those early adventurers needed every advantage they could muster. Not only were they pitting their wits against an unknown enemy, who on occasions outnumbered them by tens of thousands, they were also facing sweltering tropical heat with its accompanying foreign diseases, difficult terrain, and hundreds of miles of unexplored mountain and jungle, the haven of strange insects, reptiles and animals as well as poisonous plants and fruits. It is clear, however, that the aspect of the New World which disturbed the newly arrived Conquistadores more profoundly than anything else, was the widescale slaying of children and youths upon altars of the sun, offerings to awesomely grotesque idols in regular ceremonies of human sacrifice.

The Spanish Conquistadores are often accused of having exercised the most appalling cruelty in those early forays into the new continent, but against this must be weighed their total dedication to what they saw as a Holy Crusade, similar to the one they had left at home against the Moors. Filled with religious zeal, alongside their personal ambition, they never hesitated to question the purpose of their mission. In faith must they conquer, and where the works of the devil were being discharged, the transgressors must be put to the sword. In contrast to this, Montezuma II, Lord of the Aztecs and the lands which form Mexico as we know it today, was filled with doubt and superstition when the Spanish first landed. He half-believed that Cortés might be Quetzalcoatl, a legendary serpent-god who would one day return from the East to rule their kingdom. Some old Indians still talked of 'those animals which our fathers knew' when they first saw the horses of the Conquistadores. The Aztecs were torn, therefore, between the conflicting emotions of bowing down and worshipping the invaders, or attacking them.

Whether the Indians' pre-knowledge of horses dated back thousands of years to a period in prehistory when we now know that early *equus* did exist in the Americas, or whether it was derived from an ancient Asiatic and Mongolian ancestry is not known. Whatever this taproot of wisdom handed down from father to son, it is clear from all records that when the majority of Indians first set eyes on the Iberian horse they were frozen with fear. Upon his arrival on the Mexican mainland, Cortés galloped his horses on the beach and sent stone cannonballs crashing into the forest beyond to terrify and impress the gathering inhabitants. Totally awed by what they saw, Aztec artists made sketches of the Spaniards and their horses, and these were borne by jungle runners to Tenochtitlan, the capital of their kingdom. Here Montezuma, reigning supreme in his gleaming palace in what is now known as Mexico City, must have trembled at what he saw.

In those days, the city was built on swamp, marshland and islands, and later the Spaniards were to find riches therein beyond their wildest expectation; an abundance of gold and hammered silver, turquoise and pearls, and fine, richly dyed and woven textiles. On their 'floating gardens' the Aztecs grew corn and strange vegetables. The Spaniards marvelled at the botanical gardens, the Venetian-like waterways and 'the great towers and temples and buildings that stood in the water, and all of masonry . . . There were even some of our soldiers who asked if what they saw was in a dream.'

This, then, was the great Aztec empire which Cortés and his followers with their Spanish horses were to conquer, and because of the sheer daring and audacity of that expedition, other earlier accounts of conquest are often forgotten. Without doubt from an equestrian point of view, Cortés' adventures are by far the most accurately recorded thanks to one Bernal Diaz del Castillo, a prominent member of this campaign, whose *True History of the Conquest of New Spain* was completed fifty-five years after the event. We shall shortly return to these adventures, but let us now examine the arrival of the first Iberian horse in America and follow his course in as geographical and chronological an order as is possible to make without losing the sense of our subject.

The Very First Horses

The first horses to be seen in America for millennia arrived at the island of La Espanola, or Hispaniola, in December 1493. (Later this island was to be divided into the Dominican Republic and Haiti; the capital still bears the old name of Santo Domingo.) They formed part of Christopher Columbus' second expedition under the royal patronage of Ferdinand and Isabella. In Madrid, amongst the archives of the Indies, there still exists the original royal edict of 23rd May, 1493 which authorised ships and resources for this voyage:

> 'We command that a certain fleet be prepared to send to the islands and mainland which have newly been discovered . . . and to prepare the vessels for Admiral Don Christopher Columbus . . . and among those we command to go in the vessels there shall be sent twenty lancers with horses . . . and five of these shall take two horses each, and the two horses which they take shall be mares.'

Thus, even at the very beginning of the voyages of discovery, careful provision was made for breeding animals[2] to travel alongside the cavalry stallions. This gives an insight into the Spanish crown's firm intention to colonise the new lands and provide a foundation stock for further expeditions and conquests.

From Columbus' own writings it is certain that the intended stock for this voyage should have been made up of the finest quality of Andalusian horse, perhaps even from the royal studs themselves. However, these horses were never to arrive. Just as the stallions and mares were being embarked in Cadiz, a last-minute substitution took place by fraudulent dealers. In January, 1494 Columbus wrote to his royal patrons complaining that his crafty cavalrymen had sold the valuable bloodstock and replaced them with 'common nags'. From this and subsequent research we are led to conclude that those first horses were probably none other than the cowherder's common mount, the Sorraia, or a Sorraia Iberian cross, which could be obtained in those days at less than a tenth of the price of an Andalusian charger or top brood mare. This importation of hardy, primitive blood combining the smaller body conformation, the more pronounced convex profile and the primitive colours of dun, mouse-grey, roans and sorrels, accompanied by the distinctive dark dorsal stripe as well as faint zebra stripes on the legs, with mildness of temperament and extreme hardiness, has led to the breeding of a type of horse in America which is still found in today's feral herds of horse.

This, however, is the only reference to 'common' stock being transported to the West. Ferdinand and Isabella responded to Columbus with typical protective concern for their growing empire by initiating a royal decree in the same year

---

2. Transportation was normally paid for by the crown. In December 1507, the King ordered the Casa de Contratacion (Board of Trade) to release over 100 mares destined for the West Indies, which had been held up by officials.

Lady Conway's Spanish Jennet by Wootton. There were many instances of spotted Iberian horses in England during the sixteenth, seventeenth and eighteenth centuries. The modern name Appaloosa comes from America. (Photo by English Life Publications, by kind permission of the Marquess of Hertford)

Soldiers of the 10th Light Dragoons (1793) by George Stubbs. This magnificent oil painting was commissioned by the Prince of Wales (later George IV) on the occasion of his appointment as Colonel Commandant of the 10th (or The Prince of Wales's Own) Regiment of (Light) Dragoons. His parade horse clearly shows the gradual transition from the high-crested, powerful-necked Iberian to the more streamlined breeds of the future. (By gracious permission of Her Majesty The Queen)

stating that henceforth every ship should carry on it twelve breeding mares of '*casta distinguida*' (distinguished blood) to serve the needs of the new colonies.

The First Colonial Stud Farms

To further expansion of the empire, royal studs were set up on the first islands to be colonised for the Spanish crown in the West Indies. We read that by 1500 a stud of no less than sixty brood mares existed on Santo Domingo, and in the same year the stud was reinforced by the arrival of a new governor, Nicolas de Ovando, who brought with him ten selected Andalusian colts. In 1505 the last major importation of Spanish horses arrived in Santo Domingo, which consisted of 106 brood mares from Seville, Sanlúcar de Barrameda and Huelva – all excellent breeding grounds situated within the main Andalusian horse belt.

Cuba, conquered by Diego Velasquez in 1515, was soon to follow as an important stud base, and one amusing account is given of the Spaniards' use of the horse as a psychological as well as strategic weapon to subdue and vanquish the native Indians during Velasquez's occupation of the island. In this instance, paradoxically, it was an Andalusian mare rather than the usual stallion, which demonstrated the huge potentiality a single horse could arouse in the eyes of an enemy as a vehicle of war and superiority. One of Velasquez's lieutenants, a *hidalgo* named Narvaes, leading a mission of reconnaissance deep into the Cuban interior, found himself and his small platoon surrounded by seven hundred natives at dead of night. Clad only in his nightshirt, Narvaes acted with all the resourcefulness that seems to have come naturally to the Conquistadores of that time. He vaulted onto his horse, 'a tricky little mare', and, spurring her forward, he galloped headlong into the crowd of warriors. So terrified were they by this pale centaur-like apparition that man for man they fled and did not stop until they had covered 'fifty leagues'. This is but one of many such tales which demonstrate the havoc that the first appearance of man on a horse wreaked amongst the Indians.

From these early studs, soon to be followed by further bases on Jamaica (also discovered by Columbus) and Nicaragua (discovered by Gil Gonzales de Avila in 1522), consignment after consignment of horses was sent forth to supply the Spanish troops of Mexico, Central and South America as new lands unfolded before them in their arduous, hazardous campaigns in the years to follow.

Curiously, many people seem unaware that the West Indies played such an important role in those early days. Considering that the taproot stock of the entire horse population of America, which was to spread like wildfire from Mexico, had at some time been bred or passed through the West Indian studs, it is a pity that more relevance is not given to these.

It is also hard for us to appreciate the number and extent of the Caribbean islands as they curve from North to South America, spanning over 2,500 miles of ocean. Yet on all these islands today we still see native horses of Spanish descent. The Paso Fino is a fine example of one of the pacing horses which has been developed. Native to Puerto Rico, it is very similar to the Peruvian Ambling Horse, which is not surprising since, again, it was from the West Indian studs that Francisco Pizarro drew his first horses for his conquest of Peru.

Cortés and His Horses

Returning to the gallant Cortés, we find him serving in Cuba under the command of Velasquez. Hernan, or Hernando, Cortés was born in Extremadura in 1485 and was once a student at the University of Salamanca. He had given up his studies to enlist as a soldier and seek a life of adventure. This was to come to him perhaps more quickly than he had expected. On November 18th, 1518 Cortés was entrusted by Velasquez to set out to take possession of Mexico which had just been discovered by another Spaniard, Grijalva, who had failed to make a settlement there. Cortés set sail from Cuba with a fleet of eleven ships on which he carried six hundred foot soldiers, a number of slaves, and most important of all, sixteen horses.

Fortunately, Cortés' expeditions are well recorded not only by the diligent chronicler Diaz, but by his own hand. His letters to Emperor Charles V of Spain number five in all and are known in Spain as the *Relaciones de Cortés*. In their detail and sensitive reporting, they reveal a side to the adventurers that is often forgotten or ignored. Not only did Cortés and his men appreciate their horses, they regarded them with very deep concern and genuine affection. It is obvious also from Diaz's writing that those first hardened campaigners were all very close to the horses which carried them to Mexico. From Diaz's inventory, reproduced below, we find a very mixed assortment of animals which, after all, was only to be expected from what we have learned so far about the first horses taken to the colonies:

'I wish to put down, from memory, all the horses and mares that we disembarked:

Captain Cortés had a dark chestnut stallion which died when we reached San Juan Ulua.

Pedro de Alvarado and Hernando Lopez de Avila had a very good bright bay mare, which turned out excellent both for tilting and for racing when we got to New Spain [Mexico]. Pedro de Alvarado took his share either by purchase or by force.

Alonzo Hernandez Puertocarrero, a grey mare. She was fast, and Cortés bought her for him for a gold shoulder knot.

Juan Velasquez de Leon, another grey mare, and she was very strong. We called her *La Rabona* [Bobtail].

Christoval de Olid had a dark brown horse that was very satisfactory.

Francisco de Morla, a dark bay horse which was very fast and had a good mouth.

Francisco de Montego and Alonzo de Avila, a dark chestnut horse; he was no good for war.

Juan de Escalante, a light bay horse with three white stockings. He was not very good.

Diego de Ordas, a grey mare. She was barren and a pacer, but not very fast.

Gonzala Dominguez, an excellent horseman, had a dark brown horse, very good, and very fast.

Pedro Gonzalez de Trujillo, a good bay horse, a beautiful colour, and he galloped well.

Moron, a settler of Bayamo, had a pinto with white forefeet, and he had
    a good mouth.

Baena, from La Trinidad, had a piebald with white forefeet; he proved
    worthless.

Lares, a fine horseman, had a good horse, bay in colour, but rather light;
    he was an excellent galloper.

Ortiz, the musician, and Bartolome Garcia, who had gold mines, had
    a black horse called *El Arriero* [Drover]. He was one of the best horses
    that we took aboard the fleet.

Juan Sedeno, from the Havana, a brown mare, and this mare had a foal
    on board the ship. This Juan Sedeno was the richest soldier in the
    fleet, for he had a ship, the mare, a negro and much cassava bread
    and bacon.'

This mean list of cavalry for such an important expedition only emphasises the
strain being imposed on the studs of the Indies for the various voyages that were
being carried out in the name of Spain. Many writers have thought it odd that
a mare heavily in foal should be taken on board at all. Perhaps this only goes to
demonstrate the intrepid way in which horses were transported by sea in those
days. Sea travel had been a way of life for the Iberian cavalry for many centuries,
and as we saw in Chapters II and III not only had they transported their horses
to fight their own battles overseas, but Iberian horsemen had moved freely up
and down the Mediterranean to fight as mercenaries wherever they supported a
cause or crusade. With the modern accepted use of horseboxes and trailers, we
may express shock at the thought of a mare giving birth to a foal on a cramped
sailing boat, but for the Spanish of Cortés' time it was probably the most natural
thing in the world. Unfortunately, Diaz does not tell us what became of the foal.

The Horse's Role in the Conquest of Mexico

Not long after Cortés landed on the Mexican mainland near the town of Tabasco,
on 4th March, 1519, his own charger died. He soon appropriated the fine black
stallion of his friend Ortiz, the musician, renaming *El Arriero* by the more personal
term *Mi Morzillo* (My Black). Round the same time, Cortés heard that Velasquez
had cancelled his commission but this was not to daunt the ambitious Hernando.
He proceeded to embark on the 500-mile route to Tenochtitlan, travailling, fighting, enlisting and slaughtering for the glory of Spain every inch of the way.

Throughout this tortuous journey Morzillo displayed typical Iberian courage,
and was even to continue with Cortés on a later expedition southwards into
Guatemala.

On one occasion during the many skirmishes experienced by Cortés and his
men during their long march through the Mexican mountains to Tenochtitlan,
when as usual the Spaniards found themselves outnumbered by literally thousands
of native Indians, an ingenious display of superiority was devised by Cortés. He
knew that the Indians were afraid of the horses, but it was an explosive situation
and everyone was well aware that at any point they could be attacked. Cortés
ordered a mare, which conveniently happened to be in season, to be brought out

and hidden behind the camp. Then a black stallion, presumably Morzillo, was led forward. It did not take long for the stallion to become aware of the mare's presence and he performed with all the excitement of any horse on such occasions. 'He began to trample the ground, roll his eyes and neigh loudly, wild with excitement.' The desired effect was achieved; the Indians were terrified by the spectacle, thinking that the horse was venting his fury on them. So anxious were they for Cortés to placate the terrible beast that they pledged their support for him against Montezuma and peace was made between the two peoples. With daring such as this, the expedition continued.

Cortés' company was reinforced during the two-year campaign by Spanish forces, initially sent out by an angry Velasquez to

Eighteenth-century engraving of Cortés in Mexico. (Courtesy of Peter Newark)

capture him for usurping his authority. Thus more horses were gained and ranks swelled, ready for the final and successful assault on the great Montezuma, King of the Aztecs. By the time Cortés marched his men and cavalry through the broad streets of Tenochtitlan, where we are told eight men could ride abreast, his horses numbered eighty-six.

Despite the added numbers, the Spanish leaders still valued their cherished horses almost beyond their men. Heat and disease had taken its toll and when Diaz talks of the death of a horse one can sense his feelings of loss, even of grief, as though his had been the hand to water and caress these loyal beasts. Cortés writes with the same emotion. In one of his *Relaciones* he reports 'they [the Indians] killed a horse also, and God alone knows how great was its value to us, and what pain we suffered at its death.'

In his Third Letter to Charles V, recounting his victory over Montezuma at the end of their ninety-day siege of the great Aztec city, Cortés reveals

'We suffered no loss that day except that, during the ambush, some of the horsemen collided with each other, and one was thrown from his mare, which galloped directly towards the enemy. They wounded her severely with arrows and she, seeing the ill-treatment she got, returned to us, and that night she died. Although we grieved exceedingly at it, our grief was less than had she died in the hands of the enemy, as we feared would be the case.'

This passage shows that despite the heady sense of victory which Cortés must have been enjoying after two years' hard campaigning and some amazing escapes from death, he cared enough about each horse to include these details in his lengthy report to the King. There was a very different side to Cortés than the usual sweeping references to his cruelty and callousness would imply.

The climate of Mexico suited those early Andalusians exceptionally well. By the year 1544, Mexico was so rich in horses under the Spaniards, that a visitor, Tello de Sandoval, was received by six hundred horsemen.[3]

It is a bitter reflection of human ingratitude and fickleness that Cortés' last days were spent in near obscurity. Despite reaching the heights of Governor of Mexico and Marquis of Axaca (1529), he fell out of royal favour on many occasions, largely brought about by the fact that he became too popular a hero amongst the Spanish people at home, and his ambition brought unease to the court of Madrid. On one occasion he is said to have forced his way into Emperor Charles V's carriage and when the Emperor demanded to know who he was, he replied, 'I am a man who has given you more provinces than your ancestors left you cities.'

This brave horseman, adventurer and leader died in Seville just before Christmas 1547. For all his reputed cruelty in dealing with the Indians and rebel countrymen, we are left in no doubt of his love for the horse. And somewhere in Mexico, 9000 feet above sea-level in the Sierra Madre, where many of the natives joined him against Montezuma, the old Indians talk of him as though he is close to them still.

'Cortés?' recalls an old Indian to a modern traveller across the glow of a campfire. 'Ah, yes; a man called Cortés crossed that mountain. The grandfathers told me that he came many years ago. He brought horses.'

Brazil

Even before the Spanish were exploring Mexico and Central America, the Portuguese were establishing themselves in Brazil, the fifth greatest country in the world today.

Pedro Alvaro Cabral was the first Portuguese actually to set foot on Brazilian soil in 1500, but it was not until the reign of King Dom João III from 1521–1557 that the first coastal settlements were made, and Portuguese explorers began to push their way westward into the rugged interior with their versatile Iberian horses.

In 1541 an important consignment of Portuguese horses, reputedly from the royal stud, was landed by Alvar Nunez and, in the same way that the Spanish horse reproduced across Mexico and thence migrated northwards into the United States, so the Portuguese horses spread and bred throughout Brazil and into some parts of Argentina.

Unlike Mexico, Brazil did not at that stage yield up great treasure troves from an existing civilisation and therefore we do not hear so much of the heroic deeds of the early explorers in their quest for cities of gold. Rather, Brazil developed

---

3. Today, Mexico has some of the finest Iberian horses in the world. As well as breeding pure-bred Andalusians and Lusitanos of the finest calibre and importing the best bullfighting horses, the Mexican *charro* (cowboy) horse is famous for his versatility, and the Galiceno (similar to the Criolla) is a direct descendant from the horses of Cortés.

under the Portuguese as a country rich in forestry and agricultural resources, and by the seventeenth century Brazil was the principal source of sugar to the western world. Cattle were taken out from the old country in 1530 and by 1822 when a census was made, 5,000,000 head of cattle were counted.

The different types of horse which are native to Brazil today, the Crioulo, the Mangalarga and the Campolino, all owe their ancestry to the horses of the early Portuguese settlers which quickly adapted to the climate and terrain and proved excellent cattle horses. The versatile Lusitano was obviously well suited to this purpose, and today's breeds, although diverging into different strains from selective breeding over this huge country during the centuries, still retain all the early Iberian characteristics of stamina, strength and agility. As a result they make excellent ranch and polo horses.

Today, Brazil still imports large numbers of pure-bred Lusitanos to work with cattle and as a comfortable riding horse. They are also used for cross-breeding with Brazil's own working breeds. Bullfighting is not a national sport, in contrast to Mexico and Venezuela which attract many Portuguese *cavaleiros* during Europe's winter season.

Peru

One of the first historians of Peru, the Inca Garcilaso de la Vega, writes in his *General History of Peru*, published in 1609:

> 'In the first place, the Spaniards brought horses and mares with them and with their aid, they completed the conquest of the New World . . . The first horses were taken to the Islands of Cuba and Santo Domingo and then to the other Windward Islands, as these were discovered and conquered. Here they bred in great abundance and were taken thence for the conquest of Mexico and Peru.'

Before Cortés had ever left Spain, and several years before the Portuguese took a genuine interest in Brazil, a third movement of Conquistadores was hacking its way through the dense forests of Panama and found itself face to face with the great Pacific Ocean. The year was 1513 and under the expedition led by Vasco Nunez de Balboa of Spain, was an ambitious officer named Francisco Pizarro. Panama soon became the base from which to explore this unknown ocean and the great lands that stretched towards the southern hemisphere. By 1522 (just two years after Henry VIII left England to celebrate in the Field of the Cloth of Gold) Pizarro was sailing down the coast of Colombia, under the command of one Pascual de Andagoy. An expedition was made up the River San Juan in search of a local tribe, the *Viru* or *Biru*. This tribe was to give its name to a country lying far to the south of Colombia. From then on, Pizarro was to dream about this land: Peru . . . a land rich in silver and gold. Tales of Aztec wealth had gradually filtered southwards to Panama and it is not surprising that ambitious soldiers such as Pizarro should want to strike off independently into these new unexplored territories. They foresaw even greater El Dorados on the other side of the equator and Pizarro was convinced that it was his destiny to lay claim to these lands with their vast resources of hidden wealth.

After two reconnaissance voyages, Pizarro eventually achieved royal sponsorship. In 1530 he set sail from Seville but he did not cross from Ecuador to the Peruvian coast until the end of 1532. With only 62 horsemen[4] and 106 foot soldiers, he struck out into the Inca empire. We are left with many vivid accounts by contemporary chroniclers of how Pizarro and his officers used the Spanish horse to advantage. In exactly the same manner as Cortés had subdued the Aztecs, so Pizarro was to overpower the Incas.

In John Hemming's *Conquest of the Incas*, a detailed account of the Spaniards' tactics, armour and weaponry is given which makes compulsive reading:

> 'For the Indians, their enemies' great horses assumed a terrible value. They thought little of a Spaniard on foot, cumbersome in armour and breathless from the altitude; but the horses filled them with dread . . . The most effective Spanish weapon was a sword; either the double-edged cutting sword, or the rapier, which over the years gradually lost its cutting edge and became thinner and more rigid for thrusting. These were the weapons that slaughtered thinly protected Indians.
>
> 'In addition to his sword, and to supporting daggers and poniards, the cavalryman's favourite weapon was his lance. Along with the crouching, highly mobile jineta method of riding, came the *lanza jineta* . . . the rider could charge with the shaft resting against his chest; he could hold it down level with his thigh, parallel to the galloping horse, with his thumb pointed forward in the direction of the blow; or he could stab downwards with it. Each method was enough to penetrate Indian padded armour.'

Perhaps the most impressive story of Pizarro's use of cavalry is that relating to the capture of Atahualpa, one of the Inca leaders. This occurred shortly after the Spaniards had first arrived in Peru. At this time the Indians were at their most vulnerable to the sight of a horse.

After a number of skirmishes including one in which Pizarro killed a local Indian chief and took several Indian prisoners as bearers, the Spanish penetrated the forests of the Andes and arrived at Cajamarca. Here one of the great heirs to the Inca empire, Atahualpa, had set up his summer encampment by the springs. Pizarro and his officers were fortunate in entering Peru at a time of internal strife and power struggles, but they were unprepared for the organisation of the Incas:

> 'The Indians' camp looked like a very beautiful city . . . So many tents were visible that we were truly filled with great apprehension. We never thought that Indians could maintain such a proud estate nor have so many tents in good order . . . But it was not appropriate to show any fear, far less to turn back.'

Atahualpa greeted the reconnaissance expedition led by Hernando De Soto with civility but a lack of enthusiasm. He was unimpressed by their gifts and his only

4. According to Francisco de Xerez, secretary to Pizarro, the expedition left Panama with only 37 horses, but after their arrival at the northern coast of Peru, Pizarro requested and obtained reinforcements, so that by the time he set off to Cajamarca, he had 62 horses with him. This accounts for the often conflicting numbers given.

real interest lay in the horses. Armour, tack and weapons were minutely examined. He must have been a remarkable leader for despite the fact that he had never seen a horse in his life before, he showed no fear. The chronicler Lopez de Gomara writes that 'De Soto arrived making his horse curvet for bravery, and to amaze the Indians.' Atahualpa remained unmoved, proud upon his dais and remarked that he knew of the Christians' pillaging on the way to Cajamarca. He claimed that some of his own people had killed a horse, thus showing his understanding of the animal's mortality. This was hotly denied, and De Soto had a horse brought forward which had been trained to rear up in a bid to daunt him.

> 'The nag was spirited and made much foam at its mouth. He was amazed at this and at seeing the agility with which it wheeled. But the common people showed even greater admiration and there was much whispering. One squadron of troops drew back when they saw the horse coming towards them. Those who did paid for it that night with their lives for Atahualpa ordered them to be killed because they had shown fear.'

The outcome of the expedition to Cajamarca was that the Spaniards, realising they were in a probable trap, outnumbered by literally thousands of warriors, planned the most daring ambush. This relied totally on the effect of their horsemen and their cavalry tactics. Trumpets were sounded and giving the crusaders' battle cry '*Santiago!*', the Spanish lurched into the attack.

> 'They all placed rattles on their horses to terrify the Indians ... With the booming of the shots and the trumpets and the troop of horses with their rattles, the Indians were thrown into confusion and panicked. The horsemen rode out on top of them, sounding and killing and pressing home the attack.'

When over six or seven thousand Indians lay dead within the encampment or out in the plain where they had been pursued and cut down as they fled, and Atahualpa had been taken prisoner, the Spaniards realised they had won a huge victory against impossible odds. They thanked God for their brave horses.

Atahualpa later admitted he had plotted against them. 'He told of his great intentions ... to sacrifice some of the Spaniards to the sun and castrate others for service to his household and in guarding his women.'

As for the horses, the course of history might have been changed if Atahualpa had realised his plans. In the words of the chronicler, 'He had decided to take and breed the horses and mares – which were the thing he admired most.'

Pizarro went on to Cusco and eventually found Lima, City of the Kings, in 1535. Those first cavalry horses were to herald the arrival of thousands more from the island studs, or occasionally from mainland Spain. In fact Pizarro himself, already a hero in the eyes of the Spanish crown, sent direct to Spain for a special stallion and mare. There still exists in the archives of the Indies in Spain, a royal decree dated July 19, 1534 by which a permit is granted to one Illan Suarez De Carbajal to export these animals to Peru for the use of Captain Francisco Pizarro.

Over the centuries that followed, Peru became established as the headquarters of the conquering Spanish army in South America. Andalusian horses and mares arrived by the shipload for the remount depots of Lima, and breeding was highly

The Peruvian Ambler or Stepping Horse – Caballo de Paso. *Flor de Oro, a twelve-year-old palomino mare, demonstrates the long face, powerful neck and deeply engaged hock action of her Spanish ancestors. (Photo by kind permission of Mrs Eileen Craig)*

successful from the early arrivals which had been used for stud. By the end of the sixteenth century, only seventy years after the conquest of Peru, the Inca Garcilaso expressed the general view when he stated: 'From the horses that have multiplied in Peru, we find races as good as the best of Spain, among which we encounter some fit for the games as well as some good for the parades, work, and travel.' Many of these horses found their way into the wild and from them came the Peruvian Criollo and the Costeno.

The most famous horse of those selectively bred in Peru over the past 150 years is the Peruvian Ambler or Stepping Horse, the *Caballo de Paso*. This horse is bigger than the majority of the other Spanish-derived breeds which have become indigenous to South America, reaching at least 15 hands, and he is remarkable for his special gait. The *termino*, as this graceful, flowing, trotting action is called, when the forelegs are rolled outwards in a spectacular dish as the horse strides forward, is extremely comfortable to sit to. It can be as slow as a walk or as fast as a canter, but it enables the Paso to be ridden in comfort for hours over the rugged countryside. The Paso is noted for his ability to eat up the miles in the same smooth even gait, and over the most difficult terrain where other breeds would certainly tire and flag. Predominantly bay or chestnut, often marked with white, the Peruvian Paso is to be found in all colours like his Spanish ancestors and is held in high regard in his country for his usefulness, and kind, even temperament. Pasos are extremely sure-footed and are not shod.

Argentina

Argentina, the second largest state in South America with its huge open prairies raises more head of horse and more head of cattle with less effort than probably anywhere else in the world. But until the first Spaniards came to Argentina, this was a poor country where the Indians lived in scattered bands as uncivilised nomads picking up a precarious living by hunting small birds and animals. They had little knowledge of agriculture and when Don Pedro de Mendoza, the founder of Buenos Aires, transported one hundred Andalusian horses and mares to Argentina in 1535, the Spaniards had to combat famine and sickness, which eventually caused Mendoza's death at sea on a return voyage to Spain to bring in supplies and reinforcements.

The way in which horses and cattle were to multipy on the great Argentinian plains was to change the whole way of life for the native Indians. As pointed out by the *Encyclopaedia Britannica*:

> 'The introduction of Spanish cattle and horses into a prairie land which had been of no value at all when the Spaniards came, was the most important outcome of the conquest of Argentina. Indians of the pampa had soon learned to avail themselves of the herds and flocks and had been transformed from wretched savages into well-fed raiders.'

After a difficult beginning, the Spanish began to prosper in Argentina, but unlike Peru and Mexico, there were few precious metals to extract and the new colonies were to thrive from their own hard labour.

A new race of Spaniards whose life centred round the teeming horses and cattle of the great plains grew up, the gaucho. Typical of their forefathers in Spain, they rode superbly and the handling of the gaucho horse became a matter of great prestige and family honour.

The mount of the early settlers was named the Criolla. It is thought that these tough animals which can survive long periods on little water and food, are descended from the very first horses which came to the Americas with Christopher Columbus in 1493. Mendoza's horses, brought in after the first migratory herds had reached Argentina, were also likely to be of mixed stock. He would have needed transport and pack-horses for his exploratory trips round the River Plate, and it is known that the Spanish crown lacked the enthusiasm for the conquest of Argentina whilst the gold and silver were flowing out of Peru and Mexico in such large quantities.

Thus, the useful Criolla, which today stands at between 13.2 and 14 h.h., appears to be a closer descendant of the Sorraia type horse than of the Andalusian war-horse. Criollas are generally dun with a black dorsal stripe, but they may also be coloured, or roan, bay or brown. Zebra stripes on the legs are commonplace.

El Caballo Criollo, a book of scholastic research on the breed, by Dr Emilio Solanet, gives a full account of livestock numbers, breeding patterns and the possible ancestry of the Criolla. He suggests that 'Barb' blood is responsible for the Criolla's stamina, and whilst it is not denied that Barb genes may be present through the sources that we have already discussed in Chapter III, if we take this a stage further to the foundation stock, we arrive at the same conclusion, i.e. that the Sorraia is forefather to the Argentinian Criolla.

Argentina's famous polo ponies, reputed to be the best in the world, have evolved over the last century by careful upgrading of the Criolla with Thoroughbred blood. With the toughness and agility of their Iberian ancestors and the speed and beauty of the Thoroughbred, the Argentine polo pony has now become a separate much sought-after breed.

The United States

The horse population of North America in the sixteenth, seventeenth and early eighteenth centuries was undoubtedly the result of the Spanish colonisation of the West Indies and Mexico. There were two contributory causes to its remarkable spread throughout the land.

One was due to the Indian, whose awakening to the horse brought about a new culture within all the North American tribes. This led to a rapid expansion which initially went northwards and then fanned out to the west and east. The second was a series of important expeditions into the new territories. From Cuba, set forth that of De Soto in 1539, from Mexico went out those inspired and organised by Antonio de Mendoza (1490–1552) and Francisco Vasquez de Coronado (1500–1554). Coronado was a true Conquistador who after capturing the fabled 'Seven Cities' of New Mexico, went on to discover the Grand Canyon and reached the plains of Texas by April 1541. Despite facing every adversity on the way, and losing much of his original party of 250 horsemen when the going became too tough, he eventually penetrated the central stretch of Kansas in the same year.

Both the horses of the Indian tribes and the horses of De Soto, Mendoza and Coronado's expeditions were pure-bred Spanish originating from Cuba and Mexico City.

The first Spaniards had done all in their power to prevent the Indians from overcoming their fear of the horse, but despite attributing god-like qualities to these thundering beasts, the Indians soon discovered their mortality. Once they had realised they were more useful alive than dead, they were swift to adapt to their value not only as a vehicle of war and defence but also for hunting.

Initially employed as grooms, captive Indians built up an affinity with the animals they served, and in 1542 comes the first official record of horses being given to the Indians. This took place when the Viceroy Mendoza of Mexico City mounted allied Indian chieftains to lead their tribesmen in the Mixton War in New Mexico.

During these years of discovery, as the Conquistadores spread across the central plateau of Mexico and penetrated southwards into what is now known as Central America and northwards into the present United States, the Indian took every opportunity to acquire horses. In the beginning he resorted to night raids, capture during skirmishes, and even stealing by daylight. By the end of the sixteenth century, he was able to dispense with stealing from the Spaniards. By now, lost or abandoned horses had banded together into feral herds and such was the suitability of their newly acquired environment that they began to multiply with breathtaking rapidity.

From hereon, Nature's own miracle of regeneration would be assisted by the

An early engraving which shows Mexican vaqueros *branding cattle. The horses and saddlery are typically Spanish in appearance. (Courtesy of Peter Newark)*

nomadic Indian's delight in the horse for his itinerant way of life, and the whole process of migration received a powerful impetus.

According to American professor of anthropology, Harold B. Barclay in his book *The Role of the Horse in Man's Culture*, the Pueblo Indians may have had horses as early as 1582, but they certainly had domesticated them by 1606–1607. The Apache tribe had become mounted by 1659, the Hasinai in Texas possessed four to five horses for every household by 1690, and the Kiowa, Paiute and Utes tribes were all mounted by 1700 at the very latest. In the early eighteenth century, the Comanche were proving formidable horsemen when they appeared in New Mexico in 1705, and the Witchita tribes had horses by 1717, as did the Pawnee.

Horse culture for the Indian was to transform his very existence. Entire tribes abandoned agriculture and became totally dependent upon the wild horses they tamed and which enabled them to hunt buffalo and bison the whole year round with unprecedented efficacy. They now had almost instant food on the hoof. Not only did the buffalo provide meat, he also provided materials and the Indians became better clothed, sheltered and armoured.

The good buffalo horse, like the good cattle or bullfighting horse, had to be agile, sure-footed and courageous. The Spanish horse was tailor-made for this task with his new bareback-riding owner. All the ancient disciplines from the old country, e.g. being able to wheel sharply, stop dead in his tracks, carry double and remain close if the rider dismounted, were incorporated into the Indian's training – for which these braves had a natural talent – of the buffalo horse.

Twentieth-century mustang, a product of the feral herds which spread all over the North American continent in the sixteenth century, breeding abundantly from escaped Spanish stock. (Photo by Sally Anne Thompson)

The wild horses which they captured came to be known as mustangs, probably derived from the Mexican word *mesteno* or *mostrenco* which means roving, rough or wild.

These mustangs also became the natural mount of the early North American settlers as they arrived on the eastern seaboard. Not only was the mustang ideal for the buffalo-hunting Indian, he served equally well as an American cow pony.

The coat of the mustang often reverted to the primitive colours in the wild: duns, roans and sorrels were prevalent, but there were also pied and spotted horses descended, it is romantically suggested, from the two coloured horses in Cortés' great expedition. It is more than likely that many other pied, skewbald and spotted Andalusian horses were shipped over in those early consignments which could equally have provided the genetic colour make-up for these mustangs. Although these colours have now been bred out of Iberian stock in Spain and Portugal, we know from sixteenth- and seventeenth-century art how popular they were in Europe at the time of the first voyages to the New World.

When in 1834, Colonel Dodge and General Leventworth made an expedition into Oklahoma to see one of the principal settlements of the Comanche tribe and learn more about these 'wild' people, they left a vivid picture of mustang horses in their report:

'The country was then alive with buffaloes and bands of wild horses. Of the horses, some were milk white, some jet black, others were sorrel and bay, some cream color. Many were of an iron grey and others were pied (containing a variety of colors on the same animal). Their manes were very profuse and hanging in the wildest confusion over their necks and faces . . . and their long tails swept the ground. A small but very powerful animal; with an exceedingly prominent eye, sharp nose, high nostril, small feet and delicate leg. Undoubtedly, from stock introduced by the Spaniards at the time of the invasion of Mexico.'

American cowboy riding a bucking bronco. Engraving by Frederic Remington, 1899. (Courtesy of Peter Newark)

Superstition over colour led to many of the Indian tribes favouring a particular type. The Appaloosa breed was developed by the Nez Percé Indians who were a tribe of excellent horse breeders, unlike many of the other tribes who did nothing to improve breeding and simply removed the best specimens for their own purposes leaving the lesser strains to multiply. Living in north-eastern Oregon near the Palouse River – hence the corruption, Appaloosa – they bred selectively and developed horses of such quality that special notes were made about them in the journals of Lewis and Clark in 1804 when Thomas Jefferson sent them out to explore the territories included in the Louisiana Purchase.

The Pinto or Paint was another colour type which was specifically bred by the Indians. Colour was thought to have magical powers, but it was equally popular for its dash and impressiveness amongst the cowhands of the West particularly when the rodeo came into vogue.

It is thought, too, that the palomino originated from early Spanish stock. We know that *isabellas* and palominos were highly favoured by Queen Isabella of Spain and in selecting horses of *casta distinguida* for the Conquistadores' expeditions, Ferdinand and Isabella surely included palominos to breed in the royal stud farms of the New World. Today, American palominos bear more Arab and Thoroughbred blood than Spanish, but the early palominos were almost certainly pure Spanish.

Whilst today's American pacers contain a greater preponderance of Thoroughbred blood than any other breed, we know that the early settlers brought in palfreys and pacing horses from England and Holland which nearly always had some Iberian blood. By 1612, Spanish colonists were breeding a palfrey type horse in Florida, then known as Spanish Guale, and some of the early British settlements around Boston and New York boasted some of the finest pacers and trotters from England and Holland which all had Iberian derivations. New England preserved her pacers as Old England was discarding her Iberian horses and concentrating all her horse-breeding energy into producing a racehorse, the Thoroughbred. As we have already discussed in this book, from Roman times the horse of the Asturias was specifically regarded as a natural ambler or pacer, but to this day Spanish *jacas* and Portuguese *campino* horses often display a tendency to amble and are easily trained to other gaits. It is therefore highly probable that persistent Iberian genes governing this action, ran through the elegant standardbreds, the Tennessee Walking Horses and Canadian Pacers, however diluted this blood may have become with the passage of years.

Morgan Horse owners continually draw comparisons between the Iberian war-horse of sixteenth- and seventeenth-century Europe and their own highly popular, all-purpose pleasure mount. So far, however, it has not been possible to trace any direct link between the Morgan and the pure-bred Spanish, as the Morgan traces his bloodlines to one phenomenal stallion, the property of Mr Justin Morgan who acquired him in the early 1790s in Massachusetts. Although a large majority of native-bred horses in America were still part or pure Spanish in extraction at that period, other breeds had been imported via the eastern ports for at least 150 years before the appearance of this great stallion, so it is quite possible he was Dutch, French, Swedish or English. Many schools of thought abound[5] but conclusive evidence is still to be established. The argument for a Spanish antecedent lies only in the physical aspect of this attractive horse, and insomuch as the Morgan has a particularly powerful, high-crested neck and short-coupled back, there will always be room for speculation.

The Quarter Horse

It is often assumed that the American Quarter Horse developed in the West since the best functional horses are still to be found out on the range in Texas, Oklahoma, Ohio, and Kansas where they are unsurpassed as ranch horses with their compact, muscular conformation and their inbuilt mentality for the work of herding, separating, out-distancing and roping-in of the lumbering steers. This protective sixth sense came to be known as 'cow-savvy', and it is as highly valued today as it was in the days of the early settlers.

But it was on the eastern seaboard that the Quarter Horse first developed as a separate breed. It has since multiplied to the extent that there are more Quarter Horses registered today than any other breed.

As we have already seen, it was the peculiar role of the Indian to spread horses northwards, westwards and also eastwards throughout the United States from the mid-sixteenth century onwards. As well as the wild, feral herds of mustang tracing back to the early arrivals in Mexico, Spanish settlers in Florida[6] also imported pure-bred Iberian horses, and these were stolen by the Chickasaw and Choctaw Indians of eastern America. Through inadequate feeding and indiscriminate

5. In a letter to the author dated 20th April 1986, equestrian historian Daphne Machin Goodall puts forward the theory that the original Justin Morgan stallion was a Norfolk Roadster or English Hackney, both of which were heavily exported to the United States. This could account for some Iberian genes.
6. The first expedition to Florida took place in 1539 when De Soto set sail from Cuba carrying 300 Spanish-bred horses from the island.

breeding, these cow-ponies had lost the height of the original Spanish saddle horse and reverted directly and indirectly to many of the primitive characteristics, resulting in a tough wiry animal of little more than 14 h.h. which could exist on very meagre sustenance.

When the first English planters arrived in the Carolinas, the Indians began selling and trading these horses, which became known as Chickasaws. As some escaped and ran wild, a number migrated northwards and were gradually captured by the early Virginian colonists, who began to cross them with their imported British and French stallions 'of the blood'. These tall, elegant imports were not yet known as Thoroughbreds by name, but were bred in the Thoroughbred mould, i.e. out of English mares (which themselves had some ancestry of Iberian blood – see Chapter XIII) with a large preponderance of oriental blood from Arab and Turk sires. Thus the colonists of Virginia and the Carolinas cultivated a superior breed of their own: a horse which combined versatility on the range with pulling power for haulage or driving the family to church, and whose comfortable gaits were ideal to carry the master of the house round his property as his men hacked down the New England forests and pegged out his expanding boundaries.

The name Quarter Horse comes to us from Colonial Quarter Pather. Although life was in too much earnest in those pioneering days to clear the land exclusively for sporting purposes, the English settlers had not lost their love of racing and were content in the beginning to race their horses down the main street of a small town or village for an exciting contest often involving handsome prizes. As these dusty tracks were rarely more than a quarter of a mile, the best horses were those which could show a brilliant burst of acceleration, sustain a dazzling break-neck sprint to the post, and finally halt in a dust-raising skid at the finish.

The Colonial Quarter Pather became the most popular horse on the eastern seaboard, and horses that could 'start like a jack rabbit and stop on a dime' began to fetch high prices. However, as the colonists adapted to a more sophisticated way of life and towns turned into cities, the quarter-mile race lost its appeal and long-distance oval tracks were built which were suitable to a horse with greater staying power. More Thoroughbred blood was introduced directly from England and Janus, a Thoroughbred grandson of the Godolphin Barb, was imported to the United States in 1752 and is recognised as being one of the foundation sires of the modern American Quarter Horse, bringing extra speed and stamina to the early Quarter Pather.

Although the predominance of interest in the east of the United States was now on breeding for sprinting, other Quarter Horses were being taken westwards by their colonial owners and by crossing once again with native Spanish blood, the emphasis reverted to work with cattle. With the birth of the immense cattle ranches, for which the American mid-West is noted, the Quarter Horse with his strong Spanish ancestry reigned supreme. Not only did he possess the cow-savvy and the muscular strength for this demanding work, he could also produce brilliant turns of speed from his Thoroughbred forefathers, enough to head off the farthest, most wayward cattle. With the development of the rodeo and cowboy contests, the Quarter Horse, with his incredibly willing temperament and supreme versatility, established himself in the hearts of all Americans as a symbol of freedom, pioneering and prosperity. He is a superb example of the all-round American horse.

Courbette in hand between the pillars. During the weekly displays given at Jerez, the Andalusian School of Equestrian Art performs impressive airs above the ground with their Iberian stallions, as well as the ballet of the Quadrille and Pas de Deux. (Photo by Jane Hodge)

Above: *At Goodwood House, 1986. The eight riders of the Portuguese School of Equestrian Art, on the occasion of the International Dressage Championships at the home of the Earl and Countess of March. The Portuguese team came to England to take part in the sixth centennial celebrations of the historic Treaty of Windsor (1386) between Portugal and England. (Photo by Peter Hogan)*

Right: *The work above the ground of the Alter Real stallions at Goodwood was described by Colonel Crossley in* Horse and Hound, *June, 1986 as being 'a delightful exhibition . . . calmness and cooperation reigned and it appeared to happen easily and happily.' In the foreground the star of the capriole is seen, an* isabella *Lusitano stallion. (Photo by Peter Hogan)*

CHAPTER XVI

A Look into the Future

To ride is to aspire to gentleness . . .
Reins of silk . . .

SPANISH PROVERB

On visiting and revisiting the galleries, libraries and museums of Washington, Madrid, Florence, Lisbon, London and countless other cities, and travelling through the countryside of not only Spain and Portugal, but also of North Africa, South America and parts of the United States, I have always been very much aware of one single driving force: a burning ambition for people outside the Iberian Peninsula to understand more about the great Iberian horse, not just to recapitulate on his very honourable, historic past, but to appreciate his value to us all and to future generations.

I am convinced that the time is not far away when this ancient breed of horse will return, fully accepted for what he is, to those very countries which once had such need of him that their furtive agents rustled and hustled him through the dawn field, the afternoon market place and the dark evening sea ports of the Iberian Peninsula.

Special Contributions

There are three critical contributions that the Iberian horse can give us in this modern world:

> The first is his ability to pass on certain excellent genetic characteristics which have been proven so dominant that they are still to be found in modern breeds where Iberian blood has not been reintroduced for two or even three centuries.
>
> The second lies in this horse's unique role as a natural schoolmaster. In both temperament and conformation he is ideally suited to assist the student of equitation in the pursuit of equestrian scholarship and understanding, which he does with willingness and enthusiasm.
>
> The third is the absolutely natural and unforced way this horse enriches the art of dressage, something which is sorely needed in countries such as ours whose people have often held dressage in cool awe or even dark suspicion and have therefore failed to understand and appreciate it.

Our Research to Date

But first let us summarise all that has been learnt about this horse so far. We have charted the progress of the Royal Horse of Europe, the Iberian Great Horse, as he evolved, primarily as a war-horse, since prehistory itself. The days of the early invaders from North Africa, Carthage, Phoenicia and Greece undoubtedly brought oriental blood and considerable refinement of the horse as he developed all over the Peninsula. By the time of the Romans, the horse of the southern regions would appear to have consolidated his genetic features into a distinctive classical mould, which from this point onwards would not greatly change.

Threatened with extinction as a pure breed after the Napoleonic Wars and with more modern revolutions, the Iberian horse was also menaced by drastic change as a result of men's selective breeding for new characteristics. Despite all this, there still today remains an appreciable number of these horses which feature all the inherent classical traits of the original war-horse, and these are not only to be found in Spain and Portugal but also in growing numbers in many other countries. Costa Rica, for example, now claims to be the single largest producer of Andalusian horses after Spain and supplies all the Latin American countries as well as the United States. Australia and New Zealand have over six hundred pure-bred Andalusian horses between them and over 2,500 part-breds. In the United States there are over 2,000 registered pure-bred Andalusians and Lusitanos (both breeds are recognised under the same associations), West Germany is importing from the Iberian Peninsula well over one hundred horses annually. Traditionally France has always imported a large number of these horses throughout her history. Whilst many of these are registered in Spain and Portugal, there are innumerable Iberian-cross-French horses which are excellent saddle horses. Great Britain at present has just under a hundred pure-bred Lusitanos and Andalusians registered with their representative societies, but a number of cross-breds are now being born in this country although we have come very late into the Iberian picture.

We have discussed the significance of the *corrida* and how this sport together with its associated *fiestas*, games, carriage driving, pageantry and processions has kept alive a form of classical horsemanship as natural to the Iberian as riding across country is to us. The reader may at times have been surprised to read of the enormous influence exerted by the Iberian horse not just in ancient days when Julius Caesar introduced the first Iberian horses to the most far-flung outposts of his empire, including Britannica, but in the development of all the European breeds of the Renaissance period which received their first cross of 'blood' or 'quality' through the horses of Spain and the Barbary Coast long before pure-bred Arab horses reached Europe in any significant number.

The same pattern of a strong lasting influence was followed as we traced those dominant genes and their persistence to manifest themselves in the new warm-blood European breeds long after the Spanish horse had disappeared from the collapsing Hapsburg empire. The continuity of certain Iberian characteristics cannot be ignored throughout the centuries which followed, even after the introduction of Thoroughbred and Arab blood, with the result that still today certain hunters, show-jumpers and hackneys bear a resemblance in facial look, muscular conformation and strong hock action to their Iberian ancestors of long ago.

Finally, and most importantly, we have explored the introduction of the Spanish and Portuguese horses into the Americas, where huge herds of literally thousands of wild mustangs and Criollas sprung up from those early horses of the Conquistadores, thus providing the foundation stock for the cowboy horses of the south and west. This equally established a sound foundation for new breeds which, later crossed with imported Thoroughbred and Arab blood, was to yield a superb breeding system all over the Americas. This resulted in the emergence of many excellent and different modern riding and driving breeds with an unmistakeable American identity. No one can deny the historical significance of the Iberian horse.

A Logical Contribution to Breeding

What is less understood and constitutes an important issue which breeders should explore further is the potential that the Iberian horse offers to breeders all over the world today.

There have been moments in the last century when various breeds have suffered crises which have threatened to wipe out or drastically change a particular type. Although warning bells have been sounded, stud owners appear to have been powerless to change the downward trend of falling numbers or degeneration within their stock. On more than one occasion a well-established breed has been faced with extinction. This in fact happened in England, not only with the Yorkshire Coach Horse but with another famous carriage breed, the Norfolk Roadster. With the coming of the car, plus over-exportation, it is understandable how these horses disappeared, but now that the sport of driving has developed again worldwide into fashionable competition, it is tragic for England that horses have had to be brought in from abroad when we once produced driving horses of our own which were the envy of the world.

In the Argentine, we read that the Criolla was very nearly ruined by injudicious crossing with stallions imported from Europe and the United States which did not correspond with the progenitor make-up of the breed. These crossings, composed largely of Thoroughbred and Arab blood, produced a faster more elegant horse but one which lacked the necessary stamina and resistance to hunger and disease. Fortunately, Argentinian breeders pre-empted the problem before it was too late. By in-breeding the best of the remaining pure-bred Criollas, they were able to replenish dwindling stock and recreate herds within areas where the old Criolla had vanished.

All too often, there comes a time in the life of many a breed where it would benefit future generations if a return could be made to progenitor stock. Unfortunately, in the case of some of Britain's mountain and moorland breeds, breeders in the late 1800s and early 1900s ignored this fundamental genetic law and outcrossed to Arab stallions, perhaps in the mistaken belief that Arab blood had been there initially. As we have seen throughout this book, it is now generally accepted worldwide by equestrian historians that Arab blood did not come to Great Britain in any significant proportions until the latter half of the seventeenth century. Therefore with these new infusions of Arab blood in the last few decades before the First World War, a number of breeds were almost irrevocably changed.

The temptation to upgrade in this way was understandable, but it is tragic that, in seeking quality, the warm-blood of the horses of the Iberian Peninsula was not re-introduced into breeds such as the Welsh Cob and Connemara pony. By incorporating Iberian blood (which had once been present in the breed as we discovered in Chapter XIV) breeds would have received sufficient 'blood' to give their owners the refinement they sought, but the important characteristics of physical chunkiness, powerful hock action, balance, and superb, trustworthy temperament would not have been sacrificed.

Function should always take precedence over show-worthiness, but with the popularity of in-hand show classes, and the tendency to select miniature horses instead of round, muscular ponies, it is all too apparent that in many cases breeds are losing their individuality and beginning to look confusingly similar. The same little dished faces and daisy-cutting action are becoming too familiar a sight in pony breeds once renowned for their sensible heads and temperaments, and powerful weight-carrying ability.

Fortunately, function is still more important than mere appearance in the hunting, jumping and 'chasing world. One of the reasons German studs appear to have been so successful in terms of producing show-jumping and dressage horses is because they demand a lot of their horses, stretching them to the limit, and then breeding only from those which excel. Over the years, breeders have selected again and again for powerful hock action rather than sprinting ability, and the genetic thrust of the old Iberian blood has retained its impetus in generation after generation. Selective breeding of this type has made these horses the most sought after in the world.

Action is also required in the practical carriage horse which competes over demanding obstacle courses where balance and turning ability are of paramount importance. In England, the most popular horse amongst serious hunting folk is still the 'old fashioned hunter' with his noble, often Roman-nosed face, and his instinctive ability to get out of trouble in treacherous country. There is no phenomenon about the Irish Draught horse. His strong powerful back, ability to tuck his hocks under him and produce thrust are all a legacy from that early Iberian blood.

So why aren't people turning back to Iberian blood and reintroducing the excellent genes which have produced these worthwhile features?

The answer is that they are, but slowly. England is one of the last countries, as can be seen from her registered figures, to catch up. One of the problems has been that until recently the Iberian horse has literally been a forgotten breed. Conveniently dispatched to his country of origin when the Arab and Turk revolutionised horse breeding all over the world and the magnificent Thoroughbred horse emerged, the Iberian horse was thought by then to have completed its task. From now on, Arab crosses would provide stamina, sprinting ability and bone. The other requirements such as balance, impulsion and strong backs were taken for granted, and as a result the Iberian horse passed into murky obscurity.

But times have changed since the last World War. No one could have foreseen the growth in popularity of equestrian sport throughout the world, and the astonishing emergence of so many outlets for riders other than racing and hunting.

George III's favourite horse Adonis is typical of the Hanoverian horse of the time showing all the appearance of his Spanish ancestors. From the painting by Beechey of the King reviewing troops. (Reproduced by gracious permission of H.M. the Queen)

It is not surprising that focus has returned to the horses of the Iberian Peninsula.

The way forward is already being led by the Spanish Riding School of Vienna. Despite the firm establishment of this superior warm-blood breed, the Lipizzaner, the Stud Directors of Piber have found it prudent to return to Spain and Portugal in an attempt to reintroduce the powerful genes which have earned these horses pride of place in the hearts of all those who love the ballet of classical equitation. In-breeding within this unique breed has its pitfalls, and the significance of the School's attempts to purchase pure-bred Andalusians and Lusitanos should not be overlooked.

The French, too, are producing many beautiful riding horses by crossing Iberian stallions with French saddle breeds. We are virtually seeing a return to the palfrey within France where the emphasis is less on competition as we know it at home, but more on comfortable pleasure riding in the *bois* and the special trail rides set aside all over the country for this purpose.

In England, we now have a magnificent opportunity to avail ourselves of the very finest Iberian blood in the stud service of the Lusitano, Novilheiro. This brilliant grey stallion made famous by John Whitaker has enjoyed a very successful

Novilheiro, ridden by John Whitaker, a brilliant example of the versatility of the Veiga strain of Lusitano. Novilheiro is a full brother of Opus, pictured on page 140. (Photo by Bob Langrish)

competitive career and now stands at stud in Leicestershire, England. Novilheiro comes from what is considered by most Spaniards and certainly all Portuguese to be the top blood line in the whole Peninsula, the line which produced Alvarito Domecq's best bullfighting horse Opus (see Chapter IX) and the top horse of another famous *rejoneador*, Manuel Vidrié's Neptuno. Novilheiro exemplifies the almost magic combination of a horse out of a Veiga mare by an Andrade stallion, which is the purest link to the Andalusian war-horse of the seventeenth century that exists.

Producers of our native pony and cob breeds which trace back to an Iberian ancestor would do well to consider the merit of reintroducing this old blood, particularly where a strong back and more activity is required from a compact frame. The clean legs and 'blood' of the Iberian horse mean that showiness and flamboyance is not sacrificed; but strains that have lost the ability to track up and show signs of nappiness and a loss of kindness will benefit from sensible cross-breeding.

It is vital that an Iberian horse of the old stamp is chosen, i.e bearing the Iberian Factor which we discussed in Chapter XI. Where the modern trend has produced an Iberian which could almost be taken for an Anglo-Arab, little or nothing will be gained. Seek out the Iberian Factor and much will be gained from the progeny of such an outcross.

In this way the Iberian horse can make a logical contribution to all Iberian-related breeds, including Thoroughbreds. The Hispano-Arab or Luso-Arab is also an excellent cross, but *only as a first-time cross*. It is to be hoped that many warm-blood breeders will follow the example of the Spanish Riding School of Vienna and take advantage of this ancient blood.

Nature's Authentic Schoolmaster

Until you sit on an Iberian horse you never fully appreciate what is meant by use of the seat. A strong statement perhaps, but it is fair to say that most horses will put up with a rider who moves about in the saddle, giving inadvertent signals with one or both seat bones and/or misaligning his weight. The horse ignores the messages and continues as before.

Lucinda Prior-Palmer, now Lucinda Green, wrote[1] about the Lusitano horses she found at the Lusitano Stud and Equitation Centre in England; her words bring out clearly what an invaluable teaching horse the Lusitano or Andalusian can be and how he compares with other schoolmasters.

> 'During that short time it became painfully clear to me that I had never learnt to follow each stride of the horse's movement with my hips. By trying to learn how to relax that part of me and allow it to follow the very exaggerated movements of these Portuguese stallions *I learnt that I had the use of muscles and gears that I had never recognised sufficiently before* . . .
>
> Riding well-schooled German horses, I thought that I was using my seat properly and could never quite understand why they never felt particularly 'together' for me. Unlike the sensitive Lusitano, the German horses tolerated my irregularities and were good enough to perform the movement asked of them if only after a fashion.'

The truth is that the Iberian horse is so soft and rounded in the back that he feels every nuance of movement and weight distribution made by the rider. To ride a horse of such sensitivity for the first time can be an off-putting experience. The horse moves away from the leg into lateral movements that one is unaware of having requested; he steps backwards if there is too much forward tilt of the pelvis; he will proceed straight into canter from too strong a forward aid, and so on and so forth. In fact one of the most difficult things for a stranger to these horses to achieve at the outset is to ride forward at the walk in a straight line.

Therefore, to begin with all these rapid responses are confusing to the rider and may even be misinterpreted for disobedience. Only as things begin to improve and he becomes truly aware of what his body is doing in the saddle does the rider realise, perhaps for the first time in his life, that all of a sudden he has a score or more of 'gears' at his disposal instead of the customary five. In the apt words of Lucinda Green, one discovers the use of 'muscles and gears' one has never recognised before.

The Iberian horse, therefore, provides the key to feel and control. He teaches the rider body awareness and sharpens up the mental approach. Crude aids are gradually dispensed with and the rider learns to refine his technique to the extent that he will eventually be able to ride this horse through complicated movements without the spectator noticing any obvious movements in hand, leg or trunk. When he reaches the level of becoming 'part' of the horse, a sympathetic 'listening' stage is reached. Rider and horse learn to tune in to each other's private radar systems,

---

1. From 'Lucinda's Column' in *Riding Magazine*, written shortly before she became world three-day event champion.

and as this attunement develops, the happy climax is reached when the rider need only think a command and the horse will carry out the request.

The action of the Iberian horse, in contrast to the longer-stepping breeds such as the Thoroughbred, the Arab and the big warm-bloods, feels rather bouncy and up-and-down, yet extremely comfortable. Due to his conformation the Iberian has the shortcoming of being unable to accommodate the extreme maximum extended gaits. This shorter, more elevated gait, however, holds a special value to the dedicated dressage rider.

First and foremost, it teaches him to feel the action of the hind legs coming underneath him. As each stride is taken, the feeling is accentuated and one literally feels the horse's loins rounding up on either side of his spine as he places a hind foot on the ground. This is further emphasised by the fact that the short-backed Iberian naturally brings his hocks further underneath him. It does not take long for the rider to establish which hind leg is producing impulsion at which moment, and this enables him to follow the movement and eventually control it to his liking with his own seat. Thus the gait may be shortened, lengthened or elevated literally through the action of the rider's pelvis and seat bones.

In the non-Iberian horse it is often very hard to distinguish which leg is coming underneath at any one time, for the whole effect is muffled by the gliding forward sensation of the longer-backed horse, particularly as this horse's point of balance tends to be more forward and there is more weight in the hand which may distract from the feeling of power behind the saddle.

As collected work, elevated work, repeated lateral movements, and turns and pirouettes, are physically easy for the schooled Iberian horse, being offered readily and with enjoyment, dressage pupils may have their fill of these sensations without the horse becoming tired and nappy.

An Iberian horse that is fit and well-muscled up will happily work for an hour at a stretch in all these highly compressed exercises, which simply would put far too great a strain on the average school horse even to be considered as a daily routine.

It must be remembered that the Iberian horse has been bred for such athletic exercise for centuries, and once schooled, many Andalusians and Lusitanos spend their lives in a permanent state of collection whenever they are ridden. The other breeds we have talked of, however, are more likely to have been bred for speed and efficiency across country, and for them the 'opened-up' free movements of the working or medium gaits come most naturally. For these horses, working in collection on circles and lateral exercises is a less natural state, imposed by the rider. While many horses will adapt and comply happily to these physically demanding requests, others bitterly dislike and resist them – as can be seen all too often in dressage competitions. It is a familiar sight to see a horse which has relished with enthusiasm the cross-country and show-jumping phases at horse trials or one day events, virtually scowling down his long nose as his rider tries to make a convincing attempt at the compulsory dressage test.

Because there is a shortage of good horses outside the Iberian-derived breeds which truly enjoy and are suited to the more advanced dressage movements, we have reached a situation in many countries, Britain and the United States included, where it has become a problem to give riders experience and confidence in advanced

The late Lord Loch who achieved his vision of bringing classical equitation on fully schooled horses within the grasp of ordinary riders with the opening of his Lusitano Equitation Centre in Suffolk. No one ever guessed that Charel, his Lusitano pictured here, who was schooled to advanced level, had only one eye. His work was perfect. (Photo by Charles Hodge)

work. Once a suitable horse has been found and schooled on, there are not many owners who will submit him to the hands of a learner dressage pupil, however keen. Therefore it is extremely hard for the would-be student to know where to go to obtain a 'feel' for the more advanced areas of the sport.

Dressage books abound, and one can revel in theory, but the written word cannot replace the physical experience of riding on horses which are happy to teach you and actually enjoy giving the rider a lead into the more complicated exercises. Only by riding and reading can one acquire the knowledge and the confidence to advance into the higher echelons of classical equitation. As we know, the Iberian horse is also blessed with a superb temperament which complements his physical ability to offer advanced work, and this too is invaluable to the student.

It was with this idea in mind that my late husband, Henry Loch, and I returned to his home in England after ten happy years of running our small dressage school in Portugal. We brought with us all our old friends, a mixed complement of Lusitano stallions, geldings and mares. This was the start of a huge venture in Suffolk which was to become an all-consuming work of dedication.

For four generations the Lochs' family home has been in a remote picture post-card village in West Suffolk, miles from the nearest city and well off the nearest train route. Yet so convinced were we that we had something unique and valuable to offer all those who genuinely wanted to understand dressage better, we built an Olympic-sized indoor arena on our farm, converted the house for residential pupils and put up enough modern stabling for twenty-five horses.

There were many who, to begin with, were not wholly behind us, especially 'within the Establishment'. How could we begin to compare these chunky, high-stepping stallions with their old-fashioned, long wavy manes and tails with the great Teutonic breeds whose engineered cadence and mechanical gaits appear to have become the envy of the world?

The whole point was that we were not trying to compare. We had brought our Iberian horses to help people ride their English, German, Dutch, Swedish, Irish and Danish horses with more understanding and achieve better results. For by experimenting and capitalising on the accentuated feel of the Lusitano's action, we could begin to teach people the degree of control it was possible to achieve. By learning to regulate their own seats and bodies in accordance with the Lusitano's threshold of sensitivity, pupils began to discover the wonderful feeling of true balance in a horse – when the horse's hocks are tucked so deeply underneath him that on a fingerlight contact he can be lifted into levade or allowed forward into extended canter with the same scale of response. As one former pupil[2] of the Spanish Riding School phrased it, 'almost controlled flight'.

Neither did we wish to compete with our horses, for reasons which will shortly be explained. What we wanted more than anything was to give ordinary people in England (and they came from all over the world as well – Australia, New Zealand, Canada, Brunei, the United States, Switzerland, Saudi Arabia, Holland, Kuwait, France, etc.) the opportunity to ride horses schooled to the same refined standards (if not in all movements at least in most) as the magnificent horses of Vienna. To qualify as a student for Vienna, you have to be exceptional. Perhaps three people from Great Britain will be accepted in a year for a few weeks' training on the Lipizzaners, but strings have to be pulled, recommendations made and it is a daunting process.

By importing Iberian horses into Great Britain and setting up a school of equitation where anyone who was prepared to learn could enrol, we were bringing classical equestrianism within the grasp of the ordinary rider.

Sadly, all this came to an end with the death of my husband, Henry. With all his cavalry experience and his admiration for the equitation of Vienna, Saumur, Spain and Portugal, he was a superb trainer and knew how to get the best from his horses and pupils. I could not allow myself to let those horses remain in other hands for commercial purposes. Pupils flocked to offer homes to all the Lusitanos; they had built up a large coterie of admirers during their years in England and it was not difficult to find ideal, permanent homes. This has led to the formation of The Lusitano Breed Society[3] in England which is complementary to its sister organisation, The British Andalusian Horse Society.[4]

Today, the same horses continue to teach and to help their new owners with their dressage, and there is a growing demand amongst the British public for more such horses.

In France, there are several schools which use Iberian horses to teach pupils

2. Words used by Charles Harris, F.I.H., F.A.B.R.S., F.B.H.S., the only British rider to complete the full three-year course at the Spanish Riding School of Vienna. He regularly taught at the Lusitano Stud and Equitation Centre and greatly appreciated the contribution to teaching made by these horses.
3. Formed 1982. Address: The Secretary, 4 Jamaica Crescent, Malvern Link, Worcester.
4. Formed 1982/83. Address: The Secretary, East Cottage, Skeete Road, Lyminge, nr Folks, Kent.

Imperador, a Lusitano stallion from the Infante da Camara Stud, in a dressage competition. Here he is shown in collected trot. Note the rounded elevated action of the limbs (Photo by Philip Attwood)

more advanced work, notably that of Michel Henriquet who is France's leading High School rider and who trained under Nuno Oliveira who merited Michel's work sufficiently to mention him in his book *Reflections on Equestrian Art*. Chantilly is rich in Iberian horses and the French pursue the disciplines of High School, a legacy from the days of La Guerinière, in the peace of discreet private manèges that lie in the forests. They practise without the urge to compete, finding satisfaction in the constant quest for purity of art. The Museum of the Horse in Chantilly, with its marvellous backcloth of château and lake, is open to the public any day of the week and there we may find Lusitanos, and Andalusians and Alter Reals giving wonderful displays of the highest standard, which always includes a breathtakingly beautiful quadrille.

In Australia, there are two excellent schools where displays of High School can be seen by tourists and the general public. Both started by the late Ray Williams and both named *El Caballo*, they are situated just outside Sydney and Perth, and only use Andalusian horses.

In Germany, the famous school of Reinstitut von Neindorff uses Lusitano and Lipizzaner horses for most of the advanced work, and Herr von Neindorff is a regular visitor to Mestre Nuno Oliveira's school in Portugal and freely admits tremendous admiration for the Portuguese School's emphasis on lightness and softness in all classical equitation.

There is therefore a growing acceptance of the Baroque horse, as he is often known, all over the world which one hopes will catch the imagination of the British and American schools of thought more vividly.

The Ennoblement of the Art of Dressage in Competition

I have often been asked to explain why it is that the Lipizzaner or pure-bred Iberian horse does not excel in international dressage competition. The answer is simple enough. The specialised manège work of the horse bred for High School and the versatile competition work required of contenders for the Olympic games have evolved into two completely different concepts of achievement:

> The first is designed for work within a confined area where the horse demonstrates his suitability for the physically gymnastic exercises required in the successful execution of the martial arts. Emphasis is placed largely on courage and agility which combine to produce a spectacle of great beauty and artistry.

> The second is designed for work in a large arena wherein the horse demonstrates his suitability for covering the ground in the most economic, balanced and rhythmical way possible at the same time carrying out a logically designed series of obedience tests which at its most advanced level combine certain, but by no means all, of the exercises of the first school. Emphasis is placed on fluency and forward-going power which merge to produce a spectacle of efficiency, practicality and harmony.

With the first, which we may call the old school, covering the ground as an expression of forward movement has never been an end in itself. The idea of going forward was for a horse to develop sufficient thrust and power from the back and hocks so that he could surge forward in a series of controlled leaps and 'airs' above the ground when required. This manoeuvrability allowed the rider maximum scope for the art of attack and defence, whereas covering large tracts of ground would only be required if put to flight. Instant impulsion was displayed in full gallop – *ventre a terre* – often from the standstill or rein-back within the smallest of confines.

The pirouettes and small circles, the half and full passes, were all movements designed to be performed in tight corners – the four walls of the riding school gradually taking over from the naturally restricted confines of the battlefield. The emphasis on all training and preparation for the High School horse was (and still is where this School continues to exist) on total balance and lightness in hand. This enabled the rider to achieve any gait from the seat instantaneously without first having to follow through the interim gaits. To achieve such control it was required to bring the horse's centre of gravity as far back as possible since all movement stems from the back and the hindquarters. High School horses therefore develop extremely strong loins and often, in addition to well-muscled quarters, an over-developed second thigh, which helps to support the degree of flexion required in these athletic exercises.

Naturally, over the centuries, horses best able to adapt to this physically demanding work were selected, and so it was that the Iberian and Barb with their natural talent for this work dominated the classical schools of Vienna, Naples, Antwerp and Paris. Great classical riding masters such as Pluvinel and La Guerinière always rode their horses in collection and there are no illustrations in the books of these great masters and their contemporaries which show horses in extension or in the modern concept of riding forward 'on the bit' as interpreted by dressage judges and competitors today.

In contrast, the High School horse was not required to make a strong contact with the rider's hand. The interpretation of a balanced horse, or being 'on the bit', to the old school was when the horse had progressed far beyond the intermediate stage of stretching forward with his neck into a contact, and was sufficiently back on his hocks to heighten his poll and drop his nose into a vertical line due to his increased physical strength. This allowed his master to control him from seat, back and weight aids which gave him far greater scope for the work carried out. The reins were only to be used very lightly, often with one hand (as the other held the lance or a small firearm) and there was no loss of discipline if for one reason or another the rider dispensed with both hands, the weight of the reins alone being sufficient to keep the horse under control.

The second concept of achievement, international dressage governed by FEI rules, has never pretended or intended to emulate the martial aspect of the old school. It has evolved as a sport primarily as a test of obedience for the competition dressage and eventing horse.

When dressage was first included in the Stockholm Olympic Games of 1912, competitors had to jump over five obstacles and the last of these was a barrel which was rolled towards the horse. Until after the war, it was the Army who dominated these international competitions, and dressage, combined with cross-country and jumping events, was an excellent test for the modern cavalry horse, which had to be forward-going and fast across country. By the time dressage was being included in the Olympic Games as a separate entity (as opposed to forming a phase of three-day eventing) and more advanced movements borrowed from the old school were introduced, the emphasis was still on the concept of covering the ground and striding out rather than working in a confined space. Thus the international dressage arena was devised, measuring 20 × 60 metres. Every inch of this of this was needed by the bigger breeds being used, particularly the long-striding hunter-Thoroughbred crosses from England and Ireland, and the big carriage and jumping breeds from Germany, Holland and Scandinavia. These horses excel in the large arena; they achieve brilliant extensions with the lighter breeds, floating down the long sides, and the bigger Holsteins or Hanoverians – often measuring between 17 and 18 h.h. – covering the ground with all the piston-like automation of a Rolls-Royce engine.

The competitions currently devised for these horses accentuate their forward-going ability. The horse's point of balance is kept central, encouraging weight to flow into the hand ('on the bit') while the horse remains horizontal to the ground. Because of this emphasis, the horse has to work even harder with his back, but the developed pulling power and big rumps of the carriage breeds are able to cope with this type of locomotion. Dressage tests therefore developed to demonstrate this horse at his most useful and were built up of a logical sequence of transitions. Nothing was asked too suddenly or too quickly, and in the early preparatory tests for the novice dressage horse, even movements such as rein-back were considered too strenuous on the horse's back to be included until a higher stage was reached. The whole accent was on going forward, and only at advanced levels were changes of hand in canter and full pirouette included. Finally passage and piaffe were brought in at Grand Prix level. Movements such as levade and courbette were not included as they did not conform to the forward-going theme.

Those horses which have made their mark in international FEI competition dressage have largely been the European warm-bloods. They combine height with pulling power (from some of their driving antecedents – the Hanoverian being a notable example) and their free forward movement has come from Thoroughbred and Arab blood, whilst their powerful hock action has often been derived from long-ago Spanish blood. The development of the English Thoroughbred for dressage, in contrast to his more natural talent for racing, has been an interesting transition, and where it has worked (a notable example being Wily Trout, the mount of Christopher Bartle who rides internationally for Great Britain) it has been a joy to observe. There is perhaps nothing so graceful and elegant as a brilliantly schooled Thoroughbred floating over a dressage arena and producing a gaiety and verve that few other breeds possess. Successful cross-breds, such as Dutch Courage[5] who won an Olympic bronze for Great Britain with his trainer/rider/part owner Jennie Loriston-Clarke, have contributed to a new stamp of horse appearing on the modern equestrian scene which combines the very best of all the breeds and thus proves that with judicious breeding, the right genes can be selected and a horse of great function as well as beauty can be produced. Dutch Courage is half-Dutch warm-blood and half English Thoroughbred and I am convinced that somewhere far back in his history on both sides, Iberian blood has been present.

The real discrepancy between the two schools of equitation which we have discussed lies in the disinclination to admit that there is a difference. The FEI bases its rules on the Spanish Riding School, yet there is a definite unwillingness on the part of judges to accept the classical standards laid down by that School for the more advanced movements. We have yet to see competitors at FEI level being strictly penalised in passage and piaffe, for example, when their horse clearly does not carry out the movement as prescribed. Because of the way in which 'on the bit' is interpreted, and the importance given to extensions, competition horses are not nowadays encouraged to lower their croups to the extent required for the more elevated movements. This leads to the execution of a movement which is not clearly punctuated and fails to conform to the standard laid down. Surprisingly, however, this basic non-performance or half-performance is not heavily penalised and apologetic attempts at piaffe and passage are awarded average or even good marks.

On the other hand, and this is where disparity occurs, the Lipizzaner or Andalusian which braves the large arena will be severely penalised for the fact that his shorter, more compact frame will not allow him to cover the ground in such pronounced extension as his English or German counterpart, and where he should be able to gain advantage from his superb collected and elevated gaits, he is prevented from doing so.

There is confusion too in the judges' interpretation of contact and balance. Riders who control their horses with back and weight aids rather than excessive use of the legs are often penalised for being 'behind the movement' which discourages progress to the climax of classical training, i.e. to the point where the horse is

---

5. Dutch Courage is jointly-owned by Jennie Loriston-Clarke and Mrs R. Steele.

in total self-balance and so light in the hand that he can carry out any instruction the rider gives him instantaneously and without the need to rely on rein contact.

It would be wonderful for the noble art of dressage if these two aspects of equitation could come together and intermarry. In an ideal world, the Baroque horse of Spain, Portugal and Vienna could compete quite happily alongside the modern dressage horses of England, the United States and the Benelux countries, for where one type would excel in the collected and elevated movements, the other would shine in the extended and medium gaits. Lightness and gaiety would be as important as freedom and impulsion, and such a step forward would, I am convinced, bring a freshness and enthusiasm to the international dressage scene.

In reality, I believe the answer lies in the establishment of separate competitions for the Baroque horse. These would take place in a small arena and tests would be devised to suit the conformation of the horse. Less emphasis would be placed on covering large expanses of ground in the same gait, and more importance would be given to balance and agility, with classical movements such as the levade being reintroduced at the top of the scale.

The Kür to Music at World Championship level has proved an enormous success throughout the competing world although it is only in its early years of formation. This is largely thanks to the Earl and Countess of March of Goodwood House, home of English dressage as well as of racing, near Chichester, Sussex.

Baroque dressage competitions performed to music by horses of Iberian descent would attract many people outside the horse sphere to watch dressage as an artform, in the same way that today's interpretation of competitive ice-skating has made addicts of people who previously had no interest whatsoever in this sport.

When we consider how many people flock to watch the Lipizzaners, not only at their traditional base in Vienna but also at Kyalami in Johannesburg, South Africa, and how the art-loving tourist is drawn to watch classical performances given by Andalusians and Lusitanos in Jerez and Lisbon and across the other side of the world in Australia, it is clear that we have not yet found the magic formula. Dressage would benefit much from being released from its aura of mystique and enigma, and funds which are sorely needed to provide sponsorship and training fees to help young riders achieve the level of instruction required to take them to the Olympic Games and other international competitions, would be made more readily available from spectator interest.

Whilst the highly skilled technique of competition dressage today is not denied, it has to be said that amongst the general public, the pervading image is still one of disenchantment. The British and American public are not attracted by the intricacies of what they see as little more than obedience tests, and therefore alongside these competitions, displays and contests which encourage the horse to demonstrate joy or *allegria* are badly needed to draw the public and the media and to give the sport the prestige it deserves.

Versatility in all Spheres

Readers in Britain may wonder where it is possible to find good Iberian horses. It is not difficult to import from either Spain or Portugal, but it is essential to seek the advice of the breed societies and make the right contacts. Too many pure-

No horse possesses such courage and unquestioning faith in its rider as the Iberian. Here an Andalusian stallion completes a leap from a moving boat onto a pier during the making of a film. Iberian horses are invariably used for all stunt work.

bred horses have turned out to be cross-breds, and this is obviously disappointing for those who wish to breed and require bona fide papers.

Every year a growing number of foals are born to pure-bred Iberian horses in Great Britain. Every year, a number of 'made' schooled horses will be imported. Film makers love Iberian horses and great epic pictures such as *Ben Hur*, *El Cid*, *With a View to a Kill* of James Bond fame, and *Legend*, all used Andalusian or Lusitano horses. Photogenic and flamboyant, these horses display a remarkable sense of occasion and bring life and presence to whatever situation they find themselves in.

Now the Iberian horse is making his mark in the international driving world. He has always been the horse *par excellence* for carriage driving in Spain but now his ability for this sport is being recognised abroad and Iberian stallions will work quite happily in harness with mares.

The Iberian horse is no stranger to the circus. Bertram Mills, Billy Smart and Chipperfields have all used Iberian horses for their liberty acts, and modern experts such as Mary Chipperfield and Tanya Larrigan from established circus families within the United Kingdom believe that this breed is unsurpassable for the demands of equestrian ballet in the ring.

In stunt work, it is again the Iberian horse who will have the courage to jump through fire, leap from a lorry, and gallop out of a heaving boat at sea (see photograph). Mario Luraschi from France, one of the world's leading stunt riders, who gave an exhibition of trick riding and chariot racing at the Royal International Horse Show in 1983, now works exclusively with Iberian horses. Having started his yard with many different breeds, he gradually came to realise that only the

The influence of Iberian blood over the centuries is clearly shown in these four portraits of horses of the twentieth century. Top right: Lusitano mare. Top left: Kladruber stallion. Bottom right: Lipizzaner stallion. Bottom left: Barb stallion. (Photos by Sally Anne Thompson, except Lusitano mare)

The noble head of the horse for all seasons. Montemor-O-Novo, a Lusitano stallion now standing at stud in England. (Photo by Madeleine McCurley, courtesy of Mrs Nan Thurman)

Iberian horse has the amenity for the discipline which is required in this often hazardous work, as well as the sheer bravery.

Wherever man must work closely with his horse, the Iberian horse or his successor is first choice.

The Iberian horse's versatility knows no bounds. We have only to gaze at Novilheiro as he clears a six-foot wall, and to watch his great brother Opus quiver under saddle before a bull, and we feel awed to have had the honour of knowing, riding and loving this breed of horse.

In the same way that social barriers in the equestrian world have been broken down in recent years, the barriers of prejudice and lack of understanding about anything 'foreign' are also rightly disintegrating. People who truly love horses always admit that there is more to learn, more to experience, more to enjoy.

If I had not been convinced that the future holds great promise for the Iberian horse in countries outside the Iberian Peninsula, I would not have had the energy and determination to write this book which is the result of years of research and, of course, riding these wonderful horses. As I watch the sun go down over the eucalyptus trees, casting long purple shadows over the red earth and hear the gay clip of small, neat hooves resounding off the crumbling masonry of a nobleman's ruined *palacio* perched high on the hillside, I am tempted as always to rush out and watch the unknown *cavaleiro* riding by.

Instead, I remain on the terrace, pen in hand, looking towards the sapphire Atlantic which carried the first explorers with their Iberian horses to claim the New World for God and King. This horse will spread his wings again – of that I am certain.

c/o Quinta da Charneca
Charneca
Cascais
Portugal
20th June, 1986

Appendix – The Royal Studs of England, 1576–1624

The details reproduced in this appendix are from the only historical records known to exist which show the state of the royal studs between 1576 and 1624 and which illustrate the foundation types of the Thoroughbred horse in that period. (See Chapter XIII)

The lists below are from Prospero d'Osma's report of 1576 on the royal studs of Malmesbury and Tutbury and show the number of mares of courser, small courser and Jennet blood which were available for stud. These are the only breeds mentioned.

MALMESBURY

Courser Mares
.: A bay mare with white spot in the forehead
.: A black mare with white hind feet
.: A bay with four white feet
.: A light bay with no markings
   A dappled bay with a star
.: A bay with four white feet and a white spot
.: A black without markings
   A dark chestnut
   A light bay with a star
.: A light bay with four white feet and bald face

Half of these are already with foal; the other half will be brought to the stallion this year. Those which are not with foal, you will find indicated by this mark .: which I have made with the point of my pen. And of these 28 mares which are covered, 26 will be brought to the stallion this year, since the other two are with foal, one by the bay courser of Naples, named 'Il Superbo' (The Proud), the other, its companion, by the great dapple-grey courser of Naples, named 'Non Piu' (No More). Among these you will find 10 courser mares to which more liberty and a greater quantity of food must be given for their sustenance, since a courser mare, having a large body, needs an abundance of food to sustain it. This applies more particularly to mares with foal. For it is necessary that these have more nourishment and the care of someone who is fond of them and knows their needs, in order that he may act in conformity with what I shall say as I go along in reference to the transferring and placing of them in the place known as Ratborne Raile, which must be divided into two sections, one for the said courser mares, the other for the small courser mares.

The jennets can be kept in another section of the park, to the south called Tenraile. The stock shall remain in these three enclosures for a period of one month, each breed in its own place. In this way, the grass in the aforesaid not very fertile soil will have time to grow to the extent that when the mares are transferred from the three enclosures to others which I shall mention, some will be well nourished, since they will find themselves in a fertile place.

The Number of Small Courser Mares
.: A dark chestnut with a white spot in the forehead
.: A light gray without markings
.: A dark gray
.: A dark bay with a star
.: A light bay without markings
.: A light bay with four white feet
.: A chestnut without markings
.: A bay with a star
.: A light bay with four white feet and a star
.: A bay with a star
.: A bay with four white feet and a star

The Number of Jennet Mares
.: A light bay with a star
.: A fleabitten gray
.: A dappled bay with white fore feet and white off hind foot
.: A bay with white hind feet and white near fore feet
    A light gray
    A bay with white hind feet and white off fore foot
    A dapple gray with round spots
    A light bay with a star
The number of coursers, small coursers, and jennets which are ready to be covered is 29.

TUTBURY

The Number of Courser Mares
    A black without markings
    A fleabitten gray
    A bay with white near hind foot, white lip, and star
    A light bay with white off hind foot
    A bay without markings
These five courser mares will be sent to the stud this year. The others [there were 20 in all] you will find listed below [these have been excluded from this list] have foaled and therefore will rest this year.

    [The five above were destined] to be given this year to the gray courser stallion called 'Grison' [From his name obviously a Neapolitan].

The Number of Small Courser Mares
    A chestnut with white off hind foot and blaze
    A light bay with bald face
    A chestnut without markings
    A sorrell (sauro) with four white feet and bald face
    A dark dappled gray with round spots with four white feet
    A dark bay with white hind feet and a star
These six small coursers will be given this year to the stallion called 'Abbot' so named because of his large body.

The Number of Jennet Mares
    A dappled gray (with round spots)
    A light bay with a blaze
    A dappled bay with four white feet, bald face and black spine
    A fleabitten white

A fleabitten gray
A dark chestnut with white hind feet and white off fore foot
These six jennets will be given this year to the stallion called 'Argentina'.

In d'Osma's lengthy text which advises on the type and age of mares and stallions to be used for stud, and on the manner in which covering should be carried out (he does not recommend stallions under thirteen years of age, and mares in his opinion should not be under five) he defines his use of the word 'courser': 'we have horses for saddle which are called coursers; then another variety which are called small coursers.'

This is somewhat confusing for whilst in all probability they were imported Neapolitans (which were indeed of two types, large and small – see Chapter V) the term saddle horse indicates any riding breed. D'Osma goes on to explain that both types of courser are bigger than the Jennets, the Barb, the Sardinians and another variety, the Slavonians. He adds that 'Each one of these breeds is beautiful in itself and for its particular qualities; and pleasing because everything having taken the natural course, they are with just reason, alert, spirited and proud.'

The following are the only lists available of the royal studs at Hampton Court and have been left in their original form for historical interest. These lists contain many typographical inconsistencies as so often occurs in ancient documents. After the dispersal of the royal studs under Cromwell, apparently no Thoroughbred stock was bred there again until the reign of William III and Queen Anne. The royal studs at Tutbury and Malmesbury entirely broke up.

HAMPTON COURT STUD *c.* 1620

Note of all the mares my Lord Marques (Buckingham) appoynted to be Covered at *Hampton Court*

May	The six of May was Covered with the Barbery Sheffeeld one of the fower Spanysh Mares, a Bay with a bauld face, white feet, a black mayne and tayle.
4	The three other of the same Cumpany, Rann with them, the White Courser that the Capten of the Gard gave your Lordship, six weekes.
	The xiij^th of the same month was Covered a Bay Barbery, without white, one of the mares that my Lord Digbey sent with the lame Barbery, that my Lord Donkestor gave your Lordship.
2	The same day also was Covered, of the same cumpany another bay Barbery mare with a lyttell reach downe the face, and tow white feet, with the Barbe Cheffeld.
	Whaddon. The xxj^th of the same moneth was covered a Gray Mare with a flebytton face, with the Black Cursor.
	The same day was covered a light Dun mare, with a flexon mayne, and a small white on her Nose, with the Gray Spanysh Gennet.
	The xxiij^th was covered a Darker Dun mare with the Dapple Barbery.
4	The same day was ther another gray Mare, one of the same Cumpany, covered with the Black Coursor.
June	The fourth of June was Covered the bigger light gray Barbery Mare, that my Lord *Digbey sent with the Barbery Sheffield.
	The same day was Covered a Bay Mare, with a Coult, with the Black Courser.
3	The sixth of the Moneth was Covered a Chesnutt Mare, sumtyme my Lord Brooks, with the Barbe Sheffeeld.

The following second account is taken from C. M. Prior's research for *The Royal Studs of the 16th and 17th Centuries* and is the only other list in existence, as far as we know, of the breeding situation at Hampton Court, although unlike the first account Hampton Court is not actually named, but there are several pointers to suggest that this was the royal stud concerned. The phrase 'in the Course' is understood to indicate Hampton Court; and Mr Graham's Park, mentioned three times in the list was known to be part of Hampton Court parkland which was leased at that time to a Mr Graham by the Duke of Buckingham on behalf of the King.

HAMPTON COURT STUD 1623

'A noat of the Daie of the Month that my Lord his Mares were Covered, and with what Horses, in Anno 1623.'

Imprimis, the Bay mare that was Ednes, was covered with the Bay Jennett in Mr. Waterhouse his chardge, the 10th April, 1623.

The mare which Sir Francis Cotenton[1] gave My Lord was covered with the black Courser that was my Lord of Donkester's,[2] the 11th April 1623.

The mare that was Mr. Alles, was covered with the gray Barbery, in Mr. Waterhouse charge, the 11th April, 1623.

The Spanish mare that George Armstrong keept, was covered the 20 daie of April 1623 with the bay Jennett in Mr. Waterhouse chardge.

The Bay ball'd mare that came from Whoden,[3] was covered with the Gray Jennett that came last out of Spaine, the 22nd April, 1623.

The gray pyed mare that came from Whaddon was covered with the gray Jennett that came last out of Spaine, the 22nd April, 1623.

The Bay mare that came from Whoden, with a Blemish on her eie, was covered with the gray Barberie the 22nd daye of April, 1623.

The bright Bay mare was covered, which was Sir Frances Hedensen's, with the gray Jennett, the 26th daie of Aprill, 1623.

The dark gray Barbery mare with the white Sadley Spott on her Backe, was covered withe the little gray Barbery that Mr. Ashburnham rydes the 26th daie of Aprill, 1623.

The Bay mare wich the Captane of the Guard[4] gave my Lord [Buckingham] was covered with the little bay Jennet that came last out of Spaine, 1623 the first of May.

The whitt gray barbery mare was covered with the little gray Barbery, the 2nd daie of May, 1623.

The Bay mare that George Armstrong keept, was covered with the great bay Jennett the last daie of April, 1623.

The great bay Jennett covered the whitt mare which was in Theobalds park, the 3rd May, 1623.

The Sorell mare in the Course which had no foal was covered with the great gray Jennett the 8th May, 1623.

The Bay mare was covered with the gray barbery, the 15th May, 1623.

The Spanish mare that hath the horse colt in the Course, was covered with the gray Jennett, the 13th of May, 1623.

The Bay mare that hath the Coult in Mr. Graham's Park, was covered with the gray Jennett, the 25th Aprill, 1623.

One bright bay mare, that goethe in Mr. Graham's Park, was covered with the gray Jennett, the 25th April 1623.

The bay bald Spanish mare was covered by the great bay Jennett, the 25th April, 1623.

The Spanish mare, with the black mane and black tail, which hath the horse colt, was covered with the gray Jennett, the 15th May 1623.

The Sorrell mare, with the mare colt in the Course, was covered with the gray Jennett, 5 of June 1623.

1. Sir Francis Cottington – British Ambassador to the court of Madrid.
2. Doncaster – later known as Earl of Carlisle.
3. Whaddon (sometimes referred to as Whoden) was near Bletchley in North Bucks, an estate confiscated by James I and given to the Earl of Buckingham.
4. The Captain of the Guard was Sir Henry Rich, afterwards Lord Holland, well known British diplomat in Spain, whom with Lord Digby*, Cottington and Doncaster, was known to import Spanish horses.

C. M. Prior states: 'It will be observed that all the mares in this stud were covered either by Genets or by Barbery horses, a distinction, as usual, being drawn between the Genet of Andalusia and the Barbery from Spain or Morocco. As no pedigrees are given of the mares, save in very few cases, it cannot be said what breed they were, but the probability is they were mainly Spanish genets or Barbs.'

An Account of all his Majesty's Mares and Colts, within the Race of Tutbury in Staffordshire, and with what Horses the Breeding Mares were Covered in this Yeare, 1624.

TUTBURY RACE 1624
(From George Villiers, Duke of Buckingham's Papers)

Covered in hand with the Ambling Courser Digby, the 18th May, 1624
1. Bay Devonshire with the specke
2. Bright bay Polonia
3. Black Douglas with the Starr
4. Bay Polonia with three white feet
5. Black Emperor
6. Bay Polonia with white haires upon ye taile
7. Bay Polonia with wall eyes
8. Bay Emden
9. Chestnut Buller

The Arabian Colt covered in hand, the 18 day of May, 1624
1. Black Bullion
2. Bay Brilladore
3. Bay Polonia with a streak
4. Gray Trugg
5. Black Ginnet
6. Bright Bay Trugg

Covered in hand with the Dark gray Barbary, the 18 of May, 1624
1. Gray Savoy with the cloud in the face
2. Skewd Gilmet
3. Bay Chestnut
4. Browne bay Trugge
5. Bay Barbary with the white lipp
6. Gray Emperor
7. Bay Vadamount

Potts, the White Frensh horse, covered in hand the 18 of May 1624
1. Sorell Savoy
2. A bay mare, neither bay Embden, nor bay Brilliadore, but like them
3. Bay Polonia with the white starr, and the neere foott white
4. Dark gray Dun John
5. Black Savoy
6. Chestnut Courser
7. Skewd Barabary
8. Black Douglas with the Specke

Potts, the gray Courser, covered in hand the 18 of May, 1624
1. White Brillidare
2. Gray Robin
3. White Fortune
4. Regina the old courser
5. Gray Douglas

6. Gray Courser
7. Bay Polonia with the white heeles
8. Daple courser
9. Great gray Savoy

The Spanish Ginnet, dapled, with long Male [Mane] covered in hand the 18 of May 1624
1. Black Trubb
2. Bright bay Dun John
3. Fine gray Savoy
4. Bay Burley with the Sadle Spotts
5. White gray Burley
6. Burley with the cloud
7. Bright bay Savoy
8. Bay Polonia, with the Star onely.

It is a pity that the only information afforded about the mares is their colouring, but in those times the names given to animals usually indicated their breeding. C.M. Prior takes the viewpoint that they were mostly Barbs and Spanish. The names Savoy and Ginnet would almost certainly indicate Spanish blood, Ginnet from the word Jennet, and Savoy being a Duchy of the Spanish crown. The six stallions used were all of foreign blood. Digby could either have been a Neapolitan Courser procured by George Digby who was sent to Italy to obtain horses in 1618, or a Spanish ambling horse from his brother John Digby, Ambassador at Madrid who later became the Earl of Bristol in 1622. The 'Frensh' horse would have been a Barb horse, and gray Courser a Barb or a Neapolitan. This is the only occasion in all the records of the royal studs between the sixteenth and seventeenth centuries where an Arabian stallion is mentioned.

From the Duke of Buckingham's Papers, an account of the mares being used at Malmesbury for stud in the year 1620 is given, together with a description of the stallion being used for each. Here the names and descriptions of the mares are included as they are indicative of their breeds, although again no specific breed is given.

MALMESBURY RACE
May the 5th, 1620

Barren (and Maiden) Mares

Poland, a bright bay mare was covered by	gray Turke
Jennett, a Dunn mare was covered by	Ambling Courser
Bay Denmarke, a bay mare was covered by	white Gennett
Denmarke, a bay mare was covered by	bay Barbery
Southampton, a red Roand mare was covered by	bay Barbery
Hundsdon, a Roand mare was covered by	gray Turke
Arrabian, a bright bay mare was covered by	white Gennett
Savoy, a sorrell mare was covered by	Ambling Courser
Vadamon, a bright bay mare was covered by	Gray Turke
George, a Roand mare was covered by	White Gennett
Savoy, a young Darke gray mare was covered by	Bay Barbery
Poland, a browne bay mare was covered by	White Gennett
Frizzland, a gray mare was covered by	gray Turke
Gorge, a Roanish mare was covered by	bay Barbery
Courser, a browne mare was covered by	White Gennett
George, a brown bay mare was covered by	gray Turke
Turke, a blew Roand mare was covered by	Ambling Courser
Vadamon, a bright bay mare was covered by	White Gennett
Gennett, a gray mare was covered by	Ambling Courser
Vadamon, a black mare was covered by	White Gennett

Gray King, a bay mare was covered by	Bay Poland
Denmark, a bay mare was covered by	Ambling Courser
Barbara, a Dark gray mare, and Plunevet, a young Bay mare, of Fower yeares olde	Bay Poland
Treasurer, a young black mare of Fower yeares olde & Turk, a young Roand mare of Fower yeares olde were covered by	
Turke, a bay mare of Fower yeares olde	Bay Poland
Spanyard, a black mare	
Savoy, a bay mare of Fower yeares olde, and	
Turke, a bay mare of Fower yeares olde were covered by	

Bearing Mares

Carr, a Dappell gray mare, folled a bay horse Colte, was covered agayne by	Bay Barbara
Vadamon, a bay mare, folled a chesnut mare Colte, was covered agayne by	Gray Turke
Hundsdon, a black Roand mare, folled a Dunne horse colte, was covered agayne by	Ambling Courser
Woodstock, a Roand mare, folled a bay horse Colte, was covered agayne by	Bay Barbara
Harrison, a gray mare, folled a bay horse Colte, was covered agayne by	Ambling Courser
Denmark, a black mare, folled a bay horse Colte, was covered agayne by	White Gennett
Arrabian, a bay mare, folled a sorrell horse Colte, was covered agayne by	Bay Barbara

According to Prior: 'These 39 mares, of which only 8 had foals at foot, which suggests that many were newly imported, were covered by 5 different stallions, all of foreign blood, and presumably standing near Malmesbury (Cole Park) Stud. No pedigrees are given of these mares, and one can only guess at their nationality by their names, from which it will be gathered they were mostly of foreign descent, probably all either Genets or Barbs, the sires of the foals not being stated. It would appear that at this date that the two royal studs were mainly, if not entirely composed of imported animals, which arrived in numbers from Spain or Morocco.'

References

CHAPTER I

D'ANDRADE, Ruy, *Alrededor del Caballo Espanol*, Lisbon, 1954.

— *O Cavalo do Sorraia*, Lisbon, 1945.

— *O Cavalo Andaluz de Perfil Convexo*, Lisbon, 1941.

BLUNDEVILLE, Thomas, *The Fower Cheifest Offyces of Horsemanshippe*, London, 1565.

BRADFORD, Ernle, *The Sword and the Scimitar: The Saga of the Crusades*, Gollancz, London, 1974.

CAVENDISH, William, Duke of Newcastle, *A General System of Horsemanship*, Antwerp, 1658.

CHURCHILL, Peter, *The World Atlas of Horses and Ponies*, Sampson Low, Maidenhead, 1980.

COELHO, Alfredo Baptista (Portuguese hippologist and agronomist), letters to author, Lisbon, October 1985–June 1986.

DENT, Anthony, and MACHIN GOODALL, Daphne, *Foals of Epona*, Galley Press Ltd, London, 1962.

El Caballo en Espana, Publicaciones del Ministerio de Informacion Y Turismo, Madrid, 1975.

GLUBB, Sir John Bagot (Glubb Pasha), *The Course of Empire; The Arabs and Their Successors*, Hodder & Stoughton, London, 1965.

GLYN, Colonel Sir Richard, *The World's Finest Horse and Ponies*, George G. Harrap & Co. Ltd, London, 1971.

GOUBAUX, Armand and BARRIER, Gustave, *The Exterior of the Horse*, translated by Simon J.J. Harger, V.M.D., J.B. Lippincott & Co., Philadelphia and London, 1892.

KAMEN, Henry, *A Concise History of Spain*, Thames and Hudson, London, 1973.

LIVERMORE, H.V., *A History of Portugal*, Cambridge University Press, 1947.

MACHIN GOODALL, Daphne, *A History of Horse Breeding*, Robert Hale, London, 1977.

MATHIAS, Jorge, *Portugal e os Seus Cavalos*, Edicoes Antonio Ramos, Lisbon, 1980.

CHAPTER II

D'ANDRADE, Fernando, *A Short History of the Spanish Horse and of the Iberian 'Gineta' Horsemanship for which this Horse is Adapted*, Lisbon, 1973.

D'ANDRADE, Ruy, *O Cavalo Andaluz de Perfil Convexo*, (see above).

APPIAN, *Iberian War*, 53, 54.

DIODORUS SICILUS, Book V, Chapter XXXIII.

DOMECQ Y DIAZ, Prologue to *El Caballo en Espana* (see above).

FISHER, H.A.L., *A History of Europe*, Arnold, 1938.

HOMER, *Iliad*.

LAMB, Major A.J., *The Story of the Horse*, Alexander Maclehose & Co., London, 1938.

LIVERMORE, H., *op. cit.*

LIVY, T., Books XXV–XXVII.

MACHIN GOODALL, Daphne, *op. cit.*

POLYBIUS, Book XXXV, Chapter I.

VESEY-FITZGERALD, Brian, *The Book of the Horse*, Nicholson & Watson, 1947.

VIRGIL, *Aeneid* and *Georgics*.

XENOPHON, *Hellenics*, Book VII, 369 BC Peloponnesian War.

CHAPTER III

ANTONIUS, O., *Die Rassengliederung der quartaren Wilpferdes Europas*, 1912.

COELHO, Alfredo Baptista, *op. cit.*

DOUGALL, Neill, 'The Mount of Kings', article published in *Riding Magazine*, May, London, 1971.

DOSSENBACH, Monique and Hans D., *The Noble Horse*, Webb and Bower, London, 1985.

FUGGER, Marcus, *Von der Gestüterey*, 1527.

FURLONGE, Geoffrey, *The Lands of Barbary*, John Murray, London, 1966.

GLUBB, Sir John Bagot (Glubb Pasha), *Soldiers of Fortune*, Hodder and Stoughton, 1973.

GLYN, Colonel Sir Richard, *op. cit.*

HARTLEY EDWARDS, E., 'Saddlery' in *The Horseman's International Book of Reference*, edited by Jean and Lily Powell Froissard, Stanley Paul, London, 1980.

HITTI, Professor Philip K., (Professor Emeritus of Semitic Literature at Princeton University) *History of the Arab*, Macmillan, London, 1960.

KAMEN, Henry, *op. cit.*

LLAMAS, Colonel Juan, *Caballo Espanol – Caballo de Reyes*, Madrid, 1985.

MACHIN GOODALL, Daphne, *op. cit.*

PTOLEMY, Claudius, *Geography*, 140 AD.

READ, Jan, *The Moors in Spain and Portugal*, Faber and Faber, London, 1974.

REESE, M.M., *The Royal Office of Master of the Horse*, Threshold Books, London, 1976.

RENATUS, Publius Vegetius, *Digestorum Artis Mulomedicina Libri*, 400 AD.

RIDGEWAY, W. *The Origin and Influence of the Thoroughbred Horse*, Cambridge University Press, 1905.

SHAKESPEARE, William, *Hamlet*.

— *Othello*.

— *Richard II*.

WATT, W.M., *A History of Islamic Spain*, London, 1965.

WENTWORTH, Lady, *Thoroughbred Racing Stock*, George Allen & Unwin Ltd, London, 1938.

— *The Authentic Arabian Horse*, George Allen & Unwin Ltd, London, 1945.

YOUAT, William, *The Horse*, Baldwin & Craddock, 1831.

CHAPTER IV

BARBER, Richard, *The Knight and Chivalry*, Boydell Press, London, 1974.

BERENGER, Richard, *The History and Art of Horsemanship*, printed for T. Davis and T. Cadell, London, 1771.

BLUNDEVILLE, Thomas, *op. cit.*

CAMBRENSIS, Giraldus, *Topography of Ireland*, Dundalk, 1957 edition.

CHENEVIX TRENCH, Charles, *A History of Horsemanship*, Longman, Harlow, 1970.

DEFOE, Daniel, *A Tour through the Whole Island of Great Britain*, London, 1962 edition.

DENISON, Colonel G.T., *A History of Cavalry*, Macmillan & Co., London, 1913.

DENT, Anthony, *The Horse Through Fifty Centuries of Civilisation*, Phaidon Press.

— and MACHIN GOODALL, *op. cit.*

FROISSART, Sir John, *Chronicles of England, France, Spain and the Adjoining Countries* (translated from the 14th century French editions by Thomas Jones), Henry G. Bohn, London, 1862.

FROST, A.J., *The Battle of Hastings*, 1915.

GALTREY, Sidney, *The Horse and War*, London, 1918.

— Blenheim Papers, MSS 61101–61710, British Library, London.

HEWIT, Herbert James, *The Horse in Medieval England*, J.A. Allen, London, 1983.

KAMEN, Henry, *op. cit.*

LAMB, Major A.J., *op. cit.*

OMAN, Charles, *War in the Middle Ages*, 1885.

REESE, M.M., *op. cit.*

SIDNEY, S. *The Book of the Horse*, London, 1874.

TREVYLAN, Raleigh, *Shades of the Alhambra*, Folio, London, 1984.

CHAPTER V

ANDRADE, Manuel Carlos, *Luz da Liberal e Nobre Arte da Cavallaria*, Lisbon, 1790.

BERENGER, Richard, *op. cit.*

BLUNDEVILLE, Thomas, *op. cit.*

BRAGANZA, Diogo de, *L'Equitation de Tradition Français*, Le Livre de Paris, 1975.

DU BREUIL, General, *Le Cadre Noir*, Juilard, Switzerland, 1981.

CAVENDISH, William, Duke of Newcastle, *op. cit.*

CHURCHILL, Peter, *op. cit.*

DOLENC, Dr Milan, *Lipizzaner*, Control Data Arts, Minnesota, 1981.

GLYN, Sir Richard, *op. cit.*

HANDLER, Colonel Hans, *The Spanish Riding School in Vienna*, Thames and Hudson, London, 1972.

HERBERT, Henry, 10th Earl of Pembroke, *A Method of Breaking Horses and Teaching Soldiers to Ride, For the Use of the Army*, 1761.

HARRIS, Charles, 'The Development of Classical Equitation,' articles published in *Riding Magazine*, February, March, June issues, London, 1969.

HORE, J.P., *History of Newmarket and Annals of the Turf*, Volumes 1 and 2, 1885.

MACHIN GOODALL, Daphne, *op. cit.*

MONTEILHET, Andre, 'A History of Academic Equitation' in *The Horseman's International Book of Reference* (see above).

PRIOR, C.M., *The Royal Studs of the 16th and 17th Centuries*, Horse and Hound Publications Ltd, London, 1935.

VESEY-FITZGERALD, Brian, *op. cit.*

WALLHAUSEN, *The Art of Military Riding*, 1616.

WILKINSON, Clennel, *Prince Rupert, the Cavalier*, George G. Harrap, London, 1934.

XENOPHON, *The Art of Horsemanship* (edited by Morris H. Morgan), J.A. Allen, London, 1962.

CHAPTER VI

ADAMS, John, *Analysis of Horsemanship*, 1805.

D'ANDRADE, Fernando, *op. cit.*; also letters to author from September 1985 to February 1986.

CAMBRENSIS, Giraldus, *op. cit.*

CHENEVIX TRENCH, Charles, *op. cit.*

COOPER, Leonard, *British Regular Cavalry 1644–1914*, Chapman and Hall, London, 1965.

DIX, Carol, *The Camargue*, Victor Gollancz Ltd, London, 1975.

GALTREY, Sidney, *The Horse and War*, 1918.

El Caballo en Espana (see above).

LLAMAS, Colonel Juan, *op. cit.*

LAWFORD, James, *The Cavalry*, Sampson Low, Maidenhead.

MACHUCA, Vargas, *Teoria y exercicios de la gineta*, Madrid, 1600.

PERALTA, Juan Suarez de, *Tratado de la Cavalleria de la Gineta y Brida*, 1580.

D'URBAN, Sir Benjamin, Papers, National Army Museum, London.

Weapons and Warfare, Kingfisher Books, 1981.

CHAPTER VII

BOYD, Alastair, *The Road from Ronda : Travels with a Horse through Southern Spain*, Collins, London, 1969.

CARR, Raymond, *Spain, 1808–1939*, Oxford, 1966.

GALA, Antonio, 'The Horse in Fiesta', *El Caballo en Espana*, (see above).

HEMMING, Dr John, *Conquest of the Incas*, Macmillan, London, 1970.

KAMEN, Henry, *op. cit.*

LUARD, Nicholas, *Andalucia*, Century Publishing, London, 1984.

MITCHENER, James, *Iberia*, Secker & Warburg, London, 1968.

PILLEMENT, Georges, *Unknown Spain*, (translated from the French by Arnold Rosin) Johnson, London, 1964.

READ, Jan, *op. cit.*

The Horse, Folio no. 14, Portuguese Tourist Board, New Bond Street, London, W.1.

CHAPTER VIII

BRADFORD, Ernle, *op. cit.*

FROISSART, Sir John, *op. cit.*

HERCULANO, Alexandre, *Historia de Portugal*, Lisbon, 1914.

LIVERMORE, H.V. *op. cit.*

READ, Jan, *op. cit.*

CHAPTER IX

El Caballo en Espana (see above).
GLYN, Colonel Sir Richard, *op. cit.*
MATHIAS, Jorge, *op. cit.*
WATSON, Major J.N.P., 'Those Peerless Lusitanos', *Country Life Magazine*, June 18th, 1981.

CHAPTER X

D'ANDRADE, Fernando, letters to the author concerning general breeding methods within the Peninsula, dated December 1985.
COELHO, Alfredo Baptista, notes concerning the breeding of mares in the 17th and 18th centuries in Spain and Portugal, Lisbon, 1985.
DOMECQ Y DIAZ, Alvaro, Prologue to *El Caballo en Espana* (see above).
LUARD, Nicholas, *op. cit.*

CHAPTER XI

D'ANDRADE, Ruy, *La Crisis del Caballo Andaluz*, Lisbon, 1946.
DOMECQ Y DIAZ, Alvaro, *op. cit.*
DOSSENBACH, Monique and Hans D., *Great Stud Farms of the World*, English translation, Thames & Hudson Ltd, London, 1978.
GOUBAUX, Armand and BARRIER, Gustave, *op. cit.*
KIRKPATRICK O'DONNEL, Colonel Carlos, 'El Caballo en Espana Y Su Historia', *El Caballo En Espana* (see above).
LLAMAS, Colonel Juan, *op. cit.*
MACHUCA, Dom Barnado Vargas de, *Teoria y Ejercicios de Jineta*, 1628.
NUNEZ, Antonio Machado, *Catalogus Methodicus Mamalium*, Seville, 1869.
OETTIGEN, Burchard von, *Horse Breeding in Theory and Practice* (translated from the German), Sampson Low, Marston & Co., London, 1909.
SCHIELE, Erika, *The Arab Horse in Europe* (English translation by Anthony Dent), George G. Harrap & Co., London, 1970.
Sunday Times magazine article, April 20th, 1986.

CHAPTER XII

ANDRADE, Manuel Carlos, *op. cit.*
CROSSLEY, Colonel Anthony, 'At the Feet of the Master', *Riding Magazine*, May, London, 1977.
OLIVEIRA, Nuno, *Alta Escola, Haute Ecole*, Lisbon, 1970.
WATSON, Major J.N.P., *op. cit.*

CHAPTER XIII

CAVENDISH, William, Duke of Newcastle, *op. cit.*
DENT, Anthony and MACHIN GOODALL, Daphne, *op. cit.*
GILL, James, *Bloodstock*, Elm Tree Books, Hamish Hamilton, London, 1977.
GLYN, Colonel Sir Richard, *op. cit.*
HORE, J.P., *History of Newmarket and Annals of the Turf*, Volumes 1 and 2, 1885.
LAMB, Major A.J., *op. cit.*
MACHIN GOODALL, *op. cit.*
OETTINGEN, Burchard von, *op. cit.*
OSBORNE, Jos, *The Horsebreeder's Handbook*, 1889.
PRIOR, C.M., *op. cit.*
READE, Hubert, *Sidelights of the Thirty Years' War*.
REESE, M.M., *op. cit.*

RIDGEWAY, Professor, W., *op. cit.*

SIDNEY, S., *op. cit.*

UPTON, Roger D., *Newmarket and Arabia, An Examination of the Descent of Racers and Coursers*, London, 1873.

WEATHERBY, James, *General Stud Book*, Messrs Weatherby of London, 1791.

WENTWORTH, Lady, *Thoroughbred Racing Stock* (see above).

— *The Authentic Arabian Horse* (see above).

CHAPTER XIV

BERENGER, Richard, *op. cit.*

BLUNDEVILLE, Thomas, *op. cit.*

CAMPION, Edmund, *Historie of Ireland*, London, 1633.

CAMBRENSIS, Giraldus, *op. cit.*

CRETON, 14th-century manuscripts.

DEFOE, Daniel, *op. cit.*

DENT, Anthony, *Cleveland Bay Horses*, J.A. Allen, London, 1978.

EWART, Professor J.C., *The Ponies of Connemara*, 1900.

GILBEY, Sir Walter, *Ponies, Past and Present*, 1900.

LAMB, Major A.J., *op. cit.*

LOW, Professor, *Breeds of Domestic Animals of the British Isles*, 1842.

LYNE, Pat, *Shrouded in Mist*, Orphans Press, 1984.

MACHIN GOODALL, Daphne, *op. cit.*

O'SULLIVAN, Bartley, *The Connemara Pony*, 1939.

RIVAZ, Desmie de, The British Appaloosa Society pamphlet and information sheet, 1986.

CHAPTER XV

ALLBRIGHT, Verne R., *Caballo Peruano de Paso*, article printed in *Horse Ilustrated*, US.A., Issue no. 22, Vol. 4, no. 7.

ARCE, Juan Ruiz de, *Relacion de servicios* (1545), Boletin de la Real Academia de Historia, Madrid, vol. 102, 1933.

BARCLAY, Harold B., (American professor of Anthropology) *The Role of the Horse in Man's Culture*, J.A. Allen, London, 1980.

CONRAD, Charles W. (Editor), *Know the American Quarter Horse*, Farnham Horse Library, United States of America, 1968.

DENHARDT, Robert M., *The Horse of the Americas*, University of Oklahoma Press, 1975 edition.

DIAZ DEL CASTILLO, Bernal, *Historia verdadera de la conquista de la Nueva Espana*, (1904 edition edited by Genaro Garcia, Mexico, 2 vols.).

DOBIE, J. Frank, *The Mustangs*, Boston, 1952.

ESTETE, Miguel de, in Francisco de Xerez, *Verdadera relación de la Conquista del Perú* (1534), Biblioteca de Autores Españoles, Vol. 26, Madrid, 1947.

GRAHAM, Robert B. Cunninghame, *Horses of the Conquest*, London, 1930.

HAAS, Antonio, *Mexico*, Frederick Muller Ltd, London, 1982.

HEMMING, Dr John, *op. cit.*

MCNUTT, F.A. *Letters of Cortés*, New York, 1908.

'Mustang', The Southwest Spanish Mustang Association Newsletter, Spring, 1984.

PIZARRO, Pedro, *Relación del descubrimiento y conquista de los reinos del Perú* (1571), Colección de documentos inéditos para la Historia de España, Vol. 5, Madrid, 1844.

PRESCOTT, William H., *History of the Conquest of Mexico*, New York, 1936.

SOLANET, Dr Emilio, of the Agricultural and Veterinary Faculty of Buenos Aires, *El Caballo Criollo*, 1940.

VEGA, Inca Garcilaso de la, *General History of Peru*, Madrid, 1609.

WALLACE, Ward, Pamphlet and information sheets put together for *El Tesorillo Stud*, Arcos de la Frontera, Spain, 1985.

WILKERSON, S. Jeffrey, K., 'Following Cortés: Path to Conquest', *National Geographic Magazine*, October, 1984.

CHAPTER XVI

DOSSENBACH, Monique and Hans D., *The Noble Horse* (see above).

GREEN, Lucinda, 'Lucinda's Column', *Riding Magazine*, London, March, 1981.

OLIVEIRA, Nuno, *Reflections on Equestrian Art* (translated by Phyllis Field), J.A. Allen, London, 1976.

SMYTHE, R.H., M.R.C.V.S., *The Horse : Structure and Movement*, revised edition, C.C. Goody, J.A. Allen, London, 1986.

GENERAL REFERENCES AND FURTHER READING

I have here included those books which have helped me the most in my researches and which should be generally available through libraries etc., to the equestrian public. For ease of reference the details are quoted in full.

D'ANDRADE, Fernando, *A Short History of the Spanish Horse and of the Iberian 'Gineta' Horsemanship for which this Horse is Adapted*, Lisbon, 1973.

CHENEVIX TRENCH, Charles, *A History of Horsemanship*, Longman, Harlow, 1970.

CHURCHILL, Peter, *The World Atlas of Horses and Ponies*, Sampson Low, Maidenhead, 1980.

DENT, Anthony, and MACHIN GOODALL, Daphne, *Foals of Epona*, Galley Press, London, 1962.

Encyclopaedia Britannica, all volumes, 1949–1979 editions, USA.

FROISSARD, Jean and Lily Powell (editors), *The Horseman's International Book of Reference*, Stanley Paul, London, 1980.

GLYN, Colonel Sir Richard, *The World's Finest Horses and Ponies*, George G. Harrap & Co., London, 1971.

MACHIN GOODALL, Daphne, *A History of Horse Breeding*, Robert Hale, London, 1977.

PRIOR, C.M., *The Royal Studs of the 16th and 17th Centuries*, Horse and Hound Publications, London, 1935.

FORTHCOMING PUBLICATION OF SPECIAL INTEREST

COELHO, Alfredo Baptista, *The Horses of Lusitania and al-Andalus*, for publication 1987/8.